21世纪内容语言融合（CLI）系列英语教材

国家社会科学基金项目成果
高等教育国家级教学成果奖获奖项目成果
辽宁省普通高等教育本科教学成果奖获奖项目成果

英国国情
英国历史文化
（第3版）

UNDERSTANDING THE U.K.
BRITISH HISTORY
(THIRD EDITION)

常俊跃 夏洋 赵永青 主编

北京大学出版社
PEKING UNIVERSITY PRESS

图书在版编目(CIP)数据

英国国情：英国历史文化 / 常俊跃，夏洋，赵永青主编 . —3 版 . —北京：北京大学出版社，2023.7

21 世纪内容语言融合（CLI）系列英语教材

ISBN 978-7-301-34237-4

Ⅰ.①英… Ⅱ.①常…②夏…③赵… Ⅲ.①英语—阅读教学—高等学校—教材 ②文化史—英国 Ⅳ.① H319.37

中国国家版本馆 CIP 数据核字 (2023) 第 137695 号

书　　　名	英国国情：英国历史文化（第 3 版） YINGGUO GUOQING：YINGGUO LISHI WENHUA（DI-SAN BAN）
著作责任者	常俊跃　夏　洋　赵永青　主编
责任编辑	李　颖
标准书号	ISBN 978-7-301-34237-4
出版发行	北京大学出版社
地　　　址	北京市海淀区成府路 205 号　100871
网　　　址	http://www.pup.cn　新浪微博：@ 北京大学出版社
电子邮箱	编辑部 pupwaiwen@pup.cn　总编室 zpup@pup.cn
电　　　话	邮购部 010-62752015　发行部 010-62750672　编辑部 010-62754382
印　刷　者	三河市博文印刷有限公司
经　销　者	新华书店
	787 毫米 ×1098 毫米　16 开本　15 印张　474 千字 2010 年 1 月第 1 版　2016 年 6 月第 2 版 2023 年 7 月第 3 版　2023 年 7 月第 1 次印刷
定　　　价	69.00 元

未经许可，不得以任何方式复制或抄袭本书之部分或全部内容。
版权所有，侵权必究
举报电话：010-62752024　电子邮箱：fd@pup.cn
图书如有印装质量问题，请与出版部联系，电话：010-62756370

第三版前言

长期以来,"以语言技能训练为导向"(SOI)的教学理念主导了我国高校外语专业教育,即通过开设语音、语法、基础英语、高级英语、听力、口语、阅读、写作、翻译等课程进行语言教学,帮助学生提高语言技能。该理念对强化学生的语言技能具有一定的积极作用,但也导致了学生知识面偏窄、思辨能力偏弱、综合素质偏低等问题。

为了探寻我国外语专业教育的新路,大连外国语大学英语专业教研团队在总结西南联大等高校外语教育经验的基础上,在北美内容依托教学(CBI)的启发下,于2006年开展了校级和省级英语专业课程改革改革项目,还于2007—2022年连续开展了三个国家哲学社科项目,系统推进英语专业课程体系改革探索,推出中国特色鲜明的内容语言融合教育理念(Content and Language Integration, CLI),即"将目标语用于教授、学习内容和语言这两个重点,达到多种教育目的的教育理念"。CLI不仅具有自己独特的育人观、课程观、教材观、教学观、测评观、教师发展观,而且展示了如下特点:

(1) **教育目标**　有别于诸多外语教学理念,CLI不局限于语言教学,而是服务知识、能力和素质培养三大目标,将价值塑造、知识传授和能力培养三者融为一体,寓价值观引导于知识传授和能力培养之中,帮助学生塑造正确的世界观、人生观、价值观,着力落实立德树人根本任务。知识目标包含专业知识、相关专业知识、跨学科知识;能力目标包含语言能力、认知能力、交际能力、思辨能力等;素质目标包含人生观、价值观、世界观、人文修养、国际视野、中国情怀、责任感、团队意识等。

(2) **教学特点**　有别于单纯训练语言的教学,CLI指导下的语言训练依托内容,内容教学依靠语言;语言、内容融合教学,二者不再人为割裂。

(3) **师生角色**　有别于传统教学和学生中心理念对师生角色的期待,CLI倡导在充分发挥教师主导作用的同时发挥学生的主体作用。教师可以扮演讲授者、评估者、建议者、资源提供者、组织者、帮助者、咨询者,同时也不排斥教师的权威角色等角色。学生角色也更加多元,包括学习者、参与者、发起者、创新者、研究者、问题解决者。

(4) **教学材料**　有别于我国传统的外语教科书,在CLI指导下开发的教材具有多样化的特点,包括课本、音频资料、视频资料、网站资料、教学课件、学生作品等。教材的每个单元都围绕内容主题设计,内容具有连续性和系统性。

(5) **教学侧重**　CLI倡导教师要根据教学阶段或教学内容的特点确定教学重点,或侧重语言知识教学,或侧重语言技能教学,或侧重专业知识教学,或在语言教学和内容教学中达成某种平衡。

(6) **教学活动**　CLI主张教学活动不局限于某一种教学方法所规定的某几种技巧,倡导充分吸收各种教学方法促进语言学习、内容学习、素质培养的技巧,运用多种教学手段,通过问题驱动、输出驱动等方法调动学生主动学习;运用启发式、任务式、讨论式、结对子、小组活动、课堂展示、项目依托教学等行之有效的方法,活动与学科内容教学有机结合,提高学生的语言技能,激发学生的学习兴趣,培养学生的自主性和创造性,提升学生的思辨能力和综合素质。

(7)教学测评 CLI主张测评要吸收测试研究和评价研究的成果,开展形成性评价和终结性评价。形成性评价可以有小测验、课堂发表、角色扮演、小组活动、双人活动、项目、撰写论文、撰写研究报告、创意写作、创意改写、反馈性写作、制作张贴作品等;终结性评价可以包括传统的选择题等各种测评方法。

(8)互动性质 CLI有别于传统教学从教师向学生的单向信息传送,课堂互动包括师生互动基础上的生生互动、生师互动乃至师生与其他人员的互动。

(9)情感处理 CLI重视对学生的人文关怀,主张教师关注学生的情感反应,教学中有必要有效处理影响学生学习的各种情感因素。

(10)母语作用 CLI尊重外语环境下师生的母语优势并加以利用。不绝对禁止母语的使用,母语的使用取决于教学的需要,母语用于有效支持教育目标的达成。

(11)应对失误 CLI认可失误是学生获得语言或知识内容不可避免的现象,对学生的失误采取包容的态度。针对具体情况应对学生的失误,或不去干预,允许学生自我纠正,或有针对性地适时给予纠正。

(12)理论支撑 CLI得到语言、认知、社会互动、学习等多种理论的支撑。包括:语言是以文本或话语为基础的;语言的运用借助各种技能的融合;语言具有目的性;当人们把语言当成获取信息的工具而不是目的时学习语言更成功,作为语言学习的基础使得一些内容比另外一些内容更有用;当教学关注学生的需求时学生的学习效果会更好;教学应该以学生以前的学习经历为基础。

在CLI指导下,依托3个国家哲学社科项目,我们将教育部《高等学校英语专业英语教学大纲》规定的语言技能课程(包括英语语音、英语语法、英语听力、英语口语、英语阅读、英语写作、英语语音、英语语法、基础英语、高级英语、英语视听说、英汉笔译、英汉口译等)和专业知识课程(包括英语国家概况、英国文学、美国文学、语言学概论、学术论文写作)进行系统改革,构建了全新的英语专业课程体系,包括九个系列的核心课程:

1.提高综合英语能力的课程包括:美国文学经典作品、英国文学经典作品、世界文学经典作品、西方思想经典。依托美国、英国、世界的英语文学作品经典和西方思想经典的内容,提高学生综合运用英语的能力,丰富对文学及西方思想的认知,提高综合能力和综合素养。

2.提高英语视听说能力的课程包括:美国社会文化经典电影、英国社会文化经典电影、环球资讯、专题资讯。依托美英社会文化经典电影、环球资讯、专题资讯内容,提高学生的英语听说能力,同时增加学生对相关国家社会文化的了解。

3.提高英语口语表达的课程包括:功能英语交际、情景英语交际、英语演讲、英语辩论。依托人际交往的知识内容,提高学生的英语口语交际能力,增进对人际沟通的了解。

4.提高英语写作能力的课程包括:段落写作、篇章写作、创意写作、学术英语写作。

依托笔头交际的知识内容,提高学生的英语笔头表达能力。

5.提高英汉互译能力的课程包括:英汉笔译、汉英笔译、交替传译、同声传译、专题口译。依托相关学科领域的知识内容,提高学生的英汉笔译、交译、同传、专题口译技能,增加学生对相关领域的了解。

6.拓展社会文化知识的课程:美国社会与文化、美国自然人文地理、英国历史文化、英国社会与文化、英国自然人文地理、英国历史文化、澳新加社会与文化、欧洲文化、中国文化、古希腊罗马神话、《圣经》与文化、跨文化交际。依托相关国家区域的社会、文化、史地等知识,扩展学生的社会文化知识,增加学生专业知识的系统性,拓宽学生的国际视野,同时提高学生的英语能力。

7.提升英语文学修养的课程包括:英语短篇小说、英语长篇小说、英语散文、英语戏剧、英语诗歌。依托各种体裁的优秀文学作品内容,强化学生对英语文学文本的阅读,提高学生的文学欣赏能力及语言表达能力,提升学生的文学素养。

8.提升语言理论修养的课程包括:英语语言学、英语词汇学、语言与社会、语言与文化、语言与语用。依托英语语言学知识内容,帮助学生深入了解英语语言,增加对语言与社会、文化、语用关系的认识,同时提升学生的专业表达能力。

9.提升区域国别问题探究能力的课程包括:欧洲英语国家研究、北美英语国家研究、大洋洲英语国家研究、拉美英语国家研究、亚洲英语国家研究、非洲英语国家研究。通过指导学生获取区域国别学知识、开展区域国别问题研究项目,提高学生获取国情区情知识、拓宽国际视野、探究国别问题、进行语言沟通等综合能力和综合素养。

研究表明,CLI指导下的课程改革对学生的语音、词汇、语法、听力、口语、写作、交际、思辨、情感、知识等诸多方面产生了显著的积极影响。此外,对学生的研究、创新等能力也产生了积极影响。

CLI教育理念及其指导下的实践探索成果在国内外研讨会进行交流,产生了广泛的积极影响。CLI教育理念指导下开发的系列课程和教材在北京大学出版社、上海外语教育出版社等出版社出版并被广泛使用。培育的校级、省级和国家级教学研究成果在我国高校广泛借鉴,出版的教学研究著作及在国内外学术期刊发表的研究论文对推进外语专业教育理念变革、改善教学实践发挥了积极的作用。高校教师积极参与CLI教育教学研讨与交流,200多所高校引进了理念、课程、教材并结合本校实际开展了课程改革,取得了积极成果。

该理念不仅得到一线教师的广泛支持,也得到了戴炜栋、王守仁、文秋芳等知名专家的高度肯定。蔡基刚教授认为其具有"导向性"作用。孙有中教授认为,该理念指导的教学改革"走在了全国的前列"。教育部前外语教学指导委员会主任委员戴炜栋建议推广探索的课程。内容语言融合教育理念被作为教学要求写入《外国语言文学类教学质量国家标准》及《普通高等学校英语类专业教学指南》,用于指导全国的外语专业教育,必将对我国的外语教育产生更大的影响。

《英国国情:英国历史文化》是CLI教育理念指导下英语专业知识课程体系中英国历史文化课程所使用的教材。教材针对的学生群体是具有中学英语基础的大学生,适用于英语专业一、二年级学生,也适用于具有中学英语基础的非专业学生和英语爱好者。总体看来，本教材具有以下主要特色：

1. 打破了传统的教学理念。本教材改变了"为学语言而学语言"的传统教材建设理念，在具有时代特色且被证明行之有效的内容依托教学理论指导下，改变了片面关注语言知识和语言技能忽视内容学习的做法。它依托学生密切关注的西方文明和文化内容，结合社会文化内容组织学生进行语言交际活动，在语言交流中学习有意义的知识内容，既训练语言技能，也丰富相关知识，起到的是一箭双雕的作用。

2. 涉及丰富的教学内容。《英国国情：英国历史文化》共分为十五个单元。教材内容主要展示了从诺曼征服到英国当代的主要历史发展脉络，涵盖了较为系统的英国历史基础知识。英国历史的一般性主题和话题将贯穿教材始终，并对英国王室及相关重要历史事件有所侧重，其中包括英国各王朝的形成与更替、英国历史发展过程中的主要战争、主要君主及相关政治、社会、文化成就等诸多方面。

3. 引进了真实的教学材料。英语教材是英语学习者英语语言输入和相关知识输入的重要渠道。本教材使用大量真实、地道的语言材料，为学生提供高质量的语言输入。此外，为了使课文内容更加充实生动，易于学生理解接受，编者在课文中穿插了大量的插图、表格、照片等真实的视觉材料，表现手段活泼、形式多种多样，效果生动直观。

4. 设计了新颖的教材板块。本教材每一单元的主体内容均包括 Before You Read, Start to Read, After You Read 和 Read More 四大板块，不仅在结构上确立了学生的主体地位，而且系统的安排也方便教师借助教材有条不紊地开展教学活动。它改变了教师单纯灌输、学生被动接受的教学方式，促使学生积极思考、提问、探索、发现、批判，培养自主获得知识、发现问题和解决问题的能力。

5. 提供了有趣的训练活动。为了培养学生的语言技能和综合素质，本教材在关注英语语言知识训练和相关知识内容传授的基础上精心设计了生动多样的综合训练活动，例如头脑风暴、话题辩论、角色表演、主题陈述、故事编述等等。多样化的活动打破了传统教材单调的训练程式，帮助教师设置真实的语言运用情境，组织富于挑战性的、具有意义的语言实践活动，培养学生语言综合运用能力。

6. 推荐了经典的学习材料。教材的另一特色在于它对教学内容的延伸和拓展。在每个章节的最后部分，编者向学生推荐经典的书目、影视作品、名诗欣赏以及英文歌曲等学习资料，这不仅有益于学生开阔视野，也使教材具有了弹性和开放性，方便不同院校不同水平学生的使用。

本教材是我国英语专业综合课程改革的一项探索，凝聚了全体编写人员的艰苦努力。然而由于水平有限，还存在疏漏和补足，希望使用本教材的老师和同学们能为我们提出宝贵意见和建议。您的指导和建议将是我们提高的动力。

编者

2023 年 2 月 20 日

于大连外国语大学

Contents

Unit 1　The Birth of a Nation / 1
　　Text A　The Ancient Britons and Invasions / 2
　　Text B　Anglo-Saxon England / 10
　　Text C　King Arthur and the Knights of the Round Table / 12
　　Text D　The Venerable Bede (673—735) / 14

Unit 2　The Normans / 19
　　Text A　The Norman Monarchs / 20
　　Text B　Feudalism after the Norman Conquest / 26
　　Text C　The *Doomsday Book* / 28

Unit 3　The Early Plantagenet / 32
　　Text A　The Rule of Law / 33
　　Text B　*The Canterbury Tales* / 38
　　Text C　The Crusades / 41

Unit 4　The House of Plantagenet / 47
　　Text A　The Birth of Parliament / 48
　　Text B　The *Magna Carta* / 55
　　Text C　King John / 57

Unit 5　The 14th-century England / 61
　　Text A　The Hundred Years' War / 62
　　Text B　The Black Death and Wat Tyler Uprising / 63
　　Text C　Wat Tyler and His Revolting Peasants / 67
　　Text D　Joan of Arc—Maid of Orleans / 68

Unit 6　The House of Lancaster and York / 73
　　Text A　The Wars of the Roses / 74
　　Text B　The Mystery of the Princes in the Tower / 79
　　Text C　The Middle Ages / 81

Unit 7　The Tudor Age / 84

　　Text A　The Tudor Monarchy / 85
　　Text B　The Reformation in England (1517—1563) / 86
　　Text C　King Henry VII / 92
　　Text D　Henry VIII and His Marriage / 94

Unit 8　The Elizabethan Age / 99

　　Text A　The Reign of Elizabeth I / 100
　　Text B　Queen Elizabeth I / 106
　　Text C　Entertainment in Elizabethan Age / 108
　　Text D　Defeat of the Spanish Armada / 111

Unit 9　The House of Stuart / 115

　　Text A　The Age of Revolution / 116
　　Text B　King James VI and I / 123
　　Text C　The English Civil War / 125

Unit 10　The House of Hanover / 130

　　Text A　The Hanoverian Monarchs / 131
　　Text B　Napoleon Bonaparte (1769—1821) / 137
　　Text C　King George III / 140

Unit 11　The Industrial Revolution / 143

　　Text A　The British Industrial Revolution / 144
　　Text B　Machines for the Industrial Revolution / 149
　　Text C　The Consequences of the Industrial Revolution / 151

Unit 12　The Victorian Age (1837—1901) / 154

　　Text A　Queen Victoria and Her Reign / 155
　　Text B　Everyday Life in Victorian England / 161
　　Text C　Charles Dickens (1812—1870) / 164

Unit 13　The World at War / 169

　　Text A　The Great Britain in the World Wars / 170
　　Text B　Causes of World War I / 176
　　Text C　Winston Churchill / 178

Unit 14　Towards the New Millennium / 187

　　Text A　House of Windsor / 188
　　Text B　Queen Elizabeth II / 193
　　Text C　Margaret Thatcher / 195

Unit 15　Wales，Scotland and Ireland / 201
    Text A　The English Conquest of Wales / 202
    Text B　The Story of Scotland / 203
    Text C　The Ties between Ireland and the Great Britain / 209

Appendixes / 213
    Appendix 1：Kings and Queens of England and Britain / 213
    Appendix 2：Genealogy of the Monarchs of England / 224

主要参考文献和网站 / 226

Unit 1
The Birth of a Nation

> The charm of history and its enigmatic lesson consist in the fact that, from age to age, nothing changes and yet everything is completely different.
> —Aldous Huxley

Unit Goals

- To be familiar with the history before the Norman Conquest
- To have a glimpse at the Celtic Britain, the Roman invasion, the Germanic invasion and the Danish invasion
- To know such important figures as Julius Caesar, King Arthur, Alfred the Great and William the Conqueror during this period
- To be acquainted with the cause of the Norman Conquest
- To learn words and expressions that describe the Britain before the Norman Conquest and improve English language skills
- To develop critical thinking and intercultural communication skills

Before You Read

(1) How much do you know about the following figures in the early stage of British history? Share your knowledge about them with your partner and fill in the blanks in the following chart.

The Figure in History	What I Know about Him
Julius Caesar	
King Arthur	
Alfred the Great	

(2) Read Text A and single out the key information about the early settlers and invaders.
   The Celts: _____
   The Romans: _____
   The Anglo-Saxons: _____
   The Vikings: _____
(3) Do you know the following important cities: Gloucester, Worcester, Chester and Winchester? You may already find that these place names have something in common—the word ending "-cester" or "-chester". Figure out the origins of these words while reading Text A.
(4) Form groups of three or four students. Try to find, on the Internet or in the library, more information about William the Couqueror and the Norman Conquest. Get ready for a 5-minute presentation in class.

Start to Read

Text A The Ancient Britons and Invasions

1. The great round temple of Stonehenge stands high in the hills of southern England, where the ancient Britons built it 3500 years ago. Their remains can be seen in many places, but there is no written record of these early days until Julius Caesar, a Roman General, visited the island in 55 BC. By then, many different tribes, especially the Celts, had crossed from Europe in search of empty lands for settlement.

2. The Celts were one of the early settlers and began to move to Britain about 700 BC. The Celts lived in much of western and central Europe at the time. They defeated the natives of the islands and made them members of their tribes. Their language, the Celtic, was the earliest known language in what is now Britain.

3. For a few centuries, the Roman armies stopped the westward flow of Europe's population. In 55 BC and 54 BC, under the leadership of Julius Caesar, Romans invaded Britain twice. For nearly 400 years, Britain was under the Roman occupation, though it was never a total occupation. The Roman rule of Britain ended by 410.

4. The Romans brought Christianity to England, and their development of the country helped this religion to spread. Many of their army bases are now important cities: Gloucester, Worcester, Chester, Winchester and others. All these names are derived from the Roman word "castra", which means an armed camp.

5. From the middle of the 5th century, three Germanic (Teutonic) tribes, namely Jutes, Angles and Saxons, began to migrate from the region of Denmark and settled in Britain. The Christian Celts, in spite of their brave leaders like King Arthur, were wholly defeated. Those who escaped the sword were pushed back into the mountains of Wales and Scotland and across to Ireland.

6. The Angles and Saxons from northern Germany spoke a language which we now call Old English. The Angles gave rise to the word "England" because "England" in Old English meant "the land of the Angles". The Angles and Saxons took possession of all the land as far as the mountains in the north and west, and divided it into a handful of small kingdoms. Essex and Sussex, the kingdoms of the east and south Saxons, are still the names of English counties. Then they settled down to work their farms. But their separate kingdoms could make no organized resistance to the next wave of northern fighters, the Vikings. Some of these came from Norway and attacked the rocky coasts of Scotland and northern England; but the main body came from Denmark, sailed up the rivers of the east and south, and seized one little Saxon kingdom after another. At the last moment, the Saxons were saved by the courage of King Alfred of Wessex, who defeated the Danes and forced their army to accept the Christian faith. Then he allowed them to settle in eastern and central England.

7. Both the Saxons and the Danes had been accustomed to northern gods like Woden and Thor, whose names have given us Wednesday and Thursday. They believed that courage, loyalty and rough honesty are the greatest virtues. How did the Saxons become Christian? The question is answered by Bede, whose *History of the English Church* was written in Latin while these events were still within living memory. Bede was a Saxon but he used Latin because it was the international language of the Church. Pope Gregory, he said, was attracted by some fair-haired young slaves on sale in Rome. The Pope, who was head of the Roman Church, heard that these slaves came from England, and he decided to send a party of his priests to help the English people.

8. In 597, St. Augustine and others from Rome successfully converted the

leaders in tribes to Christianity. By the end of the 7th century, England had been Christianized. The Roman priests made their base at Canterbury, and within a hundred years all England was united under one well-organized Church. Each district had its church leader, the bishop, and its central church building, the cathedral. The head of them all was the Archbishop at Canterbury.

9. King Alfred the Great had a respect for education. He himself wrote some school books in Old English, including a translation of Bede's *History*; and he began the *Anglo-Saxon Chronicle* in which the history of the land was recorded by monks for the next three hundred years.

10. Under Alfred and his sons, the Danes and Saxons settled side by side in peace. Under Danish influence, Alfred built a navy of fighting ships to protect his shores; he also provided horses to move his soldiers quickly, though they had not yet learnt to fight on horseback.

11. Under the weak King Ethelred, there was trouble once more. Fresh waves of fierce Danish fighters attacked the south. Instead of fighting them, Ethelred collected a tax and paid them to go away, but each year they wanted more. The poor were ruined by this tax and even the rich suffered. No wonder that, when he died, the council invited the Danish leader Canute to become their king.

12. Canute worked hard to unite his Danish and Saxon peoples. He trusted great lords, who ruled various former kingdoms in his name. Canute became a Christian and used the Church to draw all men together. He kept Winchester as his capital, where English and Danish were the languages of his court.

13. Canute died and left two sons; but they were evil men, and soon Ethelred's son Edward was called from Normandy to be the king. He had been brought up in an abbey and was more like a monk than a king, so that people called him Edward the Confessor. Edward was formally married to the daughter of Godwin (the great Lord of Wessex), but he made no attempt to give her a child. He spoke Norman French. His tastes and his friends were Norman. He even appointed a Norman archbishop.

14. The council, which included both Saxon and Danish lords and bishops, was getting seriously worried. When it was reported that Edward had promised to leave the kingdom to his Norman cousin William, the council members decided to take actions. They forced Edward to dismiss his archbishop and appoint a Saxon instead; but they were too disunited to prevent the spread of

Norman influence and power.

15. At Christmas 1065, they gathered for the opening of the king's new abbey at Westminster, two miles outside the walls of London. Here Edward had already built himself a royal home. But he was too ill to attend the opening of his abbey, and a few days later he died. On his death bed he chose Harold of Wessex, his wife's brother, to be king in his place. The council approved of this choice, and Harold was crowned the next day. Like Canute, he did not belong to the royal family of England; but he was a Saxon lord, and he was chosen by Edward and the council. By English custom he was lawfully crowned.

16. The council knew well that others would claim the crown. Duke William of Normandy would claim it because of Edward's secret promise; the kings of Denmark and Norway would claim it because of their family ties with Canute. If Harold had had the full support of his lords, he could probably have saved his kingdom; but many were jealous of his position and some clearly favored his foreign rivals. When the attack came, it found England disunited.

17. When Norway's king landed and seized York, Harold rushed north and destroyed him and his army. Three days later, Duke William landed on the Sussex coast, and Harold rushed south again. Without waiting to collect support from doubtful lords, he met the Norman army near Hastings. His tired men fought bravely but they had no experience of fighting against cavalry, and the Norman cavalry were the finest fighting horsemen in Europe. When night came, King Harold and the best of his men lay dead on the hill-top. And on Christmas Day 1066, William the Conqueror was crowned in Westminster Abbey.

After You Read

Knowledge Focus

1. **Pair Work**

    Discuss the following questions with your partner.

    (1) What do you know about the Stonehenge? Share your knowledge with your partner.

    (2) Who brought Christianity to England?

    (3) What were the three Germanic tribes?

    (4) What was the origin of Old English?

    (5) Can you figure out the origins of such city names as "Essex" or "Sussex"?

    (6) How do you define the "Vikings"?

    (7) What are Wednesday and Thursday named after?

    (8) What do you know about King Alfred the Great? What made him "great" in history?

    (9) How did the Saxons become Christians?

    (10) Can you briefly retell what happened before the Norman Conquest?

2. **Solo Work**

    Tell whether and why the following are true or false according to the knowledge you have learned.

    _____ (1) When the Anglo-Saxon conquest was over, little remained of Celtic or Roman civilization on the island.

    _____ (2) The Romans brought their civilization to England, but they did not introduce a system of organized government.

    _____ (3) The Stonehenge is one of the most famous prehistoric sites in the world, which is composed of earthworks surrounding a circular setting of large standing stones.

    _____ (4) In 55BC and 54BC, Julius Caesar, a Greek general, invaded Britain twice.

    _____ (5) Edward the Confessor was the last Anglo-Saxon king in the English history. He ruled over England for twenty years.

    _____ (6) The Norman Conquest was in fact a French conquest and the imposition upon England of a ruling French aristocracy. In consequence, Norman-French of the conquerors replaced English as an authoritative language in England. English became a lower-class language.

3. Pair Work

Fill in the missing information in the following chart, which serves as a summary of major invasions.

Invaders	Time	Language	Major Figure
The Celts			N/A
Romans		Latin	
Anglo-Saxons	the 5th century		
The Vikings	the 8th century	The Old Norse	
The Norman Conquest			William the Conqueror

Language Focus

1. **Fill in the blanks with the following words or expressions you have learned in the text. Put them into appropriate forms if necessary.**

take possession of	accustom	handful	record
appoint	in search of	pour into	fierce
owe... to	approve of		

(1) She was shot by a hunter when she went out _____ firewood.
(2) Refugees have been _____ neighboring countries to escape the civil war.
(3) We've already bought the house but we will not _____ it until May.
(4) He pulled out a _____ of coins from his pocket.
(5) It'll take time for me to _____ myself to the changes.
(6) Most people no longer _____ smoking in public places.
(7) He's just been _____ director of the publishing division.
(8) We all _____ a debt of gratitude _____ Mrs. Stevenson, who kindly donated the money for the project.
(9) Two men were shot during _____ fighting last weekend.
(10) Unemployment is likely to reach the highest that has ever been _____.

2. **Find the appropriate prepositions that collocate with the neighboring words.**

(1) The Celts had crossed from Europe _____ search of empty lands for settlement.
(2) All these names are derived _____ the Roman word "castra", which means an armed camp.
(3) The Christian Celts, _____ spite of brave leaders like King Arthur, were wholly defeated.

(4) Both the Saxons and the Danes had been accustomed _____ northern gods.

(5) Pope Gregory was attracted by some fair-haired young slaves _____ sale in Rome.

(6) Canute ruled various former kingdoms _____ his name.

(7) The council approved _____ this choice, and Harold was crowned next day.

(8) The Angles and Saxons took possession _____ all the land as far as the mountains in the north and west.

Comprehensive Work

1. **Solo Work**

   Read the following introduction to the Stonehenge, and then try to appreciate the wonder of Stonehenge by comparing it with other wonders in the world like the Great Wall and the Pyramid. Write an essay of about 300 words.

   Stonehenge is a prehistoric monument located in the English county of Wiltshire, about 8 miles north of Salisbury. One of the most famous prehistoric sites in the world, Stonehenge is composed of earthworks surrounding a circular setting of large standing stones.

   Nobody knows what it was built for, perhaps Druid temple or perhaps an astronomical calculator. Work started on it in 3100 BC and it was continuously built, used and modified until 1100 BC. An amazing period of 2000 years—not many other buildings in the world have been used for so long.

   After 1100 BC, it fell into disuse. Again nobody knows why. The stones on the site were used by the local people as a convenient source for building houses and roads. Even up to 100 years ago, local farmers used the stones from Stonehenge for road building and other construction work.

   It was given to the nation in 1918, and the government has been responsible for maintaining the monument since then. The site and its surroundings were added to the UNESCO World Heritage List sites in 1986.

2. **Group Work**

   This activity will help you understand what happened when the King of England, Edward the Confessor, died.

   On the 5th of January 1066, Edward the Confessor, the King of England, died. He had no children, which meant he had no direct heir to the throne, but three men thought they should all be the new king of England, and all had good reasons too. They were Harold Godwinson, Harald Hardrada, and William Duke of Normandy.

Harold Godwinson   *Harald Hardrada*   *William Duke of Normandy*

Harold Godwinson was the Earl of Wessex at the time, and this made him the most powerful nobleman in England and the only Englishman claiming the throne, except for a relative called Edgar who was only eight and was not seriously considered for the throne for obvious reasons.

Harald Hardrada's main claim was that Canute's son promised his father the throne and that he was a descendant of King Canute, a former king of England. He also felt that he might get some support from Viking families in the North of England.

William was Edward's cousin and was promised the throne by him, and he had helped Edward in the past. William was Duke of Normandy.

On January 6, Harold Godwinson was crowned the new king of England. William and Harald were not happy.

Task 1
Answer the following questions in full sentences.
(1) Why did England need a new king?
(2) Why was there no direct heir to the throne?
(3) Who were the three men who had claims to the English throne?
(4) What roles did the three men have in their countries?
(5) What is a "claimant"?

Task 2
Discuss with your team members the reasons why these three claimants thought that they had a claim to be king.

Complete this paragraph: "I think that _____ had the best claim to the English throne. The reasons are as follows: _____
_____
_____."

Task 3
Design a poster which is entitled "Vote for..." and give reasons why we SHOULD vote for him and SHOULD NOT vote for others.

3. Writing Activity
In the time of William the Conqueror, there was no e-mail, or even postal service, so

sending a message was a slow process. Suppose that you wanted to send a message to King Harold, warning him of William's approach. What would you say in your message? How would you send it?

Read More

Text B   Anglo-Saxon England

England became England, the land of English-speaking people, at the beginning of the Middle Ages. Before that, it had been the home of Iron Age tribes known as the Celts, and for a time, part of the Roman Empire.

Then beginning in the 400s AD, tribes from the North, known as the Angles, the Saxons, and the Jutes, moved in. Some accounts called these people settlers; other accounts called them invaders. Whatever they were called, they came to England to stay.

We know about the events of that time period from the *Anglo-Saxon Chronicle*, the only written history surviving from that period. The chronicle tells of battles and invasions and all types of changes over the years of the early Middle Ages.

The most famous leader of this time period in England, as you can guess from his title, was Alfred the Great. Alfred lived in Wessex, the kingdom of the West Saxons, which was in the southern part of England. Since he had three elder brothers, he did not expect to grow up to be king. That all changed when all three of his elder brothers died. Alfred became King of Wessex in 871. He was a good leader who made his kingdom stronger. He created a system of defenses, called burhs, across the country. He built up a fleet of ships to fight off invaders. He reorganized the military so that his men had time to fight and time to farm. Alfred's efforts protected his people from Viking invaders and allowed Wessex to grow. Eventually the rulers of Wessex would rule all of England.

Alfred also made other improvements. He instituted a code of laws for his people. He encouraged learning and translated several important books into his Saxon language. This was the beginning of the language we call English today.

Two important pieces of literature from that time period are the *Anglo-Saxon Chronicle* and *Beowulf*. *Beowulf* is a long poem about a fictional hero named Beowulf. It was composed in the 8th century by an unknown storyteller and written down much later by unknown scribes. In the story, Prince Beowulf comes to Denmark to help the king get rid of a monster called Grendel. After defeating Grendel, Beowulf has to fight Grendel's mother and then a terrible dragon.

Both *Beowulf* and *the Anglo-Saxon Chronicle* were written in the language that later became known as Old English. Old English was the first of several versions of the English language. Old English lasted through most of the Middle Ages. Middle English came in during the late Middle Ages, and Modern English began about the time of the Renaissance.

Old English looks like a foreign language today. People who speak English today cannot read Old English unless they study it like a foreign language. It even has some letters that we no longer use. Nevertheless, it is the beginning of English.

England and English get their names, not from the Saxons, but from one of the other tribes, the Angles. The original name of England must have been something like Angle-land (only in Old English of course).

Today, we often say Great Britain or United Kingdom for the name of the country, but everyone still recognizes the name England as well, and English is not only the language of England now. There is the British version of English and the American version of English, but the Angles of the Middle Ages would not have recognized either one!

1. **Finish the following multiple-choice questions according to Text B.**
   (1) The Middle Ages began after _____ in what is England now.
      A. the Iron Age   B. 871 AD   C. 400 AD   D. 410 BC
   (2) All of the following, except for _____, were tribes from the north who moved into England in the 400s AD.
      A. Angles   B. Saxons   C. Jutes   D. Celts
   (3) *The Anglo-Saxon Chronicle* is a _____.
      A. poem about a hero named Beowulf
      B. newspaper
      C. historical record
      D. novel
   (4) Alfred the Great was the king of _____.
      A. Wessex   B. Great Britain
      C. the North   D. none of the above
   (5) Which happened first in the life of Alfred the Great?
      A. He created a code of laws.
      B. He protected his people from Viking attacks.

C. His brothers died.
   D. He became king.
(6) For most Americans, Old English would be _____.
   A. easy to read
   B. easy to speak
   C. a little difficult to read and speak
   D. unreadable
(7) From the information in this article, you can infer that English _____.
   A. was not spoken before the Renaissance
   B. is no longer spoken in England
   C. has changed over the years
   D. has never changed

Text C King Arthur and the Knights of the Round Table

Arthur waited in line to try pulling the great sword from the stone. He had no idea that King Uther, who had just died, was his real father. He had no way of knowing that he was the true heir to the throne.

His turn came. He gripped the huge sword, glittering with shiny metals and jewels, and slid it from its stone scabbard. That was the proof that England needed. Arthur was crowned king.

Arthur ruled England with the guidance of his long-time guardian, Merlin the magician.

He had brave and loyal knights—Lancelot, Gawain, and many others.

King Arthur's knights took their role seriously. They promised to abide by a code of rules. They promised to act bravely and with honor. They promised not to murder innocent people and they promised to rescue ladies in distress.

Arthur's knights were adventurous and ambitious. They loved to meet together and tell tales of their great feats, each one trying to out-tell the other. Sometimes the competition between the exaggerating knights got to be too much.

So Arthur, being a wise leader, came up with a solution. Into the meeting hall of Camelot Castle, he moved the huge round table that his wife, the lovely Lady Guinevere, had brought as part of her dowry. At this round table, no knight would sit in front of another one. No one would have an advantage or a favored position. Everyone would be equal.

King Arthur's court at the Round Table became known far and wide as the perfect, fair way to rule. Every knight aspired to become a Knight of the Round Table and enter the meeting hall at Camelot to the fanfare of his own clanking armor.

When their meetings were adjourned, Arthur's knights set out from Camelot for great adventures in all corners of England.

Wearing their shining suits of armor and their tin-can helmets, Arthur's knights rode out to fight whoever had done them wrong. King Arthur's red dragon painted on each shield proclaimed that they were The Knights of the Round Table.

Back at Camelot, King Arthur presided over the forces of good in his sweeping red robe and tall golden crown. Always nearby was his own trusty sword, Excalibur, given to him by the mysterious Lady of the Lake. England was in good hands.

Even good King Arthur had occasional problems to deal with. Life among so many knights and ladies could be a bit dramatic. When King Arthur's own wife, Guinevere, was stolen away by his knight Lancelot, Arthur had to act at once. He fought his nephew Mordred, who had somehow gotten into the thick of the plot.

Arthur killed Mordred.

Mordred gravely wounded Arthur too, and Arthur was swiftly carried off by his own men—never to be heard of again.

This story may or may not be true. King Arthur and his Knights of the Round Table may or may not have been real people. Many historians think that there is at least a little bit of truth in the legend. The story of King Arthur and the Knights of the Round Table, however, has become a part of history. The bravery and honor of the knights, the wisdom of King Arthur, and the magical effect of the Round Table—they have all become part of the story of England.

1. Read Text C quickly and answer the following multiple-choice questions.
   (1) Although it is not stated directly in the story, you can infer that this story takes place during the _____.
      A. Middle Ages   B. prehistoric times
      C. Civil War era   D. ancient Roman times
   (2) Lancelot was a _____.
      A. knight   B. magician
      C. king   D. all of the above

(3) Based on the story, we can say that King Arthur probably died from _____.
   A. food poisoning   B. pneumonia
   C. a gunshot wound   D. a wound from a sword
(4) The Round Table gave each knight a/an _____.
   A. fortune   B. job
   C. place to eat dinner D. equal say
(5) Excalibur was _____.
   A. a horse   B. a sword
   C. the sword in the stone D. a crown

Text D The Venerable Bede (673—735)

Within the walls of the Norman Cathedral of Durham lies the simple tomb of a Christian monk who has earned the title as "Father of English History".

Bede was born at Tyne in County Durham, and was taken as a child of seven to the monastery of Wearmouth. Shortly afterwards he was moved to become one of the first members of the monastic community at Jarrow. Here, he was ordained deacon, the religious official just below the rank of priest, when he was 19 and a priest when he was 30; and here he spent the rest of his life. He never travelled outside of this area but became one of the most learned men of Europe.

The scholarship and culture of Italy had been brought to Britain where they were transported to Jarrow. Here it was combined with the simpler traditions, devotions and evangelism of the Celtic church. In this setting, Bede learned the love of scholarship, personal devotion and discipline. He mastered Latin, Greek and Hebrew and had a good knowledge of the classical scholars and early church fathers.

Bede's writings cover a broad range including natural history, poetry, Biblical translation and detailed explanation of the scriptures. He is credited with writing three known Latin hymns.

He is remembered chiefly for his *Ecclesiastical History of the English People*. This five-volume work records events in Britain from the raids by Julius Caesar in 55 BC—54 BC to the arrival of the first missionary from Rome, Saint

Augustine in 597. Bede's writings are considered the best summary of this period of history ever prepared. Some have called it "the finest historical work of the early Middle Ages".

Bede's motive for recording history reminds us of his deepest desires. He clearly states his purpose in his writings when he says, "For if history records good things of good men, the thoughtful hearer is encouraged to imitate what is good; or if it records evil things of wicked men, the good, religious reader or listener is encouraged to avoid all that is sinful and perverse, and to follow what he knows to be good and pleasing to God".

We are indebted to Bede, as it is to this man that we owe, from his historical accounts, our dating of years from the birth of Christ.

1. **Questions for discussion or reflection.**
   (1) Who earned the title "Father of English History"?
   (2) Where did Bede spend most of his life? Can you present a brief account of his life to your partner?
   (3) What are the major topics that Bede's writings cover?
   (4) What is Bede chiefly remembered for?

Proper Names

Anglo-Saxon Chronicle 《盎格鲁-撒克逊编年史》
Bede 比德
Canterbury 坎特伯雷
Canute 卡努特
Chester 切斯特城
Edward the Confessor 虔信者爱德华
Essex 埃塞克斯
Germanic (Teutonic) tribes 日耳曼(条顿)部落
Gloucester 格洛斯特
Julius Caesar 尤利乌斯·恺撒
King Alfred the Great 阿尔弗莱德大王
King Arthur 亚瑟王
King Ethelred 埃塞雷德王

St. Augustine 圣·奥古斯丁
Stonehenge 巨石阵
Sussex 萨赛克斯
the Angles 盎格鲁人
the Celts 凯尔特人
the Danes 丹麦人
the Saxons 撒克逊人
the Vikings 维京人
Westminster Abbey 威斯敏斯特大教堂
William the Conqueror 征服者威廉
Winchester 温彻斯特
Worcester 伍斯特

Notes

1. **Stonehenge**: Stonehenge is a prehistoric monument located in the English county of Wiltshire, about 8 miles (13km) north of Salisbury. One of the most famous prehistoric sites in the world, Stonehenge is

composed of earthworks surrounding a circular setting of large standing stones. The site and its surroundings were added to the UNESCO's list of World Heritage Sites in 1986.

2. **Julius Caesar（100BC—44BC）**：Caesar was a politician and general of the late Roman republic, who greatly extended the Roman Empire before seizing power and making himself Dictator of Rome, paving the way for the imperial system.

3. **King Alfred**：King Alfred, or Alfred the Great, was one of the earliest and most important English kings. He was a pillar of light in the Dark Ages. As a boy, he went to Rome with his father and learnt much of Roman civilization. In 871 AD, he became king and took his duties very earnestly. When the Danes from North Europe began to invade the ancient England, Alfred, as the king, led his people to fight against their invasion. It is he who built a naval force and later became known as "the Father of the British Navy". This good man died in 901 and now lies buried in Winchester Cathedral, southern England.

4. **History of the English Church and People**：Bede's *History of the English Church and People*, originally written in Latin, was translated into Old English during the reign of King Alfred the Great. It became a classic and helped the people of the emerging English nation take pride in their past. *The History* itself is more than a chronicle of events. It also contains legends, lives of saints, local traditions, and stories. From Bede's writing, one can get a fairly accurate picture of Anglo-Saxon daily life.

5. **Westminster Abbey**：An architectural masterpiece of the 13th to 16th centuries, Westminster Abbey also presents a unique pageant of British history—the Confessor's Shrine, the tombs of kings and queens, and countless memorials to the famous and the great. It has been the setting for every coronation since 1066 and for numerous other Royal occasions. Today it is still a church dedicated to regular worship and to the celebration of great events in the life of the nation.

For Fun

Books to read

1. *Great English Monarchs and Their Times*, by Gina Clemen.
   This book helps to understand the English monarchs and their times. Today some of their actions seem cruel or extravagant. But remember that their times were very different from ours.

2. *Julius Caesar*, by William Shakespeare.
   Julius Caesar was a highly successful but ambitious political leader of Rome and his goal was to become an unassailable dictator. Caesar was warned that he needed to "beware the Ides of March". The prophecy came true and Caesar was assassinated.

Marcus Brutus was a well respected Roman senator who helped plan and carried out Caesar's assassination which he believed would rid Rome of a tyrant. Caesar's friend Mark Antony provided the famous funeral oration ("Friends, Romans, and countrymen..."). Brutus and Cassius met their inevitable defeat. Brutus, the noble Roman, whose decision to take part in the conspiracy for the sake of freedom, plunged his country into civil war.

Websites to visit（本书出现的网站访问日期为 2023 年 3 月 5 日）

1. http://www.etymonline.com/index.php

   This is an online etymology dictionary. If you are interested in word origins, this page is definitely your first choice.

2. http://www.bbc.co.uk/history/british/normans/after_01.shtml

   This BBC British history webpage provides a detailed account about the Norman Conquest and its aftermath.

3. http://www.britannia.com/history/h12.html

   This page is a comprehensive information resource of King Arthur.

Movie to see

1. *Julius Caesar*（1953）

   Brutus, Cassius, and other high-ranking Romans murder Caesar, because they believe his ambition will lead to tyranny. The people of Rome are on their side until Antony, Caesar's right-hand man, makes a moving speech. The conspirators are driven out from Rome, and two armies are formed: one side following the conspirators; the other, Antony. Antony has the superior force, and surrounds Brutus and Cassius, but they kill themselves to avoid capture.

2. *Camelot*（1967）

   In England, King Arthur first encounters his bride-to-be, Guenevere, in the enchanted forest surrounding his castle at Camelot. Following their royal wedding, Arthur's happiness inspires him to establish the Knights of the Round Table, an order of chivalry in which all members will be bound by a common desire to aid the oppressed, keeping faith with trust and honor. However, the romance between Guinevere and Lancelot destroys King Arthur's dream kingdom.

Song to enjoy
Will You Go to Sheriffmuir by James Hogg

Will ye go tae Sheriffmuir
Bauld John o'Innisture,
There tae see the noble Mar
And his Hieland laddies.
A' the true men o' the north,
Angus, Huntly, and Seaforth
Scouring on tae cross the Forth
Wi' their white cockadies.

There ye'll see the banners flare;
There ye'll hear the bagpipes rair,
And the trumpets deadly blare
Wi' the cannons' rattle.

There ye'll see the bauld McCraws,
Cameron's and Clanronald's raws
And a' the clans, wi' loud huzzas,
Rushing tae the battle.

There ye'll see the noble Whigs,
A' the heroes o' the brigs,
Raw hides and withered wigs,
Ridin' in array, man.
Riv'n hose and raggit hools,
Sour milk and girnin' gools,
Psaldonotuse-beuks and cutty-stools,
We'll see never mair, man.

Will ye go tae Sheriffmuir,
Bauld John o' Innisture,
Sic a day and sic an hour
Ne'er was in the North, man.
Siccan sights will there be seen,
And gin some be nae mista'en,
Fragrant gales will come bedeen,
Frae the waters o' Forth, man.

Unit 2
The Normans

> Specially marked by cunning, despising their own inheritance in the hope of winning a greater, eager after both gain and dominion, given to imitation of all kinds, holding a certain mean between lavishness and greediness—that is, perhaps uniting, as they certainly did, these two seemingly opposite qualities.
>
> —Geoffrey Malaterra

Unit Goals

- To know the succession of the Norman kings
- To understand the feudal system after the Norman Conquest
- To know the significance of the *Doomsday Book*
- To learn words and expressions that describe England after the Norman Conquest and improve English language skills
- To develop critical thinking and intercultural communication skills

Before You Read

(1) Do you know the following kings? Who are the Norman kings? Figure out what happened to them while reading Text A.

William I 1066—1087　William II 1087—1100　Henry I 1100—1135

Stephen 1135—1154　Henry II 1154—1189　Richard I 1189—1199

(2) We all know that William I is usually called "William the Conqueror" in history. Do you know that William was known as "William the Bastard" to his enemies? Figure out the reasons for such a nickname.

(3) What do you know about the feudal system that was established after the Norman Conquest? Form groups of three or four students. Try to find, on the Internet or in the library, more information about the development of feudalism after the Norman Conquest. Get ready for a 5-minute presentation in class.

Start to Read

Text A　　The Norman Monarchs

1. As soon as William had been crowned, he began to organize the government of England on the system that had been so successful in Normandy. This is called the feudal system, and it was based on the ownership of land. William took the land away from its English owners and divided it among his Norman lords, including his bishops and abbey leaders.

2. The lord's land was then divided among the 5000 knights who had fought at Hastings. Each knight had to swear loyalty to his lord; he also had to give him forty days of army service every year. The lords themselves had to swear loyalty to the king and they had to supply knights for his service. A knight's land was called his manor, and the common people belonged to the knight on whose manor they lived. They had to serve him as farm-workers but not as soldiers; only the king himself could call them out to fight in times of trouble. There was also a small class of freemen, who did not have to work on the knight's farm.

3. In Normandy, William had had much trouble with lords who grew too powerful. He was determined not to have the same trouble in England. Instead of giving each of them one large piece of land, he gave them several small pieces in different parts of the country.

4. All the lords had the right to attend the king's council, and it was his duty to ask their advice. William held council meetings nearly every day wherever he happened to be. Usually only a few lords were present besides his secretaries and state officials. But three times a year he held a ceremonial council for Christian feasts and wore his crown: in Winchester for Easter, in London for Whitsun, and in Gloucester for Christmas. Then every lord had to attend.

5. Winchester castle was still the seat of government. Here William set up his government office, which controlled the collection of taxes and kept account of all expenses. From this office, men were sent out in 1086 to make a detailed record of all the wealth of England. Their work, the *Doomsday Book*, gives us a complete description of the country.

6. The sheriff was the king's representative in each county and he held the rank of a lord. He ruled over the county courts without interference from the Church, for William had given the bishops their own courts. This was an important step, for it allowed the English Common Law to develop freely while the church courts were tied to the laws of Rome. But it also led to serious trouble because any servant of the Church could claim the right to be tried by his bishop and not by a public court.

7. County courts took important cases but manor courts dealt with local affairs and even the lords had their own courts to protect their feudal interests. When William was crowned, he swore to respect the ancient laws of England. But his Norman sheriffs and landowners did not know these laws, so a group of local people had to attend each court as advisers.

8. *The Anglo-Saxon Chronicle* of those days gives thanks for "the good peace that he made in the land", but William's troubles did not end at Hastings. The northern lords, who had not fought there, rose against him twice. His revenge was prompt and terrible. After his army had passed, no human being was left alive and no house was left standing. Norman castles were built all over the country, especially on the Welsh border, and the citizens of London were disturbed to see William's famous Tower of London rise beside their walls.

9. But castles were not his only means of controlling his new kingdom. The Church was a stronger and more effective weapon. England was already Christian, and the people were accustomed to obeying their priests. It was easy to appoint Norman bishops in place of the Saxons, and the parish priests would do what they were told. William appointed an experienced lawyer called Lanfranc as Archbishop of Canterbury, and he treated him as the head of his government. When William was away in Normandy, Lanfranc ruled for him. Meanwhile the bishops quickly made their influence felt through their new courts and their seats in council, where they held the rank of lord.

10. When William died, he left Normandy to his eldest son, Robert, and England to his second son, William Rufus. Rufus was an ugly and evil character, who scorned religion and took delight in cruelty. But he built Westminster Hall, which was the national seat of justice until the 19th century.

11. No one was sorry when Rufus was shot dead while hunting in the New Forest, and his brother Henry took his place. Henry's first thought was to reunite England and Normandy. Most of his lords owned land in both countries and they gladly supported his plan. In 1106, just forty years after Hastings, an English army under Henry's command defeated Robert and seized Normandy.

12. Henry had already done much to earn the loyalty of his English people. He was born in England and knew the English language and law. He married the daughter of King Malcolm of Scotland and Queen Margaret, who belonged to the Saxon royal house. His father had given a charter of freedom to London; he now gave charters to towns that helped him to conquer Normandy, and he let London elect its own sheriff. These charters were official papers which gave freedom from various feudal duties and allowed the towns to run their own affairs. They helped to increase trade, both at home and abroad, and coal from Newcastle began to reach France in exchange for wine, though wool and cloth were still the basis of the country's trade.

13. Henry made Normans and English equal before the law. His travelling officials checked the work of the sheriffs and their courts so that gradually the same law was applied all through the land. He was well liked because he kept the peace, but he must bear part of the blame for the terrible years that followed his death.

14. Henry was the last of the true Norman kings, for his only son was drowned at sea. He planned to leave the kingdom to his daughter Matilda, whose husband ruled all the land between Normandy and the River Loire. But England was not yet ready to be ruled by a woman, and on Henry's death the lords appointed his nephew Stephen as their king. Stephen was popular and he had an English wife, but he was weak. Matilda soon bribed half the lords to support her, and for nineteen years the two sides fought each other. Men and cattle were killed in thousands; towns and villages were destroyed; harvests were rotten in the fields.

15. At last Matilda's husband died, and the lords who had refused to accept Matilda were willing to accept her son (Henry II). The archbishop arranged a settlement, and the lords agreed to pull down all the castles—about a thousand—that they had built during the war. Stephen then conveniently died. "A mild man", said the *Saxon Chronicle*, "soft and good, but he did no justice". The *Chronicle* itself, which had begun with the great deeds of King

Alfred, now ended with the sad story of human misery under Stephen.

16. In spite of Stephen, the Normans had left to England a framework of government which a strong king could develop with success and a strong king was coming. They had also set England firmly on the path of European civilization, which would have been long delayed if they had been content to forget Normandy and settle quietly in their island. When Henry's English army defeated Robert, it was setting a pattern for the future. For five hundred years after the conquest, English kings struggled to hold and extend their French lands by battle and by marriage.

After You Read

Knowledge Focus

1. **Pair Work**
   Discuss the following questions with your partner.
   (1) In what way did William organize the government of England, after he was crowned?
   (2) Do you think we should be grateful to William because of his severe law that was hated by everybody then? Why or why not?
   (3) What did William do in order to avoid troubles he had in Normandy?
   (4) Do you know the origin of Whitsun? Share your knowledge with your classmates.
   (5) What do you know about the English Common Law? Find more information and share with your classmates.
   (6) Who was William Rufus? Why did nobody feel sorry when Rufus was shot dead?
   (7) What did Henry I do to earn the loyalty of his English people?
   (8) Who was Matilda? What happened between Matilda and Stephen after Henry's death?
   (9) Who was the last true Norman king?
   (10) What contributions did the Normans do to England?

2. **Solo Work**
   Tell whether and why the following are true or false according to the knowledge you have learned.
   ＿＿ (1) William began to organize the government of England on the system based on the ownership of land.
   ＿＿ (2) William took the land away from its English owners and divided it among his Norman lords, including his bishops and abbey leaders.
   ＿＿ (3) The common people belonged to the knight on whose manor they lived. They had to serve him as farm-workers and as soldiers.
   ＿＿ (4) William held ceremonial council for Christian feasts and wore his crown three times a year: in Winchester for Easter, in London for Whitsun, and in

Gloucester for Christmas.

_____ (5) The Church interfered with the county courts ruled by sheriff.

_____ (6) When William was crowned, he swore to respect the ancient laws of England.

_____ (7) William controlled the country only by building castles all over the country.

_____ (8) When William died, he left Normandy to his eldest son, Robert. And he built Westminster Hall, which was the national seat of justice until the 19th century.

_____ (9) In 1106, just fifty years after Hastings, an English army under Henry's command defeated Robert and seized Normandy.

_____ (10) Henry gave charters to towns and he let London elect its own sheriff. These charters gave freedom from various feudal duties and allowed the towns to run their own affairs.

Language Focus

1. Fill in the blanks with the following words or expressions you have learned in the text. Put them into appropriate forms if necessary.

under the command of	apply	prompt	conquest
bribe	in place of	scorn	disturb
in exchange for	ceremonial		

(1) They've written back already—that was a very _____ reply.

(2) Some scenes in this sitcom are violent and may _____ younger viewers.

(3) You can use margarine _____ butter in some recipes.

(4) So does he respect the press and media, or does he secretly _____ them?

(5) The soldiers who were _____ a tough sergeant-major were renowned for their bravery.

(6) Those citizens, who were involved in this non-governmental organization, were given food and shelter _____ work.

(7) The court heard how the driver had failed to _____ his brakes in time.

(8) He _____ immigration officials and entered the country illegally.

(9) A head of state may not have much political power, and may be restricted to _____ duties, for instance, meeting ambassador, laying wreath at national memorials, opening parliament, etc.

(10) Her _____ of cancer moved many to tears.

2. Find the appropriate prepositions that collocate with the neighboring words.

(1) The feudal system was based _____ the ownership of land. William took the land away from its English owners and divided it _____ his Norman lords, including his bishops and abbey leaders.

(2) The lord's land was then divided _____ the 5000 knights who had fought at Hastings.

(3) In Normandy, William had had much trouble _____ lords who grew too powerful.

(4) Winchester castle was still the seat of government. Here William set _____ his government office, which controlled the collection of taxes and kept account of all expenses.

(5) This was an important step, for it allowed the English Common Law to develop freely while the church courts were tied _____ the laws of Rome.

(6) County courts took important cases but manors courts dealt _____ local affairs and even the lords had their own courts to protect their feudal interests.

(7) Norman castles were built all over the country, especially _____ the Welsh border, and the citizens of London were disturbed to see William's famous Tower of London rise beside their walls.

(8) Henry must bear part of the blame _____ the terrible years that followed his death.

Comprehensive Work

1. Group Work

Read the following introduction to the *Doomsday Book*, and find more information about it to share with your classmates. Discuss the significance of the *Doomsday Book*.

The *Doomsday Book* is one of Medieval England's greatest treasures. It is closely linked with William the Conqueror's attempt to dominate Medieval England. Along with a string of castles throughout England, the *Doomsday Book* was to give William huge authority in England.

To further extend his grip on England, William I ordered that a book be made containing information on who owned what throughout the country. This book would also tell him who owed him what in tax and because the information was on record, nobody could dispute or argue against a tax demand. This is why the book brought doom and gloom to the people of England—hence the *Doomsday Book*.

2. Pair Work

Below is a family tree of Norman kings. Please retell to your partner what happened to these Norman kings.

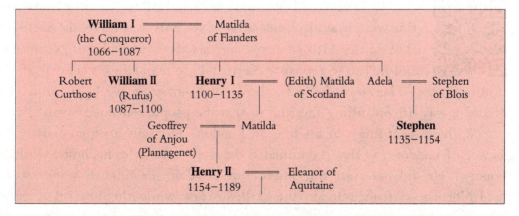

3. Writing Activity

The year 1066 was very important in history of Britain. William leapt ashore as he invaded Anglo Saxon England in September 1066. His forces met the English army led by King Harold at the Battle of Hastings. After a grueling fight, King Harold was killed and William became the first Norman King of England.

What qualities do you see in William? What qualities make a great leader out of an average person? Do leaders see the hidden opportunity in every setback? Is there really such thing as a "born leader"? Write an essay of about 300 words to air your views.

Read More

Text B　**Feudalism after the Norman Conquest**

　　Feudalism is the name given to the system of government William I introduced to England after he defeated Harold at the Battle of Hastings. Feudalism became a way of life in Medieval England and remained so for many centuries.

William I is better known as William the Conqueror. He had defeated the English army led by Harold but he had to gain control of all of England before he could be truly called King of England. He was a foreigner who had forced his way to London. He was not popular with the people of England and he had to use force to maintain his control on England.

　　William could not rule every part of the country himself—this was physically impossible. Not only was travel difficult and slow in the 11th century, he was also still Duke of Normandy and he had to return to Normandy to maintain his control of this land in France. Therefore, he had to leave the country for weeks at a time. He needed a way of controlling England so that the people remained loyal.

William spent much of his time in London. He built his own castle—the Tower of London—so that it dominated the city. It was also his home while in London. He did not trust the builders of London—or English stone—so he used Norman craftsmen to do the skilled work while the English acted as laborers and he brought in from Caen in France the stone needed for what we now call the White Tower. He also built the first castle at Windsor. Castles represented a visible threat to the people of England. Soldiers were kept in them and they could be used against the English should they cause trouble.

However, he needed a way of actually governing the country. This was the feudal system. William divided up England into very large plots of land. These were given to those noblemen who had fought bravely for him in battle. William argued that those noblemen who were willing to die in battle for him would also be loyal to him. The land was not simply given to these nobles. They had to swear an oath of loyalty to William; they had to collect taxes in their areas for him and they had to provide the king with soldiers if they were told to do so. In the 11th century, a sworn oath on the *Bible* was a very important thing that few men would dare to break as it would condemn them to Hell. The men who got these parcels of land would have been barons, earls and dukes. Within their own area, they were the most important person there. In the terms of the feudal system, these men, the barons etc., were known as tenants-in-chief.

Even these pieces of land were large and difficult to govern.

The barons etc. had to further divide up their land and these were given to trusted Norman knights who had also fought well in battle. Each knight was given a segment of land to govern. He had to swear an oath to the baron, duke or earl, collect taxes when told to do so and provide soldiers from his land when they were needed.

It was argued, that because they had sworn an oath to their baron, they had really sworn an oath to the king. These lords worked to maintain law and order. The people in their land—or manors—were treated harshly and there was always the constant threat of Norman soldiers being used against the English people wherever they lived. The lords had to do their job well as unsuccessful ones could be removed from their positions. Their job was simple—keeping the English people in their place under the control of the Normans. Under the feudal system, these men, the knights, were called sub-tenants.

Note that both groups were officially tenants—a word we associate with land that does not belong to you. Both all but rented out their land in that they had to provide money or services to the real owner of all land—William the Conqueror. At the bottom of the ladder were the conquered English who had to do what they were told or pay the price for their disobedience.

There is no doubt that William's rule was harsh. But he was a man who had conquered the country. He was not in England through the popular choice of the people and he had to ensure that he had full control over them at all times. He ensured that there were obvious signs of his power—the country saw the building of many Norman castles. He also knew what was owed to him because he ordered a survey of the whole country—the *Doomsday Book*.

1. Questions for discussion or reflection.
  (1) What did William do to the establishment of feudalism in England?
  (2) Can you describe the early feudal system in detail?

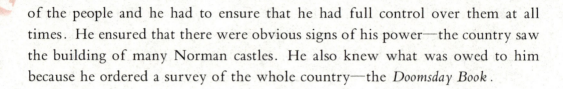

Text C   The Doomsday Book

The *Doomsday Book*, compiled in 1085—1086, is one of the few historical records whose name is familiar to most people in Britain. It is the earliest public record, the foundation document of the national archives and a legal document that is still valid as evidence of title to land.

Based on the Doomsday survey of 1085—1086, which was drawn up on the orders of King William I, it describes in remarkable detail, the landholdings and resources of the late 11th-century England, demonstrating the power of the government machine in the first century of the new Millennium, and its deep thirst for information.

It is an exercise unparalleled in contemporary Europe, and is not matched in its comprehensive coverage of the country until the population census in the 19th century—although Doomsday itself is not a full population census, and the names that appeared in it are mainly only those who owned land.

Used for many centuries for administrative and legal purposes, the *Doomsday Book* is the starting point for most local historians researching the history of their area and there are several versions in print which should be available through good reference libraries. Despite its iconic significance, it has been subjected to increasingly detailed textual analysis by historians who warn us that not everything it says should be taken at face value.

Providing definitive proofs of rights to land and obligations to tax and military service, its 913 pages and two million Latin words describe more than

13,000 places in England and parts of Wales. Nicknamed "the Doomsday Book" by the native English, after God's final Day of Judgment, when every soul would be assessed and against which there could be no appeal, this title was eventually adopted by its official custodian, known for years as the Public Record Office, and later renamed the National Archives.

The *Doomsday Book* records all land and property, as well as every mill and cottage, as well as every cow and pig. It also records the rights and duties of every landowner and every court. Such records were grouped by counties and by manors, as these were the usual groups for tax collection. The king fixed an amount for each county; his sheriff divided this amount between the manors; and the owner of each manor collected the money from his people.

1. Questions for discussion or reflection.
   (1) What is the *Doomsday Book* about? Who ordered the book should be compiled?
   (2) Why was this historical record nicknamed "the Doomsday Book"?
   (3) Why did William send his clerks to compile the property record known as the *Doomsday Book*?
   (4) Why do people think highly of the *Doomsday Book*?

Proper Names

Battle of Hastings 黑斯廷斯战役
the *Doomsday Book*《末日审判书》

Archbishop of Canterbury 坎特伯雷大主教
River Loire 卢瓦尔河（法国最长河流）

Notes

1. **Whitsun**: Whitsun is the old English for "White Sunday". It usually falls on the 49th day (7th Sunday) after Easter Sunday. In the Christian calendar, it is also known as Pentecost, commemorating the descent of the Holy Spirit upon the disciples.
2. ***The Anglo-Saxon Chronicle***: It is a collection of annals in Old English chronicling the history of the Anglo-Saxons. The annals were created late in the 9th century, probably in Wessex, during the reign of Alfred the Great. Multiple manuscript copies were made and distributed to monasteries across England and were independently updated. In one case, the chronicle was still being actively updated in 1154.
3. **Tower of London**: The Tower is a historic monument in central London, England, on the north bank of the River Thames. It is located within the London Borough of Tower Hamlets and is separated from the eastern edge of the City of London by the open space known as Tower Hill.

For Fun

Books to read

1. *The Conqueror: A Novel of William the Conqueror* by Georgette Heyer

   The narrative follows the life and achievements of William, Duke of Normandy through the eyes of one of his young knights, the fictional Raoul de Harcourt. Major events of William's life, from his illegitimate birth to his coronation as King of England in 1066, are described with fine detail.

2. *The King's Shadow* by Elizabeth Alder

   Evyn, a young Welsh serf, has dreamed all his life of becoming a storyteller. But in a cruel twist of fate, Evyn and his father suffer a brutal attack by a group of murderous ruffians. Evyn's tongue is cut off and his father is killed. Orphaned and unable to speak, Evyn assumes he is destined to a life of slavery. But Evyn is resilient and teaches himself to read and write. He is then appointed the personal companion to Earl Harold of Wessex, who later becomes King of England. The two travel the countryside together, forming a close father-son bond. Evyn chronicles all of their exciting journeys, which culminate at the Battle of Hastings, where the future of the country is decided.

Websites to visit

1. The Normans

   http://www.historyonthenet.com/Normans/normansmain.htm

   This page contains a comprehensive listing of all main factors about the Normans.

2. History of Normans

   http://www.bbc.co.uk/history/british/normans/

   On this page, you can see a well-written overview and a game based on the battle.

Song to enjoy

Song of the Shield-Wall
Words by Lady Malkin Grey, music by Lady Peregrynne Windrider

Hasten, oh sea-steed, over the swan-road,
Foamy-necked ship o'er the froth of the sea,
Hengest has called us from Gotland and Frisia
To Vortigern's country his army to be
We'll take our pay there in sweeter than silver;
We'll take our plunder in richer than gold,
For Hengest has promised us land for the fighting

Land for the sons of the Saxons to hold!

Hasten, oh fyrdsmen, down to the river
The dragonships come on the in-flowing tide
The linden-wood shield and the old spear of ash-wood
Are needed again by the cold water-side

Draw up the shield-wall, oh shoulder companions
Later whenever our story is told
They'll say that we died guarding what we call dearest,
Land that the sons of the Saxons will hold!

Hasten, oh Huscarls, north to the Dane-Law
Harold Hardrada's come over the sea
His longships he's laden with berserks from Norway
To gain Cnut's crown and our master to be
Bitter he'll find there the bite of our spear points
Hard-running Northmen too strong to die old
We'll grant him six feet, plus as much as he's taller
Of land that the sons of the Saxons will hold!

Make haste, son of Godwin, southward from Stamford
Triumph is sweet and your men have fought hard
But William the Bastard has landed at Pevensey
Burning the land you have promised to guard
Draw up the spears on the hilltop at Hastings
Fight 'til the sun drops and evening grows cold
And die with the last of your Saxons around you
Holding the land we were given to hold!

Unit 3
The Early Plantagenet

> Good order is the foundation of all things.
> —E. Burke
>
> Law is the crystallization of the habit and thought of society.
> —Woodrow Wilson

Unit Goals

- To get a general idea about the family of Plantagenet
- To know the reforms of courts and laws by Henry II
- To learn about the story of Henry II and Thomas Becket
- To learn the important words and expressions that describe the Plantagenet and improve English language skills
- To develop critical thinking and intercultural communication skills

Before You Read

(1) Do you still remember the stories about the Norman kings? Fill in the blanks based on what you have learned in Unit 2.

A. William Rufus	B. Henry I	C. Normandy	D. Robert

   William died in __(1)__ in 1087. He left Normandy to his eldest son named __(2)__, and England to his second son named __(3)__, and all his money to his third son Henry. William Rufus became known as William II, but he was killed by an arrow when he was hunting in the New Forest in 1100. His younger brother succeeded him and became known as __(4)__.

(2) How much do you know about the following terms? Share your knowledge about them with your partner.
   A. Jury System: _____
   _____

B. The Common Law: _____

C. Thomas Becket: _____
_____

(3) Form groups of three or four students. Try to find, on the Internet or in the library, more information about Henry II. Get ready for a 5-minute presentation in class.

Start to Read

Text A The Rule of Law

1. Few kings of England have done such lasting work as Henry II. He found the country in a state of ruin and confusion. He left it with a system of government and a habit of obedience that were able to keep the peace long after his death.

2. Under Henry, for the first time, conditions became settled enough for a steady increase in trade and in population. But he is best remembered for his reform of the courts and their law.

3. The new king found it absolutely necessary to limit the power of the barons. The barons had naturally regarded themselves as independent rulers within their fiefs. Their assumption was largely based on military strength without which they would not have dared to challenge the king's authority. So Henry II firstly destroyed all the fortresses which the barons had illegally built during the years. Then he ordered his barons to disband their hired foreign soldiers.

4. The new king took steps to reform the courts which had actually been left in the control of the local barons. Henry sent out his own judges, known as circuit judges, to make regular tours of the country, and any freeman could take a case to them if he did not trust the local courts. Serious offenses and land cases could only be dealt with by judges, so lords could no longer use their own courts to steal lands from their weaker neighbors. Now the on-the-spot investigation and trials could, to a certain extent, uncover their illegal actions and punish offenders.

5. Most important of all was Henry's jury system. The jury was a group of people who helped a judge in court. Nowadays they listen to witnesses and then decide whether the accused is guilty, but this practice did not develop till the 15th century. In Henry's day, the members of the jury were witnesses themselves, and no man could be tried unless a jury of twelve men swore that there was a true case against him. This was real progress, for men had often been tried with no witnesses at all. The jury system not only made it easier for the judges to collect evidence but also helped to avoid possible mistakes.

6. In criminal cases, the methods used by the jury were called "trial by ordeal" which meant corporal punishment. One of them was named "ordeal by fire". The accused held a hot iron bar and walked three paces. If the man was burnt and injured by holding the iron, he was guilty. In other cases, a man was tied up and thrown into water. If he floated, he was guilty of the crime he was accused of. The cruel practice went on until 1215, as people gradually doubted the ordeal method and replaced it with court debate.

7. There was no written law to tell judges how to punish each offender. In England now, there are two kinds of law: the laws made by the government, which are called Acts, and the Common Law. This Common Law was first gathered by Henry II. It reflects court judgments through ages. The judges made their decisions by relying on the verdicts made by a circuit court in similar cases. These verdicts were known as "precedents", which became the basis of English "Common Law". The Common Law was actually a judge-made law based on the various local customs of the Anglo-Saxons in dealing with offences.

8. Only two things spoiled Henry's peace: his quarrels with his sons and his quarrels with Archbishop Becket.

9. Henry had problems within his only family. His sons—Henry, Geoffrey, Richard and John—mistrusted each other and resented their father's policy of dividing land among them. There were serious family disputes in 1173, 1181 and 1184. The king's attempt to find an inheritance for John led to opposition from Richard and Philip II of France. Henry was forced to give way; news that John had also turned against him hastened Henry's death on 6 July, 1189.

10. It was natural that his sons should sometimes stir his temper, but the matter of Becket was more serious. Many practices of the

church courts were an insult to Henry's rule of law, for they often let even murderers go unpunished. Henry decided that criminal clerks must in future be tried by his own courts. Public opinions supported him, and most bishops agreed. So did the Pope, who was then living in France to escape the German Emperor. But Thomas Becket was a proud and fierce-tempered man like Henry himself; he refused

to agree and fled abroad. Five years later, he returned and preached against the king in Canterbury Cathedral.

11. When Henry heard of this, he lost his temper completely: "Would no one get rid of the troublesome priest?" Four knights who heard his words went straight to Canterbury and killed Becket inside his own cathedral. Henry was sincerely sorry and he let the monks of Canterbury beat him publicly for his wicked temper. But Becket's murder forced him to drop the matter of church courts, which remained a serious cause of annoyance to the common people.

12. Becket was really a rough fellow, but after his murder he was regarded as a holy man. Bottles of Canterbury water were soon sold for high prices, and men claimed that prayers to Becket had healed their sickness. Two hundred years later the poet Chaucer described in *The Canterbury Tales* how men still travelled from all England to pray at Becket's grave.

13. By the end of the 12th century, all the royal offices had been moved from Winchester to Westminster, which thus became the nation's capital. In modern times, we call London the capital because this name covers not only the old city of London but all its extensions, including Westminster. At that time, however, Westminster was quite separate.

14. The strength of Henry's work was soon proved by his sons. Richard I was only in England for ten months of his ten years' rule. The government carried on without serious trouble while he was away on the crusades. These crusades were religious wars, in which the Christian kings of Europe tried to win the control of the holy city of Jerusalem from the Turks. Earlier English kings had not joined them, but Richard was a popular and able soldier who loved adventure. His success in battle won him undying glory but it annoyed the jealous king of Austria, who seized him on his way home and imprisoned him in a castle.

15. During his absence, the government was in the hands of Archbishop

Walter, who was well supported by the knights and by the middle-class townsmen. He gave charters of freedom to towns that helped to pay for Richard's crusade. He also let London elect an independent head of its city council and gave him the title of Mayor. When Richard was imprisoned, his brother tried to seize power, but the lords and London's mayor remained loyal.

16. They helped Walter to defeat him and to buy Richard's freedom. It was a sad day for England when Richard was later killed in France. He had won the love and respect of all classes, as Sir Walter Scott had described in *Ivanhoe*.

After You Read

Knowledge Focus

1. **Pair Work**

   Discuss the following questions with your partner.

   (1) What was Henry II best remembered for?

   (2) What measures did Henry II take to reform the courts?

   (3) How do you understand the "circuit judges" during the reign of Henry II?

   (4) What was the significance of the appearance of jury system?

   (5) Can you exemplify the "trial by ordeal"?

   (6) What was the basis of the English Common Law?

   (7) What were the problems that Henry II had within his only family?

   (8) Who was Thomas Becket?

   (9) What happened between Henry II and Thomas Becket?

   (10) How do you define the crusades?

2. **Solo Work**

   Tell whether and why the following are true or false according to the knowledge you have learned.

   _____ (1) In 1162, Henry made Becket Archbishop of Canterbury, hoping he would assist him in reforming the church courts. But Becket stood firmly with the church.

   _____ (2) Henry II's rule, taken as a whole, was full of achievements. Feudal order was further strengthened and the country experienced a period of security and prosperity.

   _____ (3) During Henry II's reign, the judges had to make decisions by relying on English written laws.

   _____ (4) The barons had naturally regarded themselves as independent rulers within their fiefs.

   _____ (5) It was a sad day for England when Richard was later killed in France. He had won the love and respect of all classes, as Henry James had described in *Ivanhoe*.

____ (6) The Common Law was first gathered by William Rufus.

____ (7) In England now there are two kinds of law: the laws made by the government, which are called Acts, and the Common Law.

____ (8) In criminal cases, the methods used by the jury were called "ordeal by fire" which meant corporal punishment.

____ (9) By the end of the 12th century, all the royal offices had been moved from Winchester to Westminster, which thus became the nation's capital.

____ (10) King John quarreled with the Pope because of the choice of an archbishop, finally the king won.

Language Focus

1. Fill in the blanks with the following words or expressions you have learned in the text. Put them into appropriate forms if necessary.

confusion	obedience	offense	accused
spoil	wicked	annoyance	glory
imprison	in the hands of		

(1) The General demanded absolute _____ from his men.
(2) The designs reflect the _____ of French fashion.
(3) The knowledge of his own ingratitude convinced him that he was _____ and worthless.
(4) This matter is too important to be left _____ an inexperienced lawyer.
(5) I hope the meeting will clear up people's _____.
(6) Such considerations affect the way the courts decide on what sentence to pass on the _____.
(7) The possession of stolen property is a criminal _____.
(8) His jealousy _____ their relationship and she left him after a few months.
(9) If convicted, she will _____ for at least six years.
(10) Smoking in public places is a tremendous _____ to non-smokers.

2. Find the appropriate prepositions that collocate with the neighboring words.

(1) Henry II found the country _____ a state of ruin and confusion.
(2) He is best remembered _____ his reform of the courts and their law.
(3) Serious offenses and land cases could only be dealt _____ by judges.
(4) A man was tied _____ and thrown _____ water.
(5) If he floated, he was guilty _____ the crime he was accused _____.
(6) The judges made their decisions by relying _____ the verdicts made by a circuit court in similar cases.

(7) The king's attempt to find an inheritance for John led _____ opposition from Richard and Philip II of France.

(8) Bottles of Canterbury water were soon sold _____ high prices.

(9) _____ the end of the 12th century, all the royal offices had been moved from Winchester to Westminster.

(10) Richard I was only in England for ten months of his ten years' rule. The government carried _____ without serious trouble while he was away on the crusades.

Comprehensive Work

1. **Pair Work**

   Read the following passage and fill in the missing information in the following box. Learn more about the House of Plantagenet on the Internet afterwards.

   The early Plantagents ruled England from 1154 to 1399, and were succeeded by the rival Houses of Lancaster and York, who were themselves both direct descendants of the early Plantagenets. The surname came from the flowering broom plant (Planta genista), said to have been worn as a badge by Geoffrey, Count of Anjou between 1129—1151 who was the father of the first Plantagenet King of England, Henry II. The members of the dynasty often had fiery and violent tempers, possessed huge amounts of courage and imposed themselves fully on their kingdoms. Richard I said of his family: "From the Devil we sprang and to the Devil we shall go."

   Under the Plantagenets, huge advances were made regarding constitutional reform. The origins of Common Law originated under Henry II as did trial by jury, and the first Parliament was held in 1265, albeit against the contemporary monarch Henry III. Military conquest also featured heavily, with Wales and Ireland subjected to English rule, and inroads made into Scottish and French territory.

The origin of "Plantagenet"	
The first king of "Plantagenet"	
Characteristics of its members	
Major achievements	

Read More

Text B *The Canterbury Tales*

What do you do to pass the time on a long trip? Do you play video games or watch a DVD? Do you listen to your favorite CDs? Do you play tic-tac-toe or travel bingo?

Those are all good ways to pass the time, but travelers back in the Middle Ages could not have played even tic-tac-toe while they traveled. In medieval times, people traveled either on foot or on horseback, but there was one activity that they could enjoy to pass the time, and that was storytelling.

Sometimes medieval travelers told and retold stories that they had heard before. Sometimes they invented new stories.

Geoffrey Chaucer used this idea of a group of storytelling travelers as the frame for *The Canterbury Tales*.

The Canterbury Tales tells of a group of pilgrims traveling on horseback to the shrine of Thomas Becket at Canterbury Cathedral. They plan to take turns telling stories to pass the time.

The characters in *The Canterbury Tales* give a good picture of what life was like in the Middle Ages. They include people of all occupations and people of all social classes. This is unusual for a story written in the Middle Ages, since most literature of that time was about only the nobility or the clergy, but *The Canterbury Tales* includes many middle-class characters as well.

The pilgrims on their way to Canterbury include a knight, a squire, a clerk, a nun, a priest, a sergeant at arms, a cook, a friar, a summoner, a physician, a franklin, a haberdasher, a tapestry weaver, and a wife, among others. Each one has a distinct personality. This is another thing that makes *The Canterbury Tales* stand out among other stories of its time since medieval stories usually featured rather flat characters.

The knight is described as an honorable man who fought in the crusades. His son, the squire, on the other hand, is a young bachelor and admired by many young women. The friar in this story is not a good person; he is portrayed selfish and money-hungry. The summoner is also one of the bad guys; he is a cheater and is known for keeping bad company. The clerk is a poor student.

Each character has a story to tell.

The knight tells a romantic tale of two knights, Arcite and Palamon, fighting for the love of a young woman named Emelye.

The squire tells a tale of magic. In his story, a strange knight approaches King Arthur's court bearing gifts. He brings a brass horse that gives its owner the power to teleport to anywhere on the Earth. He also brings a mirror that reveals not just a person's face, but also his thoughts. His third gift is a ring that allows the wearer to understand the language of birds.

The friar tells a story about a summoner. In his story the summoner is sly and mean. He demands bribes from an old woman and threatens to take her to court if she does not pay.

The summoner responds by telling a tale about an evil friar. In his story, the friar goes to a sick man's house and demands that the wife cook him a feast.

The clerk's story is full of suspense. He tells of an Italian marquis who marries a girl named Griselda. He demands absolute obedience from Griselda and tests her by pretending that he is sending her children away to be killed. Then he pretends that he is going to take a new wife and has Griselda prepare a wedding for them.

These are only samples of the tales; there are many more, twenty-six all together. With all of these great stories to listen to, the pilgrims must have been in Canterbury before they knew it.

1. Finish the multiple-choice questions according to Text B.

(1) *The Canterbury Tales* was written by _____.
  A. Geoffrey Chaucer   B. Thomas Becket
  C. Palamon   D. Griselda

(2) The frame of *The Canterbury Tales* is _____.
  A. the pilgrims telling stories on their trip
  B. the conflict between the friar and the summoner
  C. King Arthur's court
  D. the differences between the knight and the squire

(3) The clerk tells a story about _____.
  A. a husband who demands total obedience
  B. a greedy friar
  C. three magical gifts
  D. two knights fighting over a lady

(4) The squire tells a story about _____.
  A. three magical gifts
  B. a husband who demands total obedience
  C. a greedy friar
  D. two knights fighting over a lady

(5) *The Canterbury Tales* is an unusual piece of literature from the Middle Ages because _____.
- A. it describes the characters' personalities
- B. it includes middle class characters
- C. both A and B
- D. neither A nor B

(6) There are _____ stories in *The Canterbury Tales*.
  A. 5   B. 26   C. 15   D. 6

2. Writing Activity

In *The Canterbury Tales*, a group of English pilgrims set out on a pilgrimage from London to Canterbury to pay their respects to the tomb of Saint Thomas Becket at Canterbury Cathedral. The group is described in detail, with characters from all classes. Harry Bailey, an innkeeper, suggests that as a game they all tell stories to each other along the way. The tale-telling begins with the knight and proceeds as the pilgrims travel to Canterbury, each person telling a story that reflects their social position, and some telling stories which are intended to make fun of others in the group.

Suppose you were one of the English pilgrims, what story would you like to tell so as to amuse others? Write your story briefly within 300 words. Your story should reflect either your personal experience or your social position.

Text C   The Crusades

Palestine, sometimes called the Holy Land, has seen more than its share of troubles. It has been at the center of many fights over the centuries. In the Middle Ages, it was the scene of the First Crusade.

The First Crusade began in 1095 when Pope Urban II made a speech in France. In his speech, he described attacks by Turkish Muslims on Christians of the Byzantine Empire. He called on European Christians to rush to defend the Holy Land from the Turks.

The offer of a papal indulgence, or forgiveness of all of a person's sins, encouraged many people to join the crusade. Serfs were allowed to leave the land they worked on to join the crusade. Crusaders were also excused from paying taxes. People from all walks of life, and from several nations, joined for a variety of reasons. Some people joined because of

religious enthusiasm. Some joined with the hope of gaining land, wealth, or power.

Soon, thousands of crusaders had joined, each wearing the red crusader's cross and shouting the battle cry, "God wills it!"

While the official armies were forming, an unofficial army of crusaders was growing larger and larger too. This throng was led by Peter the Hermit, a monk who had the gift of persuasive speech that could stir up a crowd to follow him. His group of unofficial peasant crusaders included men, women, and children. It became known as "the people's crusade" and eventually grew to a force of more than 10,000.

The official troops, commanded by Godfrey of Bouillon and other leaders, also included thousands of soldiers.

Both groups marched toward Palestine.

Along the way, some of the crusaders decided that they should begin fighting the enemies of Christianity closer to home. They attacked Muslims and Jews along the way. Many people died in these bloody fights.

By 1097, the armies arrived in the Holy Land, on the east coast of the Mediterranean Sea. They recaptured Nicaea, which had fallen to the Turks ten years earlier. The crusaders also prevailed in Antioch after a long blockade.

Eventually, they arrived at Jerusalem, a large and well-fortified city. There, the crusaders set themselves up like knights preparing to attack a castle. They built medieval siege equipment including siege towers for breaking through the city's walls and catapults for firing over them.

In an unusual move, the crusaders also marched in a solemn parade around the city's walls, possible hoping that it would crumble like the walls of Jericho in the Bible story. It did not.

The siege of Jerusalem was not meeting with much success either, until another unusual event inspired the crusaders. The inspiring event was the discovery of a lance, supposedly the very lance used to stab Christ on the cross. The discovery gave the crusaders renewed energy. They fought on, crying, "God wills it!" and were eventually victorious.

Jerusalem surrendered, and most of the crusaders went home. Others stayed and ruled lands that became known as the four Latin states of Edessa, Tripoli, Antioch, and Jerusalem.

The First Crusade was just one in a long, long series of wars in the Middle East. People all over the world are still affected by these conflicts today.

The First Crusade, in which Christian soldiers took control of Jerusalem from the Turks, was only the first in a long series of religious wars. These wars pitted Christian soldiers from western Europe against Muslim Turks. They occurred during the 11th through the 13th centuries.

Crusades were sponsored by popes and kings. Knights, peasants, and townspeople joined up, said good-bye to their families, and marched off to face death in the Middle East.

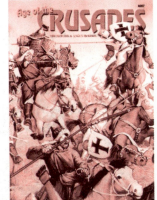

The Second Crusade occurred in 1147, after the Turks had once again begun to take back the land, known as the Latin States, which the Christians had seized in the First Crusade. This time, King Louis VII of France and King Conrad III of Germany led armies to the Holy Land. In this war, the crusaders were defeated, and after the Crusade ended, the area was united under the leadership of Saladin, the Sultan of Egypt and Syria.

In the Third Crusade, King Richard the Lionhearted of England and King Philip II of France made another attempt to retake the Holy Land. This time, they met with some successes and some failures. At the end of this crusade, King Richard made a treaty with Saladin which allowed Christian pilgrims to visit Jerusalem. This was an important step for the Christians, since the crusades had originally begun when the Turks refused to let Christians visit the Holy Land.

More crusades followed, eight major crusades in all, plus some smaller ones. As time went on, the crusades became even more about land, power, prestige, and money. Western Europe was becoming prosperous. It was increasing in military strength, and countries were anxious to fight to take over new lands.

1. Finish the following multiple-choice questions according to Text C.

(1) The First Crusade began when _____ gave a speech.
   A. Peter the Hermit   B. Godfrey of Bouillon
   C. Pope Urban II   D. none of the above

(2) _____ led "the people's crusade".
   A. Peter the Hermit   B. Godfrey of Bouillon
   C. Pope Urban II   D. none of the above

(3) The object of the First Crusade was to _____.
   A. defend the Holy Land from the Turks
   B. form new states in the Middle East
   C. defeat the Jews and the Muslims
   D. all of the above

(4) The First Crusade occurred in the _____ century.
   A. 10th   B. 9th   C. 11th   D. 19th
(5) After the siege of Jerusalem, _____.
   A. the Turks continued to rule Jerusalem
   B. religious groups were no longer involved in the rule of Jerusalem
   C. the Christians ruled Jerusalem
   D. the Jews ruled Jerusalem
(6) The crusaders fought against the _____ in the Middle East.
   A. Christians   B. Europeans
   C. Germans   D. Turks
(7) The crusades occurred _____.
   A. mostly before the 14th century
   B. mostly before the 11th century
   C. in 1147
   D. in 1100

Proper Names

Archbishop 大主教
Archbishop Walter 沃尔特大主教
Canterbury Cathedral 坎特伯雷大教堂
The Canterbury Tales《坎特伯雷故事集》
The Common Law《普通法》
The Crusades 十字军东征
Geoffrey 杰弗里
German Emperor 德国帝王

Henry II 亨利二世
Ivanhoe《艾凡赫》
Jerusalem 耶路撒冷
Philip II 菲利普二世
Plantagenet 金雀花王朝(1154—1485)
Pope 教皇
Richard I 理查一世
Thomas Becket 托马斯·贝克特

Notes

1. **Henry II (1154—1189)**: Henry II was the first Plantagenet king. He was one of the greatest Plantagenet kings, to whom the origins of the English Common Law and trial by jury can be traced. The territorial gains in Ireland and the curbing of baronial power were also hallmarks of his reign.

2. **The House of Plantagenet**: The Plantagenet dynasty ruled England for over three hundred years, from 1154—1485. They were a remarkable family, providing England with fourteen of its kings. The surname Plantagenet, one of the most famous in England, seems to have derived from a nickname adopted by Geoffrey, Count of Anjou, the father of Henry II and refers to his habit of wearing a sprig of broom or planta genista in his helmet.

3. **Thomas Becket (c. 1120—1170)**: Thomas Becket was born in around 1120, the son of

a prosperous London merchant. He was well educated and his talents were noticed by King Henry II, who made him his chancellor, and the two became close friends. In 1161, Henry made Becket archbishop. Becket transformed himself from a pleasure-loving courtier into a serious, simply-dressed cleric. The king and his archbishop's friendship was put under strain when it became clear that Becket would now stand up for the church in its disagreements with the king. In 1164, realizing the extent of Henry's displeasure, Becket fled into exile in France, and remained in exile for several years. He returned in 1170. On the 29th December 1170, four knights, believing the king wanted Becket out of the way, confronted and murdered Becket in Canterbury Cathedral. Becket was made a saint in 1173 and his shrine in Canterbury Cathedral became an important focus for pilgrimage.

For Fun

Books to read

1. **The Canterbury Tales** by Geoffrey Chaucer
   This work tells the story of a group of English pilgrims who meet by chance at the Tabard Inn in Southwark, London, and journey together to the shrine of St. Thomas Becket in Canterbury Cathedral. To pass the time along the way, they tell stories to one another with cunning wit and dry humor.

2. **Ivanhoe** by Walter Scott
   Set in the reign of Richard I, *Ivanhoe* is packed with memorable incidents. Scott explores the conflicts between the Crown and the powerful barons, between the Norman overlords and the conquered Saxons, and between Richard and his scheming brother, Prince John. At the same time he brings into the novel the legendary Robin Hood and his band, and creates a brilliant, colorful account of the age of chivalry with all its elaborate rituals and costumes and its values of honor and personal glory.

Websites to visit

1. **http://www.britannia.com/history/docs/becketnewburgh.html**
   This is largely an objective account of Henry II's struggles with his Archbishop of Canterbury, Becket.

2. **http://gbgm-umc.org/umw/bible/crusades.stm**
   You can find considerable details about the crusades on this page.

Movies to see

1. **Ivanhoe (1952)**
   The movie, based on Sir Walter Scott's 1819 novel, depicts a chivalrous knight, Wilfrid of Ivanhoe and his determination to restore Richard the Lionhearted to England's throne. It provides many beautiful panoramic scenes of the English countryside.

This movie boasts 3 Academy Award Nominations, including Best Picture.

2. *The Lion in Winter* (1968)

King Henry II of England allows his wife, Eleanor of Aquitaine, to join the royal court for the holidays, springing her from the castle in which he has imprisoned her for years for plotting against him. Discussing every aspect of their love-hate relationship, they argue the question of which of their three sons will succeed Henry, a decision that will affect both England and France.

Unit 4

The House of Plantagenet

> Henry II does not take upon himself to think high thoughts; his tongue never swells with elated language; he does not magnify himself as more than man.
>
> —Walter Map

Unit Goals

- To learn about the origin of Parliament
- To know the stories of King John, Henry III, and Edward I, Edward II
- To be familiar with the significance of the *Magna Carta*
- To learn words and expressions that describe the Plantagenet kings and the birth of Parliament and improve English language skills
- To develop critical thinking and intercultural communication skills

Before You Read

(1) Fill in the blanks in the list of England monarchs below and choose one of them to give a presentation about his life and policies.

Portrait					
Name	_____ of England	Richard I of England	_____ of England (John Lackland)	Henry III of England	_____ of England (Edward Longshanks)
From	Dec. 19, 1154	Sept. 3, 1189	May 27, 1199	Oct. 28, 1216	Nov. 20, 1272
Until	Jul. 6, 1189	Apr. 6, 1199	Oct. 19, 1216	Nov. 16, 1272	Jul. 7, 1307
Relationship with Predecessor	son of Empress Matilda	son of _____ of England	son of Henry II of England; _____ of issueless Richard I of England	_____ of John of England	son of Henry III of England

(2) What do you know about the document—*the Magna Carta*? Share your knowledge with your classmates.

Start to Read

Text A　　**The Birth of Parliament**

1. For seventy years, England suffered from weak kings who were unfit to rule, yet the troubles of Stephen's time were not repeated. Henry had taught his people the rule of law. He had set them an example of good government. In future, if any king failed to follow this example, his people were ready to remind him of it.

2. How should they remind him? Surely this was the council's duty. And if he refused to listen, clearly the council should be made stronger. There was only one answer to this problem: representatives of the people would have to join the council. Then they could resist any king's misrule without being dependent on their lords.

3. This widened council was called parliament, which was a Norman French word for a talking-place. Weak kings let its powers increase, and strong

kings kept these powers within reasonable bounds. The kings realized that a strong parliament was their own best defense against their enemies. The king and the parliament together were then at last able to control the troublesome lords and the church, whose wealth and power hindered the nation's progress. The story of the people's struggle is a long one, and it begins with Richard's brother, John.

4. King John had been his father's favorite son. He grew up to be cruel and selfish, and thoroughly unpopular. When he murdered his sixteen-year-old nephew, Prince Arthur of Brittany, King of France seized all his northern French possessions. Only the extreme south-west with its great port of Bordeaux remained loyal, not for love of John, but for the value of its wine trade with England. Without Bordeaux, the trade of John's last French lands would have been ruined.

5. Then the archbishop died, and John invited the Pope to choose between two men who both seemed suitable for the post. But the Pope chose a third man, Stephen Langton, without even asking for John's opinion. This was against custom. John refused to accept Langton, and the people supported his view. Most of the bishops fled abroad rather than take sides in such a quarrel. Other priests steered a middle course; for five years no church bell rang in all the land, but they continued to hold services outside the locked church doors. At last the Pope persuaded King of France to attack England. John yielded to this threat, for he had no army ready. He accepted Langton and promised to pay Rome a large yearly tax.

6. Two years later, for the first time in English history, the people took the side of the lords against the king. John was determined to revenge himself on France, and for this purpose he had been demanding more feudal taxes and army services than the custom allowed. He had made about seventy towns buy charters of freedom at immense cost. Now an army of angry lords marched to London, which welcomed them with open gates. Any earlier king would have called out the common people to fight for him, but no one would fight for John except his hired foreign soldiers.

7. Henry II had taught his lords to respect the law. They now taught John that a king must respect the law. At Runnymede, on the Thames near Windsor, the lords forced John on June 15, 1215 to sign the *Magna Carta*, the *Great Charter* of English freedom.

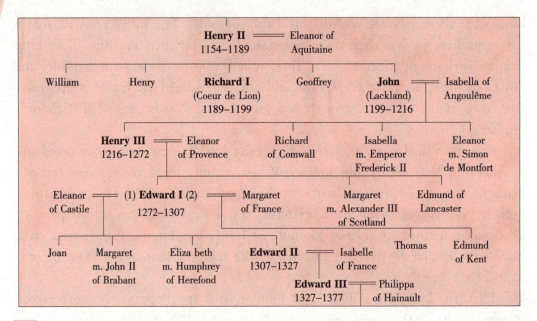

8. The charter covered a wide field of law and feudal rights, but the two most important matters were these: no tax should be made without the approval of the council, and no freeman should be arrested or imprisoned except by the law of the land.

9. John signed unwillingly and no one trusted him, so the charter itself gave the lords the right to use force against him if he broke his word. They did not have to wait for long. The Pope, whose friendship John had bought, declared the charter was unlawful and advised John to tear it up. Archbishop Langton disagreed with the Pope and begged John to listen to reason, but he begged in vain.

10. Fighting broke out again, and at first John's force was successful. But the lords asked for help from France and the King's fortunes began to turn. Then, suddenly, he died.

11. His son Henry III was only nine years old, but all parties promised him their loyalty. Under the wise influence of Langton, the charter was accepted; John's foreign army was dismissed, and all was peaceful until Henry became old enough to rule.

12. Then all the old troubles began again. Henry, like his father, hoped that, with Rome's help, he could defeat the lords and their charter. Year after year he poured English gold into the Pope's treasury and let him fill church posts with hated foreigners. He filled his own house with foreign advisers. He made expensive and useless attempts to win back the French lands that his father lost. After thirty years of misrule, his treasury was empty, and England was ready for

another Runnymede.

13. This time the scene was Oxford, and the aim was more carefully planned. The men of Runnymede had been concerned with the law and men's rights; those at Oxford were more concerned with political control. Under the leadership of Simon de Montfort, the king's brother-in-law, they forced him to dismiss his foreign advisers and to accept their own council of advisers instead.

14. De Montfort's new council took control of the Treasury, the county sheriffs and all state officials, including the Chief Justice and his staff. Then they settled down to work out their reforms. He now called the parliament that made him famous. Besides the usual lords and churchmen, it included knights from each county and representatives from each borough, which is the special name for a chartered town. The word "parliament" had been used before to describe the king's council, and such representatives had occasionally attended it to discuss their particular business. But they had never before been called to discuss the general government of the kingdom, nor had any parliament met without the king.

15. The English have always liked committees, where they can solve problems by discussion rather than by violent action; their social and political life in modern times is run entirely by committees. Parliament developed through the centuries as an expression of this national feeling. De Montfort did not invent it, but he was one of the first who helped it to take shape.

16. Edward I was the opposite of his father. He was a soldier by nature, with a towering figure and an iron will. He required strict discipline in the land under his command and he judged all men by their efficiency. He did not intend to yield any of his powers to the parliament, but he hoped to rule more efficiently by keeping in touch with popular opinion. He liked to discuss taxes with the knights and borough representatives, and he depended on them to explain his royal purposes to the people. In the days before newspaper, when travel was dangerous and difficult, their regular visits to the capital helped to develop a sense of national unity.

17. Although he was a soldier, Edward I made no serious attempt to win back the lost French lands. He aimed instead to bring Wales and Scotland under his rule. He later conquered Wales without much difficulty; but Scotland resisted more strongly, and Edward died while still fighting for control of the highlands.

18. His son Edward II was a weak and lazy king who left the work of government to his household favorites. Soon a party of lords, like de Montfort's party, was formed against him. Parliament approved of their plans, which demanded the public appointment of all the king's household as well as of the state officials. He was soon in trouble in other ways too. His father-in-law, King of France, attacked the lands around Bordeaux. The Scots rose in arms and the lords refused to fight them so that Edward's army was cut to pieces at Bannockburn. At last even the queen turned against him. For some time, she had been living with her lover, Roger Mortimer. Now she and Mortimer seized Edward with the help of foreign soldiers, and the Parliament forced him to hand over the crown to his son. A few months later, he was murdered in Berkeley Castle.

19. Edward III was only fifteen, and for three years his mother and Mortimer ruled in his name. Then Edward arrested them. He imprisoned his mother for life, and sent Mortimer to London to be hanged in public like a thief.

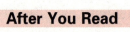

After You Read

Knowledge Focus

1. Pair Work

　　Discuss the following questions with your partner.

　　(1) What does "parliament" originally mean in Norman French?
　　(2) What made Bordeaux remain loyal to King John?
　　(3) What remarkable incident took place on June 15, 1215?
　　(4) Why did the Lords force King John to sign the *Magna Carta*?
　　(5) Where was the *Magna Carta* signed?
　　(6) Who helped the parliament in England to take shape?
　　(7) How did the Parliament develop in those years?

2. Solo Work

　　Tell whether and why the following are true or false according to the knowledge you have learned.

　　____ (1) The parliament was a French word for a talking-place.
　　____ (2) King John had been his father's favorite son. He grew up to be a popular king.
　　____ (3) King of France seized all John's northern French possessions. Only the extreme south-west with its great port of Bordeaux remained loyal for love

of John.

____ (4) Most of the bishops fled abroad because John refused to accept Langton as the archbishop, and the people supported his view.

____ (5) John accepted Langton and promised to pay Rome a large yearly tax, for King of France threatened to attack England.

____ (6) At Runnymede, on the Thames near Windsor, the lords forced John on the 15th of June 1215 to sign the *Magna Carta*, the *Great Charter* of English freedom.

____ (7) In 1215, King John was forced to sign the *Magna Carta*, a document that imposed limits on royal power and served as the basis for modern British law.

____ (8) Henry III, like his father, believed that with Rome's help he could defeat the lords and their charter.

____ (9) De Montfort's new council took control of the Treasury, the county sheriffs and all state officials, including the Chief Justice and his staff.

____ (10) Parliament developed through the centuries as an expression of this national feeling. De Montfort was the one who invented and helped it to take shape.

Language Focus

1. **Fill in the blanks with the following words or expressions you have learned in the text. Put them into appropriate forms if necessary.**

set... an example of	resist	approval	post
be more concerned with	begin with	yield to	take sides in
keep... within bounds	remind... of		

(1) The song _____ me _____ those days spent away from home.
(2) She could not _____ laughing at him in those clothes.
(3) His desire for political power apparently should be _____.
(4) The project has now received _____ from the government.
(5) Her job _____ computers, even though she's now working in the national bank.
(6) You should _____ your younger brother _____ being strong-minded.
(7) The hotel was awful! _____, our room was too small. Then we found that the shower did not work.
(8) Teaching _____ are advertised in Tuesday's edition of the paper.
(9) My mother never _____ the argument between my brother and me.
(10) It's very easy to _____ temptation and spend too much money.

2. **Fill in the appropriate prepositions that collocate with the neighboring words.**

(1) England suffered _____ weak kings who were unfit to rule, yet the troubles of Stephen's time were not repeated.
(2) A stronger council need popular support, and the people had always regarded the

king _____ their protector against the lords.

(3) The Pope persuaded King of France to attack England. John yielded _____ this threat, for he had no army ready.

(4) John was determined to revenge himself _____ France, and _____ this purpose he had been demanding more feudal taxes and army services than the custom allowed.

(5) Weak kings let the parliament's power increase, and strong kings kept it _____ reasonable bounds.

(6) The Pope declared the charter was unlawful and advised John to tear it _____. Archbishop Langton disagreed _____ the Pope and begged John to listen to reason, but he begged _____ vain.

(7) Year after year, Henry poured English gold _____ the Pope's treasury and let him fill church posts with hated foreigners.

(8) De Montfort's new council took control of the treasury, the county sheriffs and all state officials, including the Chief Justice and his staff. Then they settled _____ to work out their reforms.

(9) Edward I was the opposite _____ his father. He was a soldier by nature, with a towering figure and an iron will. He required strict discipline in the land _____ his command and he judged all men _____ their efficiency.

(10) Although he was a soldier, Edward made no serious attempt to win back the lost French lands. He aimed instead _____ bringing Wales and Scotland _____ his rule.

Comprehensive Work

1. Solo Work: The *Magna Carta*

Fill in the blanks in the text below with the words in the box.

seal	unfair	barons	unpopularity
Medieval	Magna	taxes	power
Church	England	trial	Constitution
government	Latin	Bill	military

The *Magna Carta* is an important historical document that took some _____ away from the king and gave some rights and freedoms to the people. "Magna Carta" means "Great Charter" in _____.

On June 15, 1215, the barons of _____ England confronted King John at Runnymede, and forced the king to put his _____ on the *Magna Carta*. King John had been an unpopular king who abused his power, oppressed his subjects, and angered the _____ by increasing _____ and demanding many soldiers for his _____ campaigns abroad. King John was excommunicated from the Catholic _____ by the Pope in 1209, further increasing his _____.

The barons wrote the _____ Carta, which contained 63 clauses promising all freemen access to courts and a fair _____, eliminating _____ fines and punishments, giving power to the Catholic Church in England, and addressing many lesser issues.

Although King John violated many of the clauses in the *Magna Carta*, later kings of _____ were eventually forced to comply with its terms.

The *Magna Carta* was one of the forerunners of modern British law, the US _____ and its Amendments (the _____ of Rights), and the guiding documents of many other countries that have further expanded the rights and liberties of the people and limited the power of the _____.

2. **Writing Activity**

In 1215, King John placed himself and England's future sovereigns within the rule of law by signing the *Magna Carta*. The rule of law, also called supremacy of law, means that the law is above everyone and it applies to everyone. Whether the governor or governed, the rulers or ruled, no one is above the law, no one is exempted from the law, and no one can grant exemption to the application of the law.

Write a short essay on the rule of law, with emphasis on its importance in modern society.

Read More

Text B The *Magna Carta*

The *Magna Carta* was signed in June 1215 between the barons of Medieval England and King John. "Magna Carta" is Latin and means "Great Charter". The *Magna Carta* was one of the most important documents of Medieval England.

It was signed between the barons and King John at Runnymede near Windsor Castle. The document was a series of written promises between the king and his subjects that he, the king, would govern England and deal with its people according to the customs of feudal law. The *Magna Carta* was an attempt by the barons to stop a king—in this case King John—abusing his power with the people of England suffering.

Why would a king—who was meant to be all powerful in his own country—agree to the demands of the barons who were meant to be below him in authority?

England had for some years owned land in France. The barons had

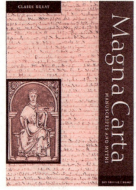

provided the king with both money and men to defend this territory. Traditionally, the king had always consulted the barons before raising taxes (as they had to collect it) and demanding more men for military services (as they had to provide the men). This was all part of the feudal system.

While kings were militarily successful abroad, relations between the kings and the barons were good. John was not successful in his military campaigns abroad. His constant demands for more money and men angered the barons. By 1204, John had lost his land in northern France. In response to this, John introduced high taxes without asking the barons. This was against feudal law and accepted custom.

John made mistakes in other areas as well. He angered the Roman Catholic Church. The Pope, angered by John's behavior, banned all church services in England in 1207. Religion and the fear of Hell were very important to the people including the barons. The Catholic Church taught the people that they could only get to Heaven if the Catholic Church believed that they were good enough to get there. How could they show their goodness and love of God if the churches were shut? What was even worse for John was the fact that the pope excommunicated him in 1209. This meant that John could never get to Heaven until the pope withdrew the excommunication. Faced with this, John climbed down and accepted the power of the Catholic Church giving them many privileges in 1214.

1214 was a disastrous year for John for another reason. Once again, he suffered military defeat in an attempt to get back his territory in northern France. He returned to London demanding more money from taxes. This time the barons were not willing to listen. They rebelled against his power. The barons captured London. However, they did not defeat John entirely and by the spring of 1215, both sides were willing to discuss matters. The result was the *Magna Carta*.

All 63 clauses of the document can be divided into sections: The first clauses concern the position of the Catholic Church in England. Those that follow state that John will be less harsh on the barons. Many of the clauses concern England's legal system.

The *Magna Carta* promised laws that were

good and fair. It states that everyone shall have access to courts and that costs and money should not be an issue if someone wanted to take a problem to the law courts. It also states that no freeman will be imprisoned or punished without first going through the proper legal system. In future years, the word "freeman" was replaced by "no one" to include everybody.

The last few sections deal with how the *Magna Carta* would be enforced in England. Twenty five barons were given the responsibility of making sure the king carried out what was stated in the *Magna Carta*—the document clearly states that they could use force if they felt it was necessary. To give the *Magna Carta* an impact, the royal seal of King John was put on it to show people that it had his royal support. This is the largest red seal at the bottom of the *Magna Carta*.

1. **Questions for discussion or reflection.**
    (1) What is the significance of signing the *Magna Carta*?
    (2) What was the baron's role in feudal system?
    (3) How did the Catholic Church assure people of their power?
    (4) What are the main points of the *Great Charter*?

Text C King John

King John was born in 1167 and died in 1216. Like William I, King John is one of the more controversial monarchs of Medieval England and is most associated with the signing of the *Magna Carta* in 1215.

John was born on Christmas Eve, the youngest son of Henry II and his wife Eleanor of Aquitaine. As a child, John tended to be overshadowed by his elder brother Richard. Like his father, John developed a reputation for violent rages. His father left no land to John when he died, so John was given the nickname John Lackland. In 1189, all of Henry's territory went to his oldest son, Richard I, better known as Richard the Lionheart.

In 1191, Richard left England to embark on the Third Crusade. He left John in charge of the country. John's reputation as a leader had been severely dented as far back as 1185 when Henry II sent him to Ireland to rule. John proved to be a disaster and within six months he was sent home.

In 1192, Richard was imprisoned by Duke Leopold of Austria as he returned from the Crusades. John tried to seize the crown from his brother but failed. In 1194, when Richard finally returned to England, John was forgiven by his brother.

In 1199, Richard was killed in France and John became the king of England. His reign started in an unfortunate way. In 1202, John's nephew, Arthur of Brittany, was murdered. Many in Brittany believed that John was responsible for his murder and they rebelled against John. In 1204, John's army was defeated in Brittany and John had no choice but to retreat. His military standing among the nobles fell and he was given a new nickname—John Softsword. The defeat in north France was a major blow for John and a costly one. To pay for the defeat, John increased taxes which were not popular with anybody other than John and his treasurers.

John also succeeded in falling out with the Pope in 1207. John quarreled with the pope over who should be Archbishop of Canterbury. The pope excommunicated John and put England under a Church law that stated that no christening or marriage would be legal until the time the pope said that they would be. Church law said that only christened people could get to Heaven while children born out of marriage were doomed to Hell. This placed people in England under a terrible strain and they blamed one person for this—John.

In 1213, John had to give in and surrender the spiritual well-being of the whole country to the pope. However, the pope never fully trusted John and in 1214, the pope proclaimed that anybody who tried to overthrow John would be legally entitled to do so. In the same year, John lost another battle to the French at Bouvines. This defeat resulted in England losing all her possessions in France. This was too much for the powerful barons in England. In 1214, they rebelled.

John was forced to sign the *Magna Carta* at Runnymede in 1215. This guaranteed the people of England rights that the king could not go back on. In 1216, John tried to go back on the *Magna Carta* but this only provoked the barons into declaring war on him. By 1216, John was ill. During the war, he suffered from dysentery. He also lost all of his treasure when he tried to take a shortcut across a stretch of water in the Wash, Lincolnshire. As the tide rose faster than he expected, his baggage train was engulfed. Just a few days later, John died and was succeeded by Henry III.

Despite the obvious failings of John, there is still some evidence that he was not as bad as some have tried to make him out to be since his death. It certainly was not uncommon for kings to have their names tarnished when they were not alive to defend themselves.

In 1994, R. Turner once commented: "John had potential for great success. He had intelligence, administrative ability and he was good at planning military campaigns. However, too many personality flaws held him back". And Matthew Paris, 13th chronicler, said, "John was a tyrant. He was a wicked ruler who did not behave like a king. He was greedy and took as much money as he could from his people. Hell is too good for a horrible person like him".

1. Questions for discussion or reflection.
   (1) How controversial is King John as one of the monarchs of Medieval England?
   (2) What brought King John the nickname "John Lackland"?
   (3) Why did King John increase the tax after 1204?
   (4) What caused England to lose all possessions in France?

Proper Names

Berkeley Castle 伯克利城堡
Bordeaux 波尔多(法国西南部城市、港口)
Parliament (英国)议会
Roger Mortimer 罗杰·莫蒂默
Roman Catholic Church 罗马天主教

Runnymede 兰尼米德
Simon De Montfort 西蒙·德·蒙特福德
Magna Carta《英国大宪章》
The Third Crusade 第三次十字军东征

Notes

1. **Roman Catholic Church**: The Roman Catholic Church, officially known as the Catholic Church, is the world's largest Christian church, representing over half of all Christians and one-sixth of the world's population. The Church's highest earthly authority in matters of faith, morality and Church governance is the Pope, currently Benedict XVI who holds supreme authority over the Church in concert with the College of Bishops, of which he is the head.
2. **Simon de Montfort**: He was Henry Ⅲ's brother-in-law and led the barons to rebel against the king. He defeated the king and summoned the Great Council in 1265. This meeting was considered the earliest Parliament. He was defeated and killed by Prince Edward the same year.

For Fun

Book to read

Henry Plantagenet: A Biography of Henry II of England
by Richard Barber

Henry II is the most imposing figure among the medieval kings of England. This readable and accessible biography offers both a study of his character and an estimate of his work as a ruler, which is in a sense the history of his life, since it occupied his entire energies from his accession at the age of twenty-one to his death thirty-five years later.

Movies to see

1. *Edward II*（1991）

This is a 1991 film by Derek Jarman based on the play *Edward II* by Christopher Marlowe. The plot revolves around Edward II of England's infatuation with Piers Gaveston, which proves to be the downfall of both of them, thanks to the machinations of Mortimer. The film is staged in a postmodern style, using a mixture of contemporary and medieval props, sets and clothing.

2. *Robin Hood*（2010）

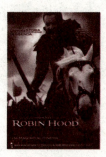

This movie is a retelling of the Robin Hood legend featuring the Gladiator star in the titular role. A bowman in the army of Richard I, virtuous rogue Robin Hood rises from an unlikely background to become a hero to the impoverished people of Nottingham and lover to the beautiful Lady Marion.

Website to visit

The Plantagenet Medieval Archery and Combat Society
http://www.the-plantagenets.freeserve.co.uk/

This is a website featuring knights, armor, archers, dancing, music, squires, swords, axes, etc.

Unit 5
The 14th-century England

> As soon as war is looked upon as wicked, it will always have its fascination. When it is looked upon as vulgar, it will cease to be popular.
>
> —Oscar Wilde

Unit Goals

- To learn about the history of the Hundred Years' War
- To be familiar with the causes and consequences of the Black Death
- To know the Wat Tyler Uprising
- To learn the useful words and expressions about the Hundred Years' War and the Black Death and improve English language skills
- To develop critical thinking and intercultural communication skills

Before You Read

(1) What do you know about the Hundred Years' War? Can you give some information about the causes of this war? Discuss with your partners.
(2) Many French peasants joined in the Hundred Years' War under the leadership of French national heroine—Joan of Arc. Retell the story about Joan of Arc to your partner.
(3) Form groups of three or four students. Try to find, on the Internet or in the library, more information about the Hundred Years' War which interests you most. Get ready for a 5-minute presentation in class.

Start to Read

Text A The Hundred Years' War

1. The Hundred Years' War (1337—1453) was not one war, but a series of wars, with victory now on one side, then on the other; and the whole contest stretched over more than a century, from 1337 to 1453.

2. The war was directly caused by the dispute over succession to the French throne. When Edward III (1327—1377) ruled England, the French king died without a legitimate successor. Edward claimed that he should succeed to the French throne because his mother was a sister of the late French king. The French nobles denied his claim. Edward could not forget that all western France had belonged to Henry II by right. Weak kings had lost most of it in war, but a strong king could regain it in the same way. If he could not get it peacefully through his claim on the crown, he was ready to fight for it. Then in 1337, Edward III landed in Normandy with an English army. The Hundred Years' War broke out, a long struggle between England and France.

3. The war continued intermittently for more than 100 years with ups and downs for both sides, though during the initial stage the English troops were on the offensive and even captured Paris and a French king. As time passed by, guns and gunpowder were used in the war. This greatly reduced the effectiveness of the English bows and arrows, the guarantee of any English victory. In addition, many French peasants joined in the war under the leadership of the famous peasant girl Joan of Arc who was a national heroine in French history. The English troops began to lose ground step by step until they were driven out of France. The war ended in failure for the Normans in 1453.

4. The Hundred Years' War deprived the English king of his possession on the Continent. But it brought unexpected benefits for the English people. After losing their territory on the Continent, the ruling Normans began to regard England as their home. By the end of the 14th century, the English language was reestablished as the official language and the French language was no longer used in daily life. The dual-linguistic period in English history came to the end.

5. The war also sped up the decline of feudalism in England. The introduction of guns and gun powder in war made castles of feudal lords easy to be stormed. Feudalist separation was becoming impossible and this was to the advantage of commercial development.

6. During the war, the English king had to hire soldiers, and gunpowder and weapons were bought. The need of money thus promoted the class with a large amount of money, including merchants, to a more important position. The feudal lords with only land could no longer sustain the revolutionized war. The change thus pushed the growing bourgeoisie onto a higher rung of social ladder in England.

Text B　The Black Death and Wat Tyler Uprising

1. The deadly plague between 1348 and 1349, commonly called the Black Death, added to the horrors of the Hundred Years' War. It originated in Italy and soon spread to France, Germany and England. Those who were stricken with it usually died in two or three days. A careful estimate shows that in England one half of the population died of this disease. As a result, certain lands were no longer of any value to the lords who could not find enough tenants to till them. Manpower became more important for the lack of it.

2. The effect of the Black Death soon made itself felt. Free labors demanded higher wages and better working conditions. When not satisfied, they repeatedly deserted one employer after another until their demand was met. The serfs also demanded reforms and improvement of their living conditions. To seek the chance for a better life, the serfs began to run away from their masters in an increasing number, for they could easily get employment once they had got away. Labor was needed everywhere.

3. In the face of such a situation, the ruling class began to take repressive measures. The first *Statute of Labors* was passed in 1351. It prohibited labors from asking for more wages. Labors were ordered to work for the established wages. Similar laws were also enacted for the same purpose. The feudal lords refused to make changes.

4. Now the peasants and serfs had only one way to achieve their goal: to get organized and fight back. The uprising broke out in Essex and Kent in 1381 when the government attempted to impose the poll tax of one shilling a head on the peasants to finance the Hundred Years' War. Wat Tyler was the most important military leader of the uprising who led the rebels in marching on London. Since many merchants were in great need of labors, they supported, to some extent, the demands of peasants. They opened the city gates for the rebel peasants.

5. Not having enough force to suppress the rebel peasants, the king decided to play a trick on them. He pretended to accept all their demands. Wat Tyler was killed in the negotiation with the king. The uprising was thus suppressed.

6. Though the uprising failed, the king was forced to make some concessions to appease the anger of peasants. The poor peasants were soon exempt from the poll tax while the rich continued to pay it. The shortage of labor resulting from the Black Death and the peasant uprising thus served to weaken the feudal bond over the peasants. The feudal relations of production were beginning to break up, paving the way for capitalist development.

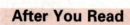

After You Read

Knowledge Focus

1. **Pair Work**

   Discuss the following questions with your partner.

   (1) Do you think young Edward had the right to claim the French crown? Why or why not?

   (2) How did the Hundred Years' War break out?

   (3) How was the war going in the initial stage?

   (4) What do you know about Joan of Arc?

   (5) How did the English people benefit from the war which ended in failure?

   (6) How serious was the disease of the Black Death?

   (7) What were the consequences of the Black Death?

   (8) The lack of manpower urged labors to demand higher wages and better working conditions. What measure did the ruling class take to deal with the situation?

   (9) How was the uprising led by Wat Tyler suppressed?

   (10) What concessions did the king make to appease the anger of peasants?

2. **Solo Work**

   Tell whether and why the following are true or false according to the knowledge you have learned.

   _____ (1) The Hundred Years' War was directly caused by the dispute over succession to the French throne.

   _____ (2) Edward Ⅱ claimed that he should succeed to the French throne because his mother was a sister of the late French king.

_____ (3) The war broke out when Edward III landed in Normandy with an English army in 1337.
_____ (4) Many French peasants joined in the war under the leadership of the famous peasant girl Joan of Arc who was a national heroine in British history.
_____ (5) The English troops were on the offensive during the initial stage, but gradually began to lose ground.
_____ (6) The English language was reestablished as the official language and the French language was no longer used in daily life by the end of the 15th century.
_____ (7) Feudalist separation promotes the commercial development.

Language Focus

1. **Fill in the blanks with the following words or expressions you have learned in the text. Put them into appropriate forms if necessary.**

in failure	compel	initial	prohibit
(be) exempt from	concession	sustain	deserted
legitimate	in addition		

(1) Mrs. Hassan was _____ by her husband and had to support four children on her own.
(2) _____, Microsoft last week appointed Rick Belluzzo as president.
(3) The government has refused to recognize the far-right group as a _____ political party.
(4) Property owners offered _____ to attract new tenants and renters.
(5) Certain religions may _____ particular types of food, alcoholic drink or restrict dress.
(6) Are students _____ from compulsory schooling or from certain courses in the curriculum on religious grounds?
(7) All the young men here were _____ to work in the coal mines.
(8) The company _____ women and minorities whenever possible.
(9) After the _____ shock, people adjusted to the new circumstances.
(10) Their first attempt to climb Mount Everest ended _____.

2. **Complete the following sentences with the right words in the brackets with their proper forms.**

(1) His heroism _____ (claim/need) our admiration.
(2) Our holidays _____ (spoil/damage) by bad weather.
(3) Whenever he's around, he always manages to _____ (stir/take) up trouble.
(4) He _____ (stretch/pull) himself out on the sofa and fell asleep.
(5) Granny _____ (be stricken with/be filled with) this disease for so long a time.

3. **Find the appropriate prepositions that collocate with the neighboring words.**

(1) The whole contest stretched _____ more than a century, from 1337 to 1453.

(2) The war was directly caused by the dispute _____ succession to the French throne.

(3) If he could not get it peacefully through his claim _____ the crown, he was ready to fight _____ it.

(4) _____ addition, many French peasants joined _____ the war _____ the leadership of the famous peasant girl Joan of Arc who was a national heroine _____ French history.

(5) The Hundred Years' War deprived the English king _____ his possession _____ the Continent.

(6) The Hundred Years' War sped _____ the decline of feudalism in England.

(7) A careful estimate shows that in England one half of the population died _____ this disease.

(8) _____ the face of such a situation, the ruling class began to take repressive measures.

(9) Wat Tyler was the most important military leader of the uprising who led the rebels _____ marching on London.

(10) The king, not having enough force to suppress the rebel peasants, decided to play a trick _____ them.

Comprehensive Work

Group Work: The Black Death on CNN

Procedure: Show a 3–5 minute videotaped segment of a typical CNN broadcast (can be on any subject). Explain how the anchor introduces the report and does a wrap-up after completion. Also explain how a correspondent gives the "who, what, when, where, why, and how" of a story and how personal/expert insights are injected via interviews on site.

Students are divided into groups of four (1 anchor, 1 field correspondent, 2 interviewees). Each group is assigned a different category.

- Spread of epidemic—causes
- Medical—what is being done (treatment, prevention)
- Economy—how is it being affected?
- Social views and attitudes—how is it changing?

Each group prepares a draft of your report and gives a CNN style report to a global audience (5 minutes maximum).

Read More

Text C Wat Tyler and His Revolting Peasants

In 1381, some 35 years after the Black Death had swept through Europe decimating over one third of the population, there was a shortage of people left to work the land. Recognizing the power of "supply and demand", the remaining peasants began to re-evaluate their worth and subsequently demanded higher wages and better working conditions.

Not surprisingly, the government of the day, comprising mainly of the land-owning bishops and lords, passed a law to limit any such wage rise. In addition to this, extra revenue was required to support a long and drawn out war with the French, and so a poll tax was introduced.

It was the third time in four years that such a tax had been applied. This tax meant that everyone over the age of 15 had to pay one shilling. Perhaps it was not a great deal of money to a lord or a bishop, but a significant amount to the average farm laborer.

In May 1381, a tax collector arrived in the Essex village of Fobbing to find out why the people there had not paid their poll tax. The villagers appeared to have taken exception to his enquiries and promptly threw him out. Joined by other villagers from all corners of the southeast of England, the peasants decided to march on London in order to plead their case for a better deal before their young king.

In what appeared to have been a well-organized and coordinated popular uprising, the peasants set off for London on the 2nd of June. As the peasants moved on to London, they destroyed tax records, and removed the heads from several tax officials who objected to them doing so. Buildings which housed government records were burned down. It was during the march that one man emerged as their natural leader—Wat Tyler (Walter the Tyler) from Kent. The rebels entered London, as some of the locals had kindly left the city gates open to them.

In an attempt to prevent further trouble, the king agreed to meet Wat Tyler. At this meeting, Richard II gave in to all of the peasants' demands and asked that they go home in peace.

Satisfied with the outcome—a promised end to serfdom and feudalism—many did start the journey home.

At this tense and highly charged meeting, the Lord Mayor, apparently angered by Wat Tyler's arrogant attitude to the king and his even more radical demands, drew his dagger and slashed at Tyler.

Whatever the king said or promised, it must have been sounded very convincing, as it resulted in the revolting peasants dispersing and returning home. By the end of the summer of 1381, just a few weeks after it had started, the peasants' revolt was over. Richard did not, or could not keep any of his promises due to his limited power in Parliament. He also claimed that they were therefore not valid in law as these promises were made under threat. The remaining rebels were dealt with by force.

The poll tax was withdrawn and the peasants were forced back into their old way of life—under the control of the lord of the manor, bishop or archbishop. The ruling classes, however, did not have it all their own way. The Black Death had caused such a shortage of labor that over the next 100 years many peasants found that when they asked for more money the lords had to give in. They were forced eventually to perhaps recognize the peasants' power of "supply and demand".

1. Discuss the following questions with your partner.
    (1) What did the government do to suppress the peasants' demand?
    (2) Can you describe the uprising by the peasants?
    (3) How did the uprising end?
    (4) What happened to Wat Tyler?
    (5) What excuses did the king make for not being able to keep his promise?

2. Tell whether the following are true or false according to the text.
    (1) The Black Death had swept through Europe decimating over one third of the population. (　)
    (2) According to the text, everyone over the age of 16 should pay one shilling. (　)
    (3) The tax had been applied twice in four years. (　)
    (4) The peasants in what appeared to have been a well organized and coordinated popular uprising set off for London on the 2nd June. (　)
    (5) At the meeting with Wat Tyler, Richard III gave in to all of the peasants, demanding and asking that they go home in peace. (　)

Text D　Joan of Arc—Maid of Orleans

In the long wars between the French and the English, not even the Black

Prince or King Henry V gained such fame as did a young French peasant girl, Joan of Arc.

She was born in the little village of Domrémy. Her father had often told her of the sad conditions of France—how the country was largely in the possession of England, and how the French king did not dare to be crowned.

She brooded over the matter so much that by and by she began to have visions of angels and heard strange voices, which said to her, "Joan, you can deliver the land from the English".

At last these strange visions and voices made the young girl believe that she had a mission from God, and she was determined to try to save France.

Little by little, people began to believe in her mission. At last, all stopped trying to discourage her and some who were wealthy helped her to make the journey to the town of Chinon, where the French king, Charles VII, was living.

When Joan arrived at Chinon, a force of French soldiers was preparing to go to the south of France to relieve the city of Orleans which the English were besieging.

King Charles received Joan kindly and listened to what she had to say with deep attention. The girl spoke modestly, but with a calm belief that she was right.

"Gracious King," she said, "my name is Joan. God has sent me to deliver France from her enemies. You shall shortly be crowned in the cathedral of Rheims. I am to lead the soldiers you are about to send for the relief of Orleans. So God has directed and under my guidance victory will be theirs".

The king and his nobles talked the matter over and finally it was decided to allow Joan to lead an army of about five thousand men against the English at Orleans.

When she left Chinon at the head of her soldiers, in April, 1429, she was in her eighteenth year. She inspired the whole army with courage and faith as she talked about her visions.

When she arrived at the besieged city of Orleans, she fearlessly rode round its walls, while the English soldiers looked on in astonishment. She was able to enter Orleans, despite the efforts of the besiegers to prevent her.

She aroused the city by her cheerful, confident words and then led her soldiers forth to give battle to the English. Their success was amazing. One after another the English forts were taken.

When only the strongest remained and Joan was leading the attacking force, she received a slight wound and was carried out of the battle to be attended by a surgeon. Her soldiers began to retreat. "Wait," she commanded, "eat and drink and rest; for as soon as I recover I will touch the walls with my banner and you shall enter the fort." In a few minutes, she mounted her horse again, rode rapidly up to the fort and touched it with her banner. Her soldiers almost instantly carried it. The very next day the enemy's troops were forced to withdraw from before the city and the siege came to an end.

The French soldiers were jubilant at the victory and called Joan the "Maid of Orleans". By this name, she is known in history. Her fame spread everywhere, and the English as well as the French thought she had more than human power. Among all the men of her time none did nobler work than Joan.

1. Finish the following multiple-choice questions according to Text D.

(1) Joan of Arc lived during the _____ century.
    A. 14th   B. 15th   C. 16th   D. 13th

(2) Joan lived and fought in _____.
    A. Greece   B. France   C. Rome   D. England

(3) When Joan led the French army to victory, she was _____.
    A. a teenager   B. in her 20s
    C. Queen of France   D. ten years old

(4) According to Joan, she was told to lead the French army by _____.
    A. the army commander   B. the king
    C. the queen   D. Saints

(5) Which happened first?
    A. Joan was executed.
    B. Joan ended the siege of Orleans.
    C. Joan marched to Rheims.
    D. Joan was escorted to see Charles.

(6) Because of Joan's actions, Charles _____.
    A. became King of England
    B. was removed from the throne of France

C. became King of France
D. was executed for heresy

(7) Joan is an inspiration to many because of her _____.
A. obedience   B. bravery   C. style   D. creativity

2. **Discuss the following questions with your partners.**
   (1) Suppose that you were Joan, trying to convince Charles to let you lead his army. What would you have said to convince him?
   (2) Why do you think Charles' army began to win battles once Joan took charge?

Proper Names

the Black Death 黑死病   Joan of Arc 圣女贞德
the Channel 英吉利海峡   *The Statute of Labors*《劳工法令》
the Hundred Years' War 百年战争   Wat Tyler 瓦特·泰勒

Notes

1. *Edward III*: He is King of England (ruled 1327—1377), son of Edward II. He was skillful in politics and war. His claim to the French crown initiated the Hundred Years' War in which his reputation was made by spectacular successes in various battles. His later years were marked by financial difficulties and decline. Edward's reign also witnessed the outbreak of the Black Death.
2. *The Statute of Labors*: *The Statute of Labors* was a law enacted by the English Parliament under King Edward III in 1351 in response to a labour shortage. It was introduced by Sir John Halles.
3. *Wat Tyler*: He was an English rebel, whose given name appeared in full as Walter. He came into prominence as the leader of the rebellion of 1381, known as the Peasants' Revolt. The revolt had its origins in the plague of 1348—1349.

For Fun

Websites to visit

1. http://www.vlib.us/medieval/lectures/hundred_years_war.html
   It is a website about the development of Hundred Years' War.
2. http://en.wikipedia.org/wiki/Hundred_Years'_War
   This website provides you with comprehensive information about Hundred Years' War.

Movie to see

The Messenger: The Story of Joan of Arc (1999)

This is a 1999 historical drama film directed by Luc Besson. *The Messenger* portrays the story of St. Joan of Arc, the famous French war heroine of the 15th century and religious martyr. The story begins with young Joan witnessing the atrocities of the English against her family, following her through her visions to her leadership in battle, and finally to her trial and execution.

Song to enjoy

My Heart Calling

This is a song in Eric Serra's album—*The Story of Joan of Arc*. It is also the postlude of the film *The Messenger: The Story of Joan of Arc*.

My Heart Calling

By Eric Serra

Tell me who I am
Tell me what I'm hearing
Is it God or man
Leads us to our fate

Tears cried through the night
So much we've been fearing
I know I can fight
Soon will be too late

It's my heart calling
It's my heart calling
It's my heart seeing
What it wants to see

It's my heart crying
It's my heart flying
It's my heart trying
To set me free

Darkness turns to light
While my soul is healing
I know I must fight
This war deep inside

It's my heart calling
It's my heart calling
It's my heart seeing
What it wants to see

It's my heart crying
It's my heart flying
It's my heart trying
To set me free

Waving banners, swinging swords
Queens and kings, and other lords
And the battles of our pride
Greed and hunger deep inside

All the sorrow born of pain
Cruelty and cruelty again
Who will stop this vicious spin
Open arms and let love in
Open arms and let love in
Open arms and let love in
Open arms and let love in

Unit 6
The House of Lancaster and York

> Once more unto the breach, dear friends, once more;/ Or close the wall up with our English dead./ In peace there's nothing so becomes a man/ As modest stillness and humility;/ But when the blast of war blows in our ears,/ Then imitate the action of the tiger;/ Stiffen the sinews, summon up the blood.
>
> —William Shakespeare

Unit Goals

- To learn about the causes of the Wars of the Roses
- To know the stories about House of Lancaster and York
- To learn words and expressions that describe House of Lancaster and York and the Wars of the Roses and improve English language skills
- To develop critical thinking and intercultural communication skills

Before You Read

Look at the pictures below and discuss the following questions in pairs.

(1) Do you think a war can be somehow romantic? What is the origin of the romantic name "the Wars of the Roses"?
(2) Were the Wars of the Roses civil wars or transnational wars?

(3) What was the outcome of the Wars of the Roses?

Start to Read

Text A　The Wars of the Roses

1. The Wars of the Roses were a series of civil wars fought in medieval England from 1455 to 1487 between the House of Lancaster and the House of York. The name "Wars of the Roses" is based on the badges used by the two sides, the red rose for the Lancastrians and the white rose for the Yorkists.

2. Although there were no battles fought until 1455, the causes of the wars dated back to the reign of Edward III and the power struggle between his sons after his death.

3. The four eldest sons of Edward III (1327—1377) were Edward the Black Prince (heir to the throne), Lionel of Antwerp (Duke of Clarence), John of Gaunt (Duke of Lancaster) and Edmund of Langley (Duke of York).

4. Edward III died in 1377. His eldest son, Edward, the Black Prince had died of the plague in 1376. As a consequence, his grandson, Richard (son of the Black Prince) aged ten, became king. As Richard II was only ten years old, his uncle, John of Gaunt, Duke of Lancaster, ruled the country. As Richard grew older he rebelled against his uncle and made decisions that were not popular with the most powerful men in the country.

5. In 1399, John of Gaunt died and Richard II confiscated the land he had owned. John of Gaunt's son, Henry, raised an army and took the throne as Henry IV, when Richard surrendered. Richard was imprisoned in a castle and mysteriously died in February, 1400.

6. Henry IV faced a number of challenges to his place on the throne because he was not the natural successor to Richard II. However, Henry managed to keep his place on the throne and when he died in 1413, the country was at peace and his son, Henry V, succeeded without problem.

7. Henry V, a member of the House of Lancaster, was crowned king in 1413 at the age of 26. Henry spent most of his reign campaigning in France in order to regain territories claimed by his ancestors. He won many battles, including the Battle of

Agincourt in 1415 and conquered Normandy and Rouen for England. In 1420, Henry married the daughter of the king of France and it was agreed that their children would be the heirs of both England and France. When Henry V died in 1422 from dysentery, his son, Henry VI, became the only king to be crowned king of England and France.

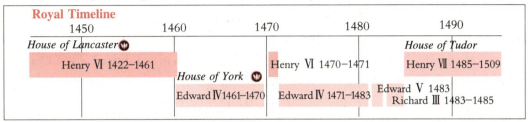

8. Henry VI was four months old when he became king and his father's brothers ruled England and France in his place. France was soon lost when Joan of Arc raised an army against the English and restored the French monarchy. As Henry grew older, it became apparent that he was a weak king, totally dominated by his French wife Margaret of Anjou. The king had mental illness that was hereditary in his mother's family. He was also prone to bouts of insanity. The House of York challenged Henry VI's right to the throne and began plotting to take his place on the throne. England was plunged into a civil war—The Wars of the Roses.

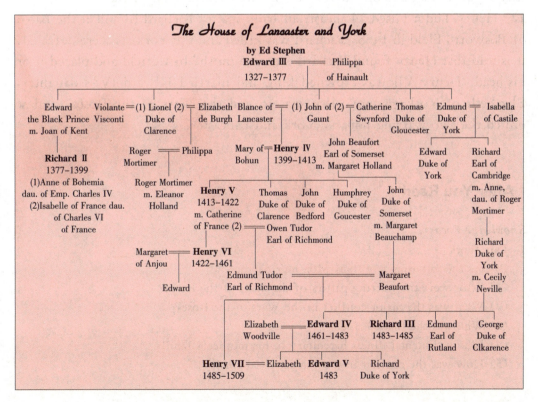

9. The first battle of the Wars of the Roses took place at St. Albans on 22nd May 1455. The Yorkists led by Richard Duke of York easily defeated the king's army. Henry VI was injured and taken prisoner. In 1455, Henry suffered another bout of insanity and Richard Duke of York was made Protector of England. In 1456, Henry recovered and retook the throne. There were further battles and in 1459 Richard was killed at the Battle of Wakefield.

10. In 1461, Richard's son Edward, Earl of March, defeated the king's army, took the king prisoner and made himself King Edward IV. Queen Margaret took her son and fled to Wales where they were taken in by the king's half-brother Jaspar Tudor. In 1470, Henry regained the throne but in 1471 was defeated by Edward's army at the Battle of Tewkesbury and taken prisoner. Henry's son, Edward, Prince of Wales was killed during the battle. With no other Lancastrian heir to challenge him, Edward IV remained king until his sudden death in 1483.

11. Edward IV had two sons, Edward and Richard, both of whom were too young to rule, so their uncle Richard Duke of Gloucester ruled England. The two princes were taken to the Tower of London and in the summer of 1483 mysteriously disappeared. It is believed that their uncle murdered them. Richard was crowned Richard III. He was not a popular king and faced many challenges to his place on the throne, notably from Henry Tudor.

12. Henry Tudor raised a Lancastrian army against Richard III and at the Battle of Bosworth Field in 1485, Richard was killed and the Yorkists were defeated. It is told that Henry found Richard's crown on the battlefield and placed it on his head. Henry VII was crowned king and married Edward IV's daughter, Elizabeth of York—a move that was to end the Wars of the Roses, and so united the two warring houses, York and Lancaster.

After You Read

Knowledge Focus

1. **Pair Work**

    Discuss the following questions with your partner.

    (1) What were the warring parties of the Wars of the Roses?

    (2) What was the major conflict in the Wars of the Roses?

    (3) Who was the Black Prince?

    (4) Who had mental illness hereditary in his mother's family?

    (5) How was the conflict in the war resolved finally?

Unit 6 The House of Lancaster and York

2. Fill in each blank with the word that best completes the following passage.

| discontent | medieval | dynasty | claimed | reign |
| battlefield | mental | emblem | corrupt | opposing |

Like (1) _____ football teams or rival gangs, the House of Lancaster and the House of York, both royal families, each had its color. The House of Lancaster's color was red, and their (2) _____ was a red rose. The House of York's color was white, and their emblem was a white rose. So, when the Houses of Lancaster and York fought for 30 years over who would rule England, it became known as the Wars of the Roses.

Both Lancaster and York based their claim to the throne on an ancestor that they had in common, King Edward III. Henry VI, a descendant of Edward III and a member of the House of Lancaster, was king in the 1450s, but he would not (3) _____ unopposed. (4) _____ was growing among Henry's subjects. They no longer had much faith in their king after England's losses in The Hundred Years' War. Some people also (5) _____ that Henry's government was (6) _____.

Henry was having personal troubles too; he suffered from (7) _____ illness. From time to time, this illness became so severe that he was unable to rule his country.

The House of York believed that someone from its side of the family would make a better king. They led the opposition to Henry's rule and used the public's discontent with Henry to rally support for their side.

In 1455, Richard of York led an attack on King Henry. He organized his knights and led them on a march to London. When King Henry heard that they were coming, he mustered his own troops and set out to stop the Yorks.

The two armies met in the town of St. Albans. Swords and shields clashed. This time, Henry was defeated, but the war had just begun. St. Albans was the first battle of a long war.

During the 30 years that the war lasted, England went from Lancaster rule to York rule, back to Lancaster, and back again to York. When the Lancasters were in power, Henry VI was king. When the Yorks were in power, Edward IV ruled. Later, Edward IV was succeeded by Edward V and Richard III.

In 1485, while Richard III was king, Henry Tudor, a Lancaster, planned another attack. The armies of Henry Tudor and Richard III met in the village of Bosworth. Once again, the sounds of (8) _____ knights at war rang out on the (9) _____. By the end of the Battle of Bosworth, Henry Tudor had defeated Richard III.

Henry Tudor was crowned King Henry VII.

Then Henry, the Lancaster king, married Elizabeth. Elizabeth was Edward IV's daughter and a member of the House of York. The marriage of Henry and Elizabeth united the two sides at last. After 30 years, there was no more need for war.

A new (10) _____, the House of Tudor, began. A red and white rose, named the Tudor Rose, became the emblem of England's new royal family.

Language Focus

1. Fill in the blanks with the following words or expressions you have learned in the text. Put them into appropriate forms if necessary.

reign	consequence	confiscate	surrender	a bout of
insanity	plunge into	restore	hereditary	recover

(1) It was sheer _____ to try to drive through the mountains in that thunderstorm.

(2) Pain and illness are sometimes thought to be the unavoidable _____ of growing old.

(3) The building has been carefully _____ after the fire.

(4) Many of the most-feared militants were shot, and more than 700 of them _____.

(5) It took a long time for the British economy to _____ from the effects of the war.

(6) I was drunk for _____ drinking with company colleagues last night.

(7) This _____ factor means that there is often a connection between the physical appearance of an individual and his/her temperament.

(8) The airplane's engines failed and it _____ the ocean.

(9) An increasing number of guns have been _____ in schools recently.

(10) They say that relics of Hitler's _____ should be destroyed, not sold for profit.

2. Complete the following sentences with the proper forms of the words in the brackets.

(1) The man must be totally _____ (insanity) to do that foolish thing.

(2) According to the laws of _____ (hereditary), tall parents tend to have tall children.

(3) His decision of _____ (surrender) implied the failure of the battle.

(4) She made a quick _____ (recover) from her headache.

(5) His long time _____ (imprison) led to the divorce.

(6) Most of children like stories full of _____ (mysteriously).

3. Find the appropriate prepositions that collocate with the neighboring words.

(1) The name "Wars of the Roses" is based _____ the badges used _____ the two sides, the red rose _____ the Lancastrians and the white rose _____ the Yorkists.

(2) Although there were no battles fought _____ 1455, the causes of the wars dated back _____ the reign of Edward III and the power struggle _____ his sons _____ his death.

(3) Edward, the Black Prince had died _____ the plague in 1376.

(4) As Richard grew older he rebelled _____ his uncle and made decisions that were not popular _____ the most powerful men in the country.

(5) Henry IV faced a number of challenges to his place _____ the throne because he was not the natural successor _____ Richard II.

(6) The country was _____ peace and his son, Henry V, succeeded

_____ problem.

(7) When Henry V died in 1422 _____ dysentery, his son, Henry VI became the only king to be crowned king of England and France.

(8) Henry VI was four months old when he became king and his father's brothers ruled England and France _____ his place.

(9) England was plunged _____ a civil war—the Wars of the Roses.

(10) Queen Margaret took her son and fled to Wales where they were taken _____ by the king's half-brother Jaspar Tudor.

Comprehensive Work

1. Comparison and Contrast

The Hundred Years' War and the Wars of the Roses were two consecutive series of wars in the history of England. With your knowledge about the history during this period, can you possibly make a comparison between the Hundred Years' War and the Wars of the Roses? You may fill in the chart first and write a composition on this topic.

	The Hundred Years' War	The Wars of the Roses
The Duration		
The Reason for Its Name		
The Warring Parties		
The Causes		
The Outcome		
Major Kings Involved		

2. Read the summary concerning the causes of the conflict in the wars and surf the Internet to find materials to back up the points below.

Major causes of the conflict include: 1) both houses were direct descendants of King Edward III; 2) the ruling Lancastrian king, Henry VI, surrounded himself with unpopular nobles; 3) the civil unrest of much of the population; 4) the availability of many powerful lords with their own private armies; and 5) the untimely episodes of mental illness by King Henry VI.

Read More

Text B The Mystery of the Princes in the Tower

In 1933, the skeletons of two young boys, one aged about 10 and the other 13, were disinterred from Westminster Abbey.

These bones had been re-buried in an urn in 1674 and placed in the Henry VIII Chapel in the Abbey. The skeletons aroused much interest and debate as they were believed by many historians to be the bones of the two princes who were murdered in the Tower of London in the 15th century.

The princes were Edward V and his brother Richard Duke of York, the sons of Edward IV and his queen, Elizabeth Woodville. Their uncle, Richard of Gloucester, later Richard III, came after them in the succession.

In his *History*, Sir Thomas More was quite sure that these young boys were murdered by their uncle Richard of Gloucester and Shakespeare also portrayed Richard III as the evil murderous uncle.

Sir Thomas More stated that the princes were smothered with the pillows on their beds by Sir James Tyrell, John Dighton and Miles Forest. Tyrell was reported to have confessed to the crime in 1502 when under sentence of death for treason.

Richard III is the name most associated with the mystery of the two little princes. It is said that he had them killed as their right to the throne was stronger than his. Shakespeare certainly decided that he had given the order for the boys to be killed.

But Henry Tudor, who later became Henry VII in 1485 after defeating Richard III at the Battle of Bosworth, had an even shakier claim to the throne. His claim was based on the right of conquest.

If the princes were alive in 1485, they would have been a great embarrassment to Henry, and Henry had as much to gain as Richard by the death of the young boys.

There is no proof of Henry's guilt any more than there is of Richard's.

Immediately after Henry gained the throne, he accused Richard of cruelty and tyranny but strangely did not mention the murder of the little princes. Henry did not announce that the boys had been murdered until July 1486, nearly a year after Richard's death.

The only conclusion to the mystery of the princes in the tower is that nobody now will be able to prove who killed them, and what happened all those years ago will remain one of the most intriguing whodunit of all time.

1. Questions for discussion or reflection.
   (1) Who gave the order to Tyrell and his accomplices?
   (2) Did Henry have the princes in the Tower murdered?
   (3) What happened to the princes?

2. Tell whether and why the following are true or false according to the text.
   (1) The skeletons of the two princes were discovered in 1674. (   )
   (2) The princes Edward V and his brother Richard Duke of York, were the sons of Richard of Gloucester. (   )
   (3) According to Sir Thomas More, the princes were smothered with the pillows on their beds by Sir James Tyrell, John Dighton and Miles Forest. (   )
   (4) Thomas More certainly decided that Richard III had given the order for the boys to be killed. (   )
   (5) Henry announced that the boys had been murdered in July 1486. (   )

Text C   The Middle Ages

The medieval period in history was between the 5th and 15th centuries. Also called the Middle Ages, it was a time of change in western Europe. It began with the fall of the Roman Empire to invading Germanic tribes. Western Europe broke into many separate kingdoms. Trade collapsed; people made their living from the land; and the feudal system began. The early Middle Ages are called the "Dark Ages" because the learning and culture of ancient Greece and Rome almost disappeared. The medieval period ended when the Renaissance swept across Europe.

Before medieval times, all of western Europe was part of the Roman Empire. Exact dates for the beginning and end of these eras do not exist. Rather the fall of the Roman Empire happened over a period of several hundred years as the Roman Empire weakened and Germanic tribes from the Scandinavian regions were able to conquer, eventually leading to a new way of life.

Compared to the citizenry of Ancient Rome, most Germanic people were uneducated. They were a rough-looking people clothed in animal skins and coarse linen. Called barbarians, these fierce people lived in tribes governed by a chief. They lived mainly by hunting and employing a crude level of farming. Their laws were based on tribal customs and superstition rather than a strong system of laws. They were fierce and bold warriors, battling with spears, clubs, and shields.

The barbarian invasions destroyed most of the European trade. The stone road system that was developed to connect prosperous cities of the Roman Empire was abandoned. Communication slowed and money almost went completely out of use. By the 9th century AD, most of western Europe was carved into large manor estates ruled by landlords. Most people became poor

peasants who worked the land. Some towns were completely abandoned and disappeared as the people moved to the countryside. Each manor was supported almost entirely by the production of its inhabitants. Most of the state and city schools closed and education and cultural activities ceased. Few people could read or write and the developments of ancient literature, architecture, painting, and sculpture were forgotten.

Medieval life eventually combined the ways of Germanic people with practices of ancient Rome and Greece, but was also influenced by the Muslims of Spain and the Middle East and the Byzantine Empire of southeastern Europe. Some adopted elements of their Roman neighbors, accepting Christianity as their religion, farming the land, and trading with merchants. The church became the single great force that bound Europe together during this feudal period.

1. Questions for discussion or reflection.
   (1) What does the term "the Middle Ages" usually refer to in history?
   (2) What do you know about the "Dark Ages"?
   (3) Do you think the Medieval Ages were a crucial period in the history of Europe? And why?

Proper Names

the Battle of Wakefield 威克菲尔德战役　　the House of Lancaster 兰开斯特家族
the Battle of Agincourt 阿让库尔战役(1415)　the House of York 约克家族
the Battle of Bosworth Field 博斯沃思原野战役

Notes

1. **Henry VII**: (Henry Tudor, January 28, 1457—April 21, 1509) Henry VII was King of England and Lord of Ireland from his usurpation of the crown on August 22, 1485 until his death on April 21, 1509, as the first monarch of the Tudor dynasty.
2. **Queen Margaret**: Margaret of Anjou was the queen consort of Henry VI of England from 1445 to 1471 and led the Lancastrian contingent

in the Wars of the Roses. Due to the king's frequent bouts of insanity, Margaret virtually ruled the kingdom in lieu of her husband.

For Fun

Website to visit

http://en.wikipedia.org/wiki/Wars_of_the_Roses

It is a comprehensive website about the Wars of the Roses, where you can find more information about the names and symbols, key figures, and their family tree, etc.

Movies to see

1. *Princes in the Tower* (2000)

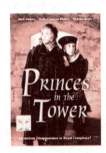

The historical drama *Princes in the Tower* recreates the strange 15th-century disappearance of two European royals—12-year-old Edward V and his 10-year-old brother, providing one possible explanation for their fates.

2. *Henry V* (1989)

During The Hundred Years' War, Henry V of England with some 6,000 men defeated a French army six times that size on Oct. 25, 1415. The victory enabled the English to conquer much of France. The battle of Agincourt is the central scene of Shakespeare's drama *Henry V*.

3. *The Hollow Crown* (2012)

The Hollow Crown is a lavish new series of filmed adaptations of four of Shakespeare's most gripping history plays: Richard II, Henry IV, Part 1, Henry IV, Part 2 and Henry V. The films — chronicling a bloody tale of family, politics and power — tell the rise and fall of three Kings and how their destiny shaped English history.

4. *The White Queen* (2013)

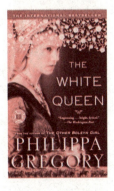

The White Queen is a British television drama series in ten parts, based on Philippa Gregory's historical novel series *The Cousins' War*. The series is set against the backdrop of the Wars of the Roses and presents the story of the women involved in the long conflict for the throne of England. It starts in 1464; the nation has been at war for nine years fighting over who is the rightful king as two sides of the same family, the House of York and the House of Lancaster contest the throne.

Unit 7
The Tudor Age

> They wrote in the old days that it is sweet and fitting to die for one's country. But in modern war, there is nothing sweet nor fitting in your dying. You will die like a dog for no good reason.
> —Ernest Hemmingway

Unit Goals

- To be familiar with the Tudor Monarchy
- To learn about the history of the English Reformation
- To know the Dissolution of Monasteries
- To learn the important words and expressions that describe the Tudor Age and improve English language skills
- To develop critical thinking and intercultural communication skills

 Before You Read

(1) Have you ever heard of the story about Henry VIII and his six wives in the history of England? Retell the story to your partner.
(2) Do you know anything about Thomas More's *Utopia*? Why is it so influential?
(3) What do you know about the Reformation in England?
(4) Form groups of three or four students. Try to find, on the Internet or in the library, more information about the English Reformation. Get ready for a 5-minute presentation in class.

Start to Read

Text A The Tudor Monarchy

1. The Tudors, as a family, ruled over England from 1485 until 1603. They brought peace to England after many years of war. There had been the Wars of the Roses for 30 years in England. The Lancastrians had a red rose as a symbol, and the Yorkists had a white. At the end of the war, Henry Tudor, a Lancastrian, married Elizabeth of the Yorks. They put the white rose and the red rose together as a symbol of unity.

2. The ending of the Wars of the Roses ushered in a new age in English history. English children are commonly told that the Middle Ages ended in 1485 when the Wars of the Roses were over and the House of Tudor ascended the throne in the person of King Henry VII. The Tudor Monarchy was known as the new monarchy because it differed from the old ones in many aspects.

3. A lot of nobles had lost their heads during the Wars of the Roses and many big feudal households had been destroyed. As a result, the position of the Tudor Monarchy was greatly strengthened and the influence of the new-born bourgeoisie increased. To protect the interests of the commercial and landed middle class, on which the Tudors themselves relied for their power and popularity, the monarchy emphasized the need to promote the development of trade and industry. It was also during the Tudor Monarchy that America was discovered and the Renaissance spread into England. All these helped to prepare the conditions for the establishment of the capitalist mode of production in England. Meanwhile, large amounts of wealth needed for capitalist development was being accumulated. The day for the English bourgeoisie to take over political power was not far off. The Tudor Monarchy thus served as the transitional stage from feudalism to capitalism in English history.

4. The fast development of the clothing industry was of great significance during the Tudor Monarchy. Towards the end of the Hundred Years' War in the 15th century, the clothing industry began to develop and England turned from a producer of wool into a manufacturer of cloth. With the development of the profitable clothing industry, more wool was needed. Many landowners soon realized the sheep-farming was far more profitable than growing crops. Besides, sheep-farming was less vulnerable to bad weather and required less labor. As a result, England witnessed what has been called the Enclosure. Landowners expelled their tenants and enclosed their fields. The separate small fields were combined into a consolidated farm which was turned into grazing land for the use of sheep-breeding. The situation caused much suffering to the tenants and resulted in social unrest. It was a period in which "sheep devour men", as was described in Thomas More's *Utopia*.

Text B The Reformation in England (1517—1563)

1. The English Reformation started in the reign of Henry VIII. The English Reformation was to have far-reaching consequences in Tudor England. Henry VIII decided to rid himself of his first wife, Catherine of Aragon, after she had failed to produce a male heir to the throne. He had already decided who his next wife would be—Anne Boleyn. By 1527, Catherine was considered too old to have anymore children.

2. However, a divorce was not a simple issue. In fact, it was a very complicated one. Henry VIII was a Roman Catholic, and the head of this church was the Pope based in Rome.

3. The Roman Catholic faith believed in marriage for life. It did not recognize, let alone support, divorce. This put Henry VIII in a difficult position. If he went ahead and announced that as King of England he was allowing himself a divorce, the Pope could excommunicate him. This meant that under Catholic Church law, your soul could never get to Heaven. To someone living at the time of Henry, this was a threat which the Catholic Church used to keep people under its control.

4. Another approach Henry used was to make a special appeal to the Pope so that the Pope would agree to Henry's request for a divorce purely because Henry was King of England, but it would not affect the way the Catholic Church banned divorce for others. The Pope refused to grant Henry this and by 1533 his anger was such that he ordered the Archbishop of Canterbury to grant him a divorce so that he could marry Anne Boleyn. The Archbishop

granted Henry his divorce—against the wish of the Pope. But what else could the Archbishop do if he wanted to remain on good terms with Henry? This event effectively led to England breaking away from the Roman Catholic Church based in Rome. Henry placed himself as head of the church and in that sense, in his eyes, his divorce was perfectly legal.

5. How did the people of England react to this? In fact, the vast bulk of the population was very angry at the way the Roman Catholic Church had used them as a source of money. To get married you had to pay; to get a child baptized (which you needed to be if you were to go to Heaven—so the Catholic Church preached) you had to pay; you even had to pay the Church to bury someone on their land (which you had to do as your soul could only go to Heaven if you were buried on Holy Ground). Therefore, the Catholic Church was very wealthy while many poor remained just that poor. Their money was going to the Catholic Church. Therefore, there were no great protests throughout the land as many felt that Henry would ease up on taking money from them. Henry sensed the Catholic Church's unpopularity and therefore used this to his advantage. Henry was made Supreme Head of the Church by an Act of Parliament in 1534. The country was still Catholic but the Pope's power had been ended.

6. The most wealthy Catholics in England were the monasteries where monks lived. They were also the most loyal supporters of the Pope. This made them a threat to Henry.

7. By the time of Henry, many monks had grown fat and were lazy. They did not help the community as they were meant to do. All they seemed to do was take money from the poor. Also some monasteries were huge and owned vast areas of land.  So here were monks not loyal to Henry who were also very wealthy. Henry decided to shut down the monasteries of England. The monasteries were to disappear like sugar dissolves in hot liquid. This is why Henry's attack on the monasteries is called the "Dissolution"—they were to be dissolved.

8. Some monastery buildings were reduced to ruin as the local population was allowed to take what they wanted as long as the silver and gold in the monastery went to the Crown. This meant that things like expensive building bricks could be acquired for free.  This alone made the Dissolution popular with the majority of the people who tended to dislike lazy monks anyhow.

9. However, the vast bulk of the wealth of the monasteries went to Henry. Some was spent building defenses against France on the south coast around Portsmouth; a small amount went on paying pensions to monks and abbots.

10. To reform means to change. This is why this event is called the English Reformation as it did change the way the church was run throughout England. However, the death of Henry in 1547 did not see an end of the religious problems of England.

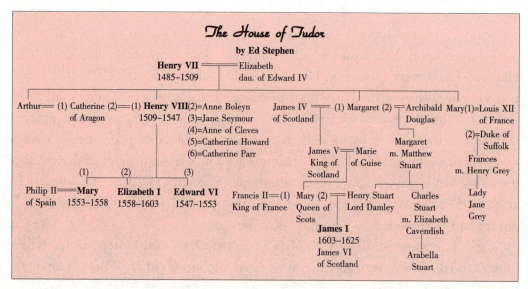

After You Read

Knowledge Focus

1. Pair Work

Discuss the following questions with your partner.

(1) Who was the first king of the House of Tudor?

(2) Why was the Tudor Monarchy known as a new monarchy different from former ones?

(3) What do you know about the Enclosure Movement in England?

(4) How do you understand "sheep devour men"?

(5) Who was in the reign when the English Reformation started?

(6) What were the far-reaching consequences of the Reformation in Tudor England?

(7) What was the Roman Catholic faith about marriage?

(8) How did the people of England react to England breaking away from the Roman Catholic Church?

(9) Why was the attack on the monasteries called the "Dissolution"?

(10) How do you comment on the English Reformation?

2. **Solo Work**

   Tell whether and why the following are true or false according to the knowledge you have learned.

   ____ (1) The Wars of the Roses lasted for 30 years in England.

   ____ (2) At the end of the war, Henry Tudor, a Yorkist, married Elizabeth of the Lancastrian. They put the white rose and the red rose together as a symbol of unity.

   ____ (3) It was also during the Tudor Monarchy that India was discovered and the Renaissance spread into England.

   ____ (4) The Tudor Monarchy served as the transitional stage from feudalism to capitalism in English history.

   ____ (5) Towards the end of the Hundred Years' War in the 15th century, England turned from a producer of silk into a manufacturer of cloth.

   ____ (6) Sheep-farming was more vulnerable to bad weather and required less labor.

   ____ (7) The period in which "sheep devour men" was described in Thomas More's *Utopia*.

   ____ (8) The English Reformation started in the reign of Henry VII.

   ____ (9) Henry VIII decided to rid himself of his first wife, Anne Boleyn, after she had failed to produce a male heir to the throne.

   ____ (10) During the reign of Henry VIII, many monks did not help the community as they were meant to do and took money from the poor.

Language Focus

1. **Fill in the blanks with the following words or expressions you have learned in the text. Put them into appropriate forms if necessary.**

be on good terms with	accumulate	let alone	usher in
ascend	be vulnerable to	reduce... to	bulk
differ from	consolidate		

   (1) Many thousands of poor children had never even seen, _____ owned a pair of leather shoes.

   (2) He seemed to _____ the people behind the bar.

   (3) The great _____ of the evidence from the town concerns pottery production.

   (4) By the late 1950s, scientists had already _____ enough evidence to show a clear link between smoking and cancer.

   (5) The discovery of oil _____ an era of employment and prosperity.

   (6) Scottish law has always _____ English law.

   (7) This short case study shows these medium-sized factories _____ continuing change.

   (8) He acquired it partly by accident, for war was near when he _____ the throne.

   (9) Successful advertising helped them to _____ their position as the

largest computer company in Europe.

(10) A massive earthquake _____ the city _____ ruins.

2. **Complete the following sentences with the proper forms of the words in the brackets.**
   (1) I've made an _____ (accumulate) of work while I was ill.
   (2) You may move cards off in _____ (ascend) order from Ace to King to their respective piles off the playing area.
   (3) Somalia was again crippled by a drought that _____ (threat) to kill hundreds of thousands more.
   (4) One of her weak points is _____ (vulnerable).
   (5) He is so arrogant that he is _____ (popular) in this party.

3. **Find the appropriate prepositions that collocate with the neighboring words.**
   (1) The Tudors ruled _____ England from 1485 until 1603.
   (2) The ending of the Wars of the Roses ushered _____ a new age in English history.
   (3) The House of Tudor ascended the throne _____ the person of King Henry VII.
   (4) The Tudor Monarchy was known _____ the new monarchy because it differed _____ the old ones _____ many aspects.
   (5) The Tudors themselves relied _____ the commercial and landed middle class _____ their power and popularity.
   (6) The day for the English bourgeoisie to take _____ political power was not far _____.
   (7) The Roman Catholic faith believed _____ marriage _____ life.
   (8) But what else could the archbishop do if he wanted to remain _____ good terms _____ Henry?
   (9) There were no great protests _____ the land as many felt that Henry would ease up _____ taking money from them.
   (10) Some was spent building defenses _____ France _____ the south coast around Portsmouth; a small amount went _____ paying pensions to monks and abbots.

Comprehensive Work

1. **Team Work**

   The story of the Tudors has it all—love, betrayal, war, death, humor, and lots of juicy details. If the Tudor story was the basis of a television story today, what would it be?

   Work with your team member and decide: Which aspect of Tudor Monarchy is getting you interested in the story? One possible story is entitled "Days of My Wives", a soap opera on Henry VIII. With due preparation, you can have a show of various stories of Tudor family in class.

2. Pair Work

Link Past with Present

Read the statements in the left column in terms of life in Tudor age, and supply relevant information about your life today in the right column. Discuss the changes or transformations with your partner.

Life in Tudor Age	Life Today
Girls could marry at the age of 12, boys at the age of 14! They still had to live with their parents until they were 16 though.	
Nine out of ten people died before they were 40. There was so much disease and they had no idea how to cure any of them or how to be hygienic.	
Baths were not considered healthy, so Tudors just covered up the awful smell with strong perfume.	
Toilets were called "privies" and were not very private at all. They were often just a piece of wood over a hole in the ground and might have room for up to 6 people to go at the same time.	
Open sewers ran in the streets and passed many of the diseases on.	
An average person drank about 8 pints of weak beer a day, which had very little alcohol and even children drank; it was safer than the water. It was called "small beer".	
They knew that sugar rotted their teeth, and since sugar was so expensive, women used to deliberately black their teeth out to look rotten, because it showed they could afford to buy sugar.	
A popular "cure" for illness was bloodletting. People believed that illness was caused by too much blood in the body. So they would cut a slit and let some of the blood out. Sounds like you'd feel worse after that.	
Water came from village pumps, and they got the water from the local stream, which was most likely full of sewage from the town. No wonder they got so ill!	

3. Writing Activity

As for Thomas More, probably most people are familiar with his *Utopia*, which is now to describe any real or imaginary state or place believed to be ideal, perfect and excellent. Probably far fewer are familiar with Sir Thomas More's most enduring image of sheep devouring men—a commentary on the practice of "enclosure", whereby common land was taken for profitable sheep-farming, for wool, but depriving peasants of their land, livelihood and food.

Write a short essay within 300 words to comment on the phenomenon "sheep devouring men".

Read More

Text C — King Henry VII

King Henry VII ruled England from 1485 to 1509. During his reign, he made important decisions that helped to modernize England, or to bring it into what we call the Renaissance today. He made improvements in government and education. He also sponsored important voyages of exploration.

Henry Tudor became king through a dramatic event in 1485. He defeated the reigning king, Richard III, at the Battle of Bosworth. As soon as the old king was killed, the soldiers on the battlefield proclaimed Henry the new king of England. He became King Henry VII.

Later, back in London, his coronation was made official in a ceremony full of kingly pageantry and splendor.

In 1486, Henry married Elizabeth of York. This was an important move for the English monarchy, because it united Henry's family, known as Lancaster, to Elizabeth's family, known as York. At that time, royal marriages were often arranged to unite countries or parts of countries.

Some of the first problems that Henry had to deal with as king were conflicts that continued to arise among the lords of his kingdom. King Henry set up a court, known as the Star Chamber. This court had the power to take nobles to court if they got out of hand. Then, the court would decide who was right.

There were still conflicts going on between England and France. Early in his reign, Henry decided to try an invasion of

France. His invasion was not successful. After a while, Henry and the French king sat down at a peace conference. There they decided to settle the problem with money instead of with more battles. England withdrew its forces from French territory, and France paid a large sum of money to England.

With all of this money, King Henry's government was in a good position to take on other projects.

Henry spent some of England's money on education. He brought in scholars from France who could pass on their knowledge to people in England. In his court, scholars from Italy and other countries were welcome too. Through these scholars, the Renaissance began to spread to England.

King Henry was also interested in exploration. Everyone had heard about Christopher Columbus's voyage in 1492. Columbus had sailed for Spain, but Henry thought that it would be a good idea for England to get in on some explorations too. After all, England had excellent ships and was known as a seafaring nation.

Then, King Henry heard that John Cabot was looking for someone to sponsor a voyage of exploration. Cabot was from Italy; his real name was Giovanni Cabotto. His home country had not been interested in sending him on an exploration. So Cabot had gone to Spain, the country of Christopher Columbus, but Spain was not interested in his plan either. Finally, Cabot went to England. There, King Henry was happy to see the explorer, and signed him on to sail for England. Cabot set sail on his famous voyage to North America flying the English flag.

King Henry VII was the first king of the Tudor dynasty. Throughout the following years, the reign of the Tudor dynasty also became known as the time of the Renaissance in England.

1. **Finish the following multiple-choice questions according to Text C.**
    (1) Henry VII became king in _____.
        A. 1509   B. 1486   C. 1885   D. 1485
    (2) Henry VII succeeded King Henry VI. This statement is _____.
        A. false   B. true
    (3) King Henry VII defeated King Richard III in the Star Chamber. This statement is _____.
        A. false   B. true

(4) The conflict over land between England and France was settled when _____.
   A. France gave land to England
   B. France gave money to England
   C. England gave land to France
   D. England gave money to France

(5) King Henry VII sponsored the voyage of exploration of _____.
   A. Richard III   B. Christopher Columbus
   C. Queen Elizabeth   D. John Cabot

(6) Cabot sailed to _____ under the flag of _____.
   A. South America, Spain   B. South America, England
   C. North America, Spain   D. North America, England

(7) The Renaissance in England occurred during the _____ dynasty.
   A. Tudor   B. York   C. Stuart   D. Lancaster

Text D Henry VIII and His Marriage

Henry VIII was never meant to be king. His elder brother, Arthur was destined to rule over England, but that was not to be. When Henry was 12, Arthur died. Henry's father immediately betrothed Henry to Catherine. When his father died in April, 1509, Henry became King of England. One of his first decisions as king was to marry Catherine of Aragon, his dead brother's wife. The wedding took place on June 11. Catherine was 23 and Henry not 18 yet.

But all was not happy in Henry and Catherine's marriage. Out of nine pregnancies, only one child, Mary, lived. Believing that God was showing his divine displeasure at their marriage, he asked the Pope for an annulment of his marriage to Catherine. The Pope refused. In 1532, Henry VIII took matters into his own hands by declaring the church in England separate from the church in Rome. Free of Rome, Henry had his own clergy renounce his marriage to Catherine. He and Anne were married in 1533, with Anne already pregnant with Henry's longed-for heir.

Henry had already decided before the child was born that the baby would be named either Henry or Edward. However, the baby turned out to be a daughter. Henry was greatly disappointed, as was Anne. Anne had at least one more child, a male who was born dead on the same day Anne's nemesis, Catherine of Aragon, was buried. The termination of that pregnancy resulted in her death.

Henry wanted Anne out of the way, and he wanted her out of the way quickly and permanently. In May of 1536, Anne was arrested with five men, one of whom was her brother, George, and taken to the Tower of London. She was charged with adultery. She and the other men, accused as her lovers, were also charged with plotting the king's murder. Anne herself denied all charges, but it did not matter. She was convicted and sentenced to burning or beheading "at the king's pleasure". Henry was planning his next wedding by the time Anne's body was buried.

Henry was engaged to be married to Jane Seymour, a former lady in waiting to Anne Boleyn (just as Anne had been a lady in waiting to Catherine of Aragon) the day after his second wife's execution. They were married on May 30. On October 12, Jane gave birth to a healthy baby boy. Twelve days later, she was dead of childbed fever.

Soon after his third wife's death, Henry began a sort of beauty contest with the big prize. In 1539, Henry attempted to find the fourth lucky woman to be his bride. Her name was Anne of Cleves, the twenty-three-year-old sister of Duke of Cleves, and Henry VIII signed the marriage contract without laying eyes on her first, which was a mistake. When she arrived in England, he found her not to his taste, to say the least. The marriage was annulled six months later.

In December of 1540, Henry married his fifth wife, Catherine Howard. She was pretty and young—not yet twenty when she married Henry—and unfortunately, "bird-brained". After the couple had been married almost two years, it came to light that not only had Catherine apparently entered into a marriage contract with another man years before, and was therefore considered legally married to that man, Francis Dereham, but she was also carrying on in a very un-queen-like way with a member of her court. Catherine and the two men who were charged as her lovers were put to death in December of 1542.

The king married again, this time on July 12 of 1543 after a period of almost seven months (waiting much more to remarry than he did after the last wife he had executed). This time he married a woman who was already twice-widowed, Catherine Parr. She was a good woman who brought a sense of family to the dysfunctional Tudor brood, including Mary and Elizabeth, who were often estranged from their father. Catherine also took into her charge her great-niece by marriage, Jane Grey.

Henry died on 28th January 1547 in Whitehall, London, at the age of 56. His son, Edward, succeeded him.

1. **Questions for discussion or reflection.**
   (1) How many wives did Henry VIII marry in his lifetime?
   (2) Henry VIII broke away from the church in Rome. What else do you know about it?
   (3) Who succeeded Henry VIII after his death?

Proper Names

the Enclosure Movement 圈地运动   the Roman Catholic 罗马天主教
the English Reformation 英国宗教改革   the Tudor Monarchy 都铎王朝

Notes

1. **Henry VII:** He was King of England and Lord of Ireland from his usurpation of the crown on August 22, 1485 until his death on April 21, 1509, as the first monarch of the Tudor dynasty.
2. **Henry VIII:** Henry VIII, King of England and Ireland (June 28, 1491—January 28, 1547) was King of England from April 21, 1509 until his death. He was also Lord of Ireland (later King of Ireland) and claimant to the Kingdom of France. Henry was the second monarch of the House of Tudor, succeeding his father, Henry VII. He was a significant figure in the history of the English monarchy. Although in the great part of his reign he brutally suppressed the Protestant Reformation of the church, a movement having roots with John Wycliffe of the 14th century, he is more popularly known for his political struggles with Rome. These struggles ultimately led to his separating the Anglican Church from the Roman hierarchy, the Dissolution of the Monasteries, and establishing himself as the Supreme Head of the Church of England. He is noted for his six marriages.

For Fun

Website to visit
http://www.brims.co.uk/tudors/tudors.html
This is an interactive website with information about the Tudors, Henry VIII and his wives, etc.

Movies to see

1. The Tudors (2007)

This is a British-Irish-Canadian historical fiction television series set primarily in sixteenth-century England. *The Tudors* premiered in April 2007, and it was the highest-rated Showtime series in three years. The series, although named after the Tudor dynasty as a whole, is based specifically upon the reign of King Henry VIII of England.

2. The Other Boleyn Girl (2008)

The movie is loosely based on the life of 15th-century aristocrat Mary Boleyn, the sister of Anne Boleyn, about whom little is known. Inspired by the life of Mary, Gregory depicts the annulment of one of the most significant royal marriages in English history (that of King Henry VIII and Catherine of Aragon) and conveys the urgency of the need for a male heir to the throne. Much of the history is highly distorted in the movie. Some said it was a brilliantly claustrophobic look at palace life in Tudor England, while others are troubled by the lack of historical accuracy. It has enjoyed phenomenal success and popularity since its publication.

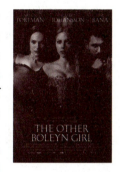

Books to read

1. The Terrible Tudors by Terry Deary

This book recollects the history with the nasty bits. It includes details of Tudor life from horrendous beheadings to mysterious murders and cruel kings and queens. History has never been so horrible!

2. Even More Terrible Tudors by Terry Deary

This book takes you back for another look at the mad Tudor monarchs and their suffering subjects, who just could not help losing their heads.

Song to enjoy

The most famous song associated with Elizabethan Age is undoubtedly "Greensleeves". This song has been attributed to King Henry VIII who was believed to have composed this song for his second wife, and the mother of Queen Elizabeth I, Anne Boleyn. This is a highly romantic notion but there is no proof that King Henry really did compose this famous Elizabethan song.

Greensleeves

Alas my love, ye do me wrong
to cast me off discurteously:
And I have loved you so long,
Delighting in your companie.

Greensleeves was all my joy
Greensleeves was my delight:
Greensleeves was my heart of gold,
And who but my Ladie Greensleeves.

I have been readie at your hand,
to grant what ever you would crave

I have both waged life and land,
your love and good will for to have.

Thou couldst desire no earthly thing,
But still thou hadst it readily,
Thy musicke still to play and sing,
And yet thou wuldst not love me.

Greensleeves now farewell adieu
God I pray to prosper thee,
For I am still thy lover true
Come once again and love me.

Unit 8
The Elizabethan Age

> We don't go to Shakespeare to find out about life in Elizabethan England; we go to Shakespeare to find out about ourselves now.
> —Jeanette Winterson

Unit Goals

- To learn about the history in the Elizabethan age
- To know the English Renaissance
- To be familiar with the achievements in the Elizabethan age
- To learn the useful words and expressions that describe the Elizabethan age and improve English language skills
- To develop critical thinking and intercultural communication skills

Before You Read

(1) What do you know about Elizabeth I, Queen of England? Fill in the missing information in the following box.

Her Father	
Her Mother	
The Royal Family She Belonged To	
Her Marital Status	
Major Achievements during Her Reign	

(2) What do you know about the English Renaissance?

(3) William Shakespeare is a household name. Can you name some of his masterpieces?

Comedy	History	Tragedy	Poetry

(4) Form groups of three or four students. Try to find, on the Internet or in the library, more information about the English Renaissance which interests you. Get ready for a 5-minute presentation in class.

Start to Read

Text A The Reign of Elizabeth I

1. Elizabeth I was 25 years old when she became Queen of England in 1558. Her 45-year reign, which ended with her death in 1603, saw England's emergence as a nation of tremendous political power and unparalleled cultural achievements. Because so much of the English Renaissance is directly attributable to Elizabeth's personal character and influence (as well as to the unprecedented length of her reign), it is appropriate that the last half of the 16th century in England is identified as the Elizabethan Age.

2. The daughter of Henry VIII and his second wife, Anne Boleyn, Elizabeth was third in line of succession, following her younger half-brother Edward (son of Henry VIII and Jane Seymour) and her elder half-sister Mary (daughter of Henry VIII and Catherine of Aragon). Under normal circumstances, it would be unlikely that she would ever assume the throne.

3. However, as has often happened throughout history, events did not follow their predicted course. The nine-year-old Edward became King Edward VI on the death of Henry VIII in 1547, but he had little opportunity to establish himself as a monarch, dying at the age of 15. He was succeeded by Mary I (1553—1558), whose efforts to return England to Catholicism brought about a true reign of terror and stifled any possibility of forward movement in the nation. When Mary died suddenly in 1558, Elizabeth I became Queen.

4. In both intellect and character, Elizabeth was well-suited for the role of monarch. She was exceptionally well-educated, having been taught at her father's court by Roger Ascham, one of the most outstanding scholars and thinkers of the age. Her intellectual interests were broad, ranging from history and science to art, literature, and philosophy, and she was a remarkably astute political strategist.

5. Not only did she return the country to internal political and religious stability in the wake of "Bloody Mary's" reign, she also directed England's course as it became a powerful force among European nations. Both Spain and France felt England's growing strength and audacity under Elizabeth's rule.

6. Sir Francis Drake's circumnavigation of the globe (1577—1580) added to the nation's prestige in navigation and exploration. However, the peak of England's power at sea was the triumph over the mighty Spanish Armada in 1588, which secured the nation's position as a world power. Eleven years later, in 1599, England entered the arena of world trade and colonization, which it would dominate for the next three centuries, with the chartering of the East India Company.

7. Elizabeth was an enormously popular monarch, one of western civilization's first true cult figures. The Queen's tastes in fashion set the standard for the aristocracy and the rest of society; her love of music, drama, and poetry fostered an atmosphere in which many of England's greatest writers found encouragement and financial aid. Under Elizabeth's leadership, England experienced the true cultural reawakening or renaissance of thought, art, and vision which had begun in Italy a century earlier. And at the Queen's direction, Oxford and Cambridge universities were reorganized and chartered as centers for learning and scholarly endeavor.

8. The great literary achievement of the Elizabethan Period was the drama, a form which was rooted in centuries of popular folk entertainment and which had been adapted into the religious plays of the Middle Ages. As the 16th century progressed, playwrights increasingly moved their plots from the religious to the worldly, weaving into their dramas such diverse elements as legend and myth, classical dramatic forms and intense exploration of character.

The dramatic form allowed playwrights to simultaneously develop plot, theme, complex characters, and poetic language which pushed the English language to new heights of imaginative achievement. Everyone, regardless of social class, enjoyed the spectacle of the Elizabethan theatre, and playwrights found themselves writing for highly diverse audiences which reflected the ever-changing society.

9. The greatest dramatist of the age was William Shakespeare (1564—1616). In more than 30 comedies, tragedies and histories, Shakespeare gave the fullest expression of England in the transitional period from feudalism to capitalism. The best of his plays—*Hamlet*, *Othello*, *King Lear* and *Macbeth*, etc.—have become permanent pieces in the world's literature.

10. The last years of Elizabeth's reign were not always politically smooth; in fact, by the 1590s there was at least one serious threat of rebellion, as well as a series of bitter parliamentary conflicts. But Elizabeth was steadfast as a monarch and held things firmly in control until her death in 1603. She was succeeded by her cousin, King James VI of Scotland, who united the two nations as King James I.

11. England during the reign of Elizabeth I was a country of tremendous ambition, achievement, and promise. The accomplishments and spirit of the age can be traced back to many sociological and cultural factors, but foremost among these is the leadership of the forceful, resourceful, and shrewd Queen Elizabeth I. Her death marked not only the end of the Tudor line, but also of a glorious era in English history.

After You Read

Knowledge Focus

1. **Pair Work**

    Discuss the following questions with your partner.

    (1) How do you define "the Elizabethan Age" in the history of England?

    (2) Do you think Elizabeth could be a natural successor of the throne? If not, what made her become Queen of England?

    (3) What qualities do you find in Queen Elizabeth I?

(4) What contribution could be ascribed to Elizabeth and her reign?
(5) What added to the nation's prestige in navigation and exploration in the Elizabethan Age?
(6) When was the Spanish Armada defeated?
(7) What do you know about the drama—the great literary achievement of the Elizabethan Age?
(8) Can you name several plays written by William Shakespeare?
(9) Who succeeded the throne after Elizabeth I?
(10) How do you comment on the reign of Elizabeth I?

2. Solo Work
   Tell whether and why the following are true or false according to what you have learned.
   ____ (1) Elizabeth I became Queen of England in 1558.
   ____ (2) It is appropriate that the last half of the 15th century in England is identified as the Elizabethan Age.
   ____ (3) It would be likely that she would ever assume the throne under normal circumstances.
   ____ (4) The efforts of Mary I stifled any possibility of forward movement in the nation.
   ____ (5) Elizabeth I was a remarkably astute scientist.
   ____ (6) Both Spain and France felt England's growing strength and audacity under Elizabeth's rule.
   ____ (7) The Renaissance of thought, art, and vision had first begun in England because of Elizabeth's wise government.
   ____ (8) Lyrics are the great literary achievement of the Elizabethan Period, which had been adapted into the religious plays of the Middle Ages.

Language Focus

1. **Fill in the blanks with the following words or expressions you have learned in the text. Put them into appropriate forms if necessary.**

be attributable to	unprecedented	stifle	astute	prestige
in the wake of	range from... to	foster	endeavor	diverse

(1) The president's wife is often politically _____, ambitious and very influential in White House policy decisions.
(2) Hosting the Olympic Games would add to our country's international _____.
(3) How can this party _____ debate on such a crucial issue?
(4) Much of this trend _____ a strong economy, but there are other forces at work.
(5) All five kids, _____ in age _____ 10 to 19, were in this wedding.
(6) An _____ boom in tourism brought prosperity to this faraway town.
(7) It is difficult to design a program that will meet the _____ needs of

all our users.

(8) Recent studies show that advertising usually _____ competition and therefore lower prices.

(9) The businessmen always _____ to please our customers.

(10) _____ Thailand's economic troubles, Malaysia's currency also sank.

2. **Complete the following sentences with the proper forms of the words in the brackets.**

(1) The sun _____ (emergence) from the clouds.

(2) Honesty is one of his many _____ (attributive).

(3) My calculations were based on the _____ (assume) that house prices would remain steady.

(4) Our topics are varied, _____ (range) from education to juvenile delinquency.

(5) I could mention the names of several persons whose influence over their flocks was solely _____ (attribute) to this circumstance.

(6) He had the _____ (audacious) to tell me that I was too fat.

(7) Most parents expect to send their children to those _____ (prestige) universities.

(8) His mother did not tell him that he is a _____ (foster) child until he grew up.

(9) The manager is expected to use his or her best _____ (endeavor) to promote the artist's career.

(10) "It is _____ (stifle) here. Can we open the window?"

3. **Find the appropriate prepositions that collocate with the neighboring words.**

(1) Elizabeth I's 45-year reign ended _____ her death in 1603.

(2) She was third _____ line of succession.

(3) _____ both intellect and character, Elizabeth was well-suited _____ the role of monarch.

(4) Her intellectual interests were broad, ranging _____ history and science _____ art, literature, and philosophy.

(5) The great literary achievement of the Elizabethan Age had been adapted _____ the religious plays of the Middle Ages.

(6) Everyone, regardless _____ social class, enjoyed the spectacle of the Elizabethan theatre.

(7) As the 16th century progressed, playwrights increasingly moved their plots _____ the religious _____ the worldly, weaving _____ their dramas such diverse elements as legend and myth, classical dramatic forms and intense exploration of character.

(8) Elizabeth was steadfast _____ a monarch and held things firmly _____ control _____ her death in 1603.

Comprehensive Work

1. **Pair Work**

The Renaissance was a period in western European history from 1300 to 1600. Increased trade between European cities and the rest of the world weakened the feudal manor and helped cities grow. Local lords were not as powerful as they were during the Middle Ages and peasants found new freedoms at home and in the cities. The decline of feudalism and the movement of people and ideas made the Renaissance a time of great advances in western history. Inventions such as the printing press and fast production of books helped disseminate knowledge of ancient Greece and Rome and of science and medicine. The arts also flourished as people created new techniques and discovered new subjects to paint and sculpt. Artists, scientists, inventors, writers, philosophers, and others examined and explored their world with a new outlook.

The chart below lists accomplishments from the Renaissance period. Use the names below to identify the person responsible for each accomplishment. Work with your partner and write the names in the column on the left next to the appropriate accomplishment. Visit your library or use the Internet to learn about each person in the list.

Christopher Columbus	Ambrose Paré	Galileo Galilei	Andreas Vesalius
Robert Hooke	Nicolaus Copernicus	John Calvin	Johannes Gutenberg
Aretmisia Gentileschi	Sir Thomas More	William Shakespeare	Martin Luther
Pieter Brueghel	Niccolò Machiavelli	Filippo Brunelleschi	Leonardo da Vinci
Miguel de Cervantes	Michelangelo	Prince Henry of Portugal	Louise Labé

Name	Accomplishment
	Painted *The Peasant Dance*, a painting that relied on detail and realism.
	Wrote a book called *The Prince*.
	Designed and built a dome for the Florence Cathedral.
	Invented and sketched early tanks and cars.
	Wrote *Don Quixote*.
	Painted the ceiling of the Sistine Chapel.

(Continued)

Name	Accomplishment
	Established a center of navigation and exploration.
	Author who encouraged women to write books.
	Invented moveable type printing press.
	Painted pictures of strong women including a self-portrait.
	Wrote a book titled *Utopia* in which he shared a vision of a society of equals.
	Wrote the play *Romeo and Juliet*, among others.
	Wrote the *Ninety-Five Theses* challenging the Catholic Church.
	Preached about reforming the church. Geneva became the center of the Calvinist religion.
	Published the theory that the Earth was not the center of the universe.
	Developed the compound microscope.
	Published detailed descriptions of the human anatomy.
	Created a powerful telescope and was the first to observe and record sunspots.
	Surgeon who developed the use of bandages.
	Traveled to the Caribbean Sea, explored, and claimed large areas for Spain.

2. **Writing Activity**

The Elizabethan era is associated with Queen Elizabeth I's reign (1558—1603) and is often considered to be the golden age in English history. Choose one of the following topics and write an introductory essay.

(1) Why is the Elizabethan era considered to be a Golden Age in English history?
(2) What were some popular Elizabethan festivals and celebrations?
(3) What were some scientific achievements of the era?
(4) How is the Elizabethan era romanticized today?
(5) How did people entertain themselves during the Elizabethan era?
(6) What were the laws and illegal systems like?
(7) What were medicine and science like in the Elizabethan era?

Read More

Text B　　Queen Elizabeth I

Elizabeth Tudor grew up in a time of change in Europe. Kings and queens of European countries were constantly fighting for power and territory. The Reformation was well underway, and England had changed to a Protestant country under King

Henry VIII, and then back to a Catholic one under Queen Mary I.

England had dreams of expansion too, and at the same time had to fight off neighboring countries, like Spain, which tried to take over England.

England had been ruled by King Henry VIII, Elizabeth's father, and then by the young King Edward, Elizabeth's brother, who died while still a teenager. Edward was succeeded by Lady Jane Grey who ruled for only a few days, and then by Mary, Elizabeth's elder sister. When Mary died, Elizabeth became ruler of England, "Queen Elizabeth I".

England needed a good ruler. It had been through some hard times under its last four monarchs. Henry VIII's reign had been a time of controversy and unrest. Edward had been only a child during his brief reign, and that time had been full of rivalries among relatives who wanted to rule in Edward's place. Lady Jane Grey never even had time to rule, and Mary's short rule had been marked by bloody conflicts between Catholics and Protestants.

During Queen Mary's rule, Elizabeth had faced some of her worst troubles. During one of the many conflicts between Catholics and Protestants, her sister Mary had imprisoned Elizabeth in the Tower of London.

Elizabeth, however, would soon become not just the new ruler, but the ruler that England needed. She was well suited for the job of queen, in that she was well educated, able to speak several languages, and familiar with the ways of British royalty.

In her hand-embroidered gowns decorated with brilliant gems and pearls, and her starched neck ruffs, Elizabeth was the picture of royalty. She became a popular queen who loved sports, music, dancing, plays, and pageantry. The people of England loved and admired Queen Elizabeth.

Elizabeth was also popular among the royalty of Europe. Once she became queen, she received many proposals of marriage. Queen Elizabeth, however, chose to stay single.

In 1588, King Philip of Spain sent his fleet of ships to England, not to pay a royal visit, but to attack. Elizabeth sent Philip home in defeat and became even more popular with her subjects.

The conflict between Protestants and Catholics was another challenge for Queen Elizabeth. During her reign, England once again became a Protestant country.

Elizabeth faced many conflicts during her long reign, some from outside like King Philip's attack, and some from political fighting within her own country. She remained a strong ruler, however, and handled whatever problems came her way. She ruled with both power and dignity, so it is no surprise that the time of her reign, known as the Elizabethan Age, was one of the best in English history.

By the time of Elizabeth, the European Renaissance had already produced many great accomplishments. During her reign, some very famous Englishmen made their contributions to the Renaissance. William Shakespeare wrote during the Elizabethan Age, and Sir Francis Drake made the first voyage around the world during Elizabeth's reign too. All in all, the Elizabethan Age was a great time for England.

1. Tell whether the following statements are true or false according to Text B.
   (1) Elizabeth succeeded Edward VI to the throne of England. (   )
   (2) Under the rule of Queen Elizabeth I, England was a Protestant country. (   )
   (3) Elizabeth married King Philip of Spain. (   )
   (4) Elizabeth was a popular ruler. (   )
   (5) Elizabeth's reign was part of the time period known as the Renaissance. (   )

2. Team Work
   After you finish reading Text B, share your views on the following topics with your team members.
   (1) Why do you think Elizabeth was able to rule so successfully even though previous kings and queens had not been able to accomplish as much?
       Reason 1: _____
       Reason 2: _____
       Reason 3: _____

   (2) Suppose that you suddenly became ruler of your own country. What would your priorities be? Make a list of things that you would like to accomplish for your country.
       Accomplishment 1: _____
       Accomplishment 2: _____
       Accomplishment 3: _____

Text C Entertainment in Elizabethan Age

Long before the invention of modern technologies, such as radios and televisions, CDs and videos, video games and the Internet, the Elizabethans created an elaborate system of activities and events to keep themselves entertained. Although there was work to be done, leisure was an important part of the lives of the English people during the Elizabethan Age. Most of this leisure came either after church on Sundays or on the holidays.

During the Elizabethan Age there were great cultural achievements, particularly in the area of music and drama. In that time, musical literacy was expected in the upper class of society. Many Elizabethans made their own music. The laborers would sing while they worked, and the townspeople would sing or play music after meals. The lute, virginals, viola, recorder, bagpipe and the fiddle were favored instruments of that time. A popular form of entertainment in the countryside was the ringing of church bells. Elizabethans also loved to hear music. Since there was no access to a recording studio, the music had to be performed. In the major towns, official musicians gave free public concerts. The wealthy people hired musicians to play during dinner.

In the Elizabethan Age, drama was at the high peak of its cultural achievement for all time. There were a variety of plays including action, humor, violence, and plays with musical interludes. This period witnessed the first entertainment industry, especially in theater. Although the first performances were done in the courtyards of large inns, the very first public theater in London was built in 1576. Theaters were mostly to be found in London, near the court.

Elizabethan theater was the work of a few men: proprietors, actors, playwrights and workmen. The actors creating theater often received rewards, became respectable and would slowly move up in social standing. The brilliant playwrights included Christopher Marlow, William Shakespeare, and Ben Johnson. The rise, maturity and decline of Elizabethan Theater coincided with Shakespeare's dramatic career. By the year of Shakespeare's death, there was a transition from plays to literature. Elizabethan drama owed its strength and richness to the fusion of many elements. It was a mirror of the whole society.

Sports played a major role in the leisure time of the Elizabethan Age. Some of the indoor games included dice, chess, checkers and a variety of card games. If the cards and dice were too passive for the men, wrestling was an alternative for them. With wrestling, however, came injuries like broken ribs, internal injuries, broken necks and more.

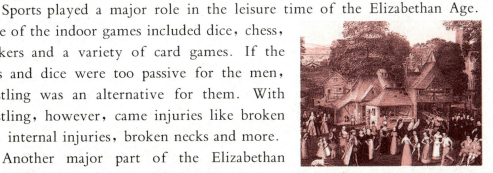

Another major part of the Elizabethan

lifestyle had to do with feasts and festivals. Every season of the year had special days that drew the people together to celebrate. In the spring, Shrove Tuesday was one of the festivals observed in the Lenten season. Feasts and a carnival were held and bell ringing, masking, gaming, and begging were among the activities. One of the greater festivals of the year was held at Easter time. The May Day celebration consisted of the decorating of the maypole and dancing around it. In the summer, bonfires were burned and dances were held to celebrate Midsummer's Eve on June 24. Also in June, St. John the Baptist's Festival was an important civic occasion. In the fall, harvest festivals were held. On All Hallow's Eve, Elizabethans celebrated by ducking for apples, dancing and bell ringing. The winter holidays began with Christmas, ran through New Year's Eve and ended on January 5.

From the beginning to the end of each year, Elizabethans found ways to keep themselves entertained. They were a creative group of people who pursued leisure activities with great passion.

1. **Questions for discussion or reflection.**
   (1) What do you know about the achievements in the area of music and drama during the Elizabethan Age?
   (2) In the Elizabethan Age drama was at the high peak of its cultural achievement for all time. Could you cite examples to illustrate the point?
   (3) What were the indoor games during the Elizabethan Age?

2. **Fill in the blanks with words you have learned in the passage above.**
   Long before the invention of _____, the Elizabethans created an elaborate system of _____ and _____ to keep themselves entertained.
   During the Elizabethan Age there was great cultural achievement, particularly in the area of _____ and _____. In that time, _____ was expected in the upper class of society. A popular form of entertainment in the countryside was _____. In this Age, _____ was at the high peak of its cultural achievement for all time. This period witnessed the first _____ industry, especially in _____. By the year of _____ death, there was a transition from _____ to _____. _____ was a mirror of the whole society. _____ played a major role in the leisure time of the Elizabethan Age. Another major part of the Elizabethan lifestyle had to do with _____ and _____. One of the greater festivals of the year was held at _____ time. In short, Elizabethans were a _____ group of people who pursued _____ activities with great passion.

Text D   Defeat of the Spanish Armada

In the 16th century, Europe was becoming organized into countries as we know them today. Now, armies were larger, and the stakes were higher as countries fought each other for power and territory. A few of the large, seafaring countries fought for even larger prizes. England and Spain were two of these large countries. Both had ambitions to extend their power beyond their own borders.

At one time, Spain and England had been on friendly terms. Trade had been established between the two countries. King Philip II of Spain and Queen Elizabeth I of England had worked together at times. However, conflicting goals soon threatened any alliance between the two rulers.

Some of the problems were commercial. English privateers had attacked Spanish merchant ships and even Spanish colonies in America. These attacks fueled Spanish anger at the English.

Some of the differences were religious. Spain had been trying to put down an uprising by Protestants in the Netherlands. England, under the Protestant Queen Elizabeth, supported the rebels. This made Spain angry at England.

In 1588, Spain had troops in the Netherlands, but their leader, Duke of Parma, feared that their safety was being threatened by England. So, Spain sent a fleet of warships, an armada, to escort them.

The meeting with Parma's troops would not be easy to coordinate. Radios had not yet been invented. The Armada, when it arrived, would have to wait out beyond the small harbor for Parma's troops to come out to them. It would take time to move Parma's troops, assembled on barges, out to the fleet. In the meantime, the Armada would be vulnerable to attack.

The Spanish Armada ran into trouble even before it met up with Parma's troops. It was spotted off the coast of England and was soon under attack by the British forces led by Lord Howard.

In one battle, Lord Howard set fireships floating towards the Armada. These were old wrecked ships that the English filled with wood, tar, and pitch. Then they set them on fire and released them to sail in the direction of the Armada. The Spanish sailors were forced to cut their own anchor chains to escape.

The next day, the two sides met in the Battle of Gravelines, France. The

Spanish troops had been trained in the seize and grapple technique that had been used in previous sea battles. In this technique, sailors used grappling hooks to latch onto an enemy ship. Then the sailors boarded the enemy ship for hand-to-hand combat. At Gravelines, however, the English attacked from a distance using their new long-range cannons. The Spanish never even had a chance to fight back.

The Spanish were good soldiers and sailors, and so were the English. Both sides regrouped and prepared for another day. Battles between the two sides continued for about a week. Finally, the Spanish gave up their plans to meet Parma and set sail for home, going the long way around the north of England to avoid the enemy ships still in the English Channel.

Then, Spain was struck another blow, this time by nature itself. A huge Atlantic storm blew the ships and drove some of the ships onto shore. Many ships were lost. Losses were even heavier than they had been in battle. Many sailors were never heard from again.

The remains of the Spanish Armada returned to Spain.

The Spanish Armada had been defeated; however, both sides regrouped once again, and the war between Spain and England continued for many more years. Spain remained a great seafaring nation, and it continued its colonization of America as well. England too remained a great seafaring nation, and would begin colonizing America too in the years to come.

Both nations had also learned a new lesson about warfare. They had learned that battles can be won with technology. In the defeat of the Spanish Armada, the newest technology, long-range cannons, had won the day. Both sides would now enter into a new competition, which was the competition to have the newest and best-equipped warships on the sea.

1. Finish the following multiple-choice questions according to Text D.
   (1) The battles between the English ships and the Spanish Armada occurred in the _____.
      A. English Channel   B. English countryside
      C. Pacific Ocean   D. Atlantic Ocean
   (2) How was the Netherlands involved in the defeat of the Spanish Armada?
      A. It was the location of the major land battles.
      B. England and Spain supported opposite sides of a religious conflict there.
      C. Both England and Spain hoped to establish colonies there.
      D. Spain's ships were all built in the Netherlands.
   (3) Duke of Parma was the leader of _____.
      A. the English fleet of sailing ships
      B. Spanish troops in the Netherlands

C. England

  D. Spain

(4) After the defeat of the Spanish Armada, _____.

  A. England claimed all of Spain's ships

  B. Spain ended its colonization of America

  C. Spain no longer had any ships

  D. Spain once again built a strong fleet

(5) One effect of the defeat of the Spanish Armada was the new importance of _____ in warfare.

  A. technology   B. hand-to-hand combat

  C. sailing   D. metal armor

2. **Pair Work**

   Share your views on the following topics with your classmates.

(1) Explain two reasons why the defeat of the Spanish Armada was an important historical event.

(2) Suppose that the Spanish Armada had not been defeated by the British in 1588. What effect do you think this would have had on future events in history?

Proper Names

Francis Drake 弗朗西斯·德雷克　　　　　the East India Company 东印度公司

Spanish Armada 西班牙无敌舰队　　　　　the Renaissance 文艺复兴

Notes

1. **Bloody Mary**: Mary I, Queen of England and Ireland (Feb. 18, 1516—Nov. 17, 1558), was Queen of England and Queen of Ireland from July 19, 1553 until her death. The fourth crowned monarch of the Tudor dynasty, she is remembered for restoring England to Roman Catholicism after succeeding her short-lived half brother, Edward VI, to the English throne. In the process, she had almost 300 religious dissenters burned at the stake in the Marian Persecutions, earning her the sobriquet of "Bloody Mary". Her re-establishment of Roman Catholicism was reversed by her successor and half-sister, Elizabeth I.

2. **Sir Francis Drake**: Francis was an English sea captain, privateer, navigator, slaver, and politician of the Elizabethan era. Queen Elizabeth I awarded Drake a knighthood in 1581. He was second-

in-command of the English fleet against the Spanish Armada in 1588, subordinate only to Charles Howard and the Queen herself. He died of dysentery in January 1596 after unsuccessfully attacking San Juan, Puerto Rico. He is famous for sailing around the world, returning to England in 1580.

For Fun

Websites to visit
1. http://www.teacheroz.com/renaissance.htm
   This page provides hyperlinks of a wide range of topics about the Renaissance.
2. http://www.elizabethan.org/
   This website helps you to explore the world of Elizabethan England.

Movies to see
1. *Shakespeare in Love* (1998)

   It was directed by John Madden. The stars in this film are Judi Dench, Gwyneth Paltrow, Geoffrey Rush and Joseph Fiennes.

   William Shakespeare (Joseph Fiennes) is on a cold streak. Not only is his writing for Philip Henslowe (Geoffrey Rush), owner of "The Rose," a theatre whose doors are about to be closed by sadistic creditors, but he's got a nasty case of writer's block. Shakespeare has not written a hit in years. In fact, he has not written much of anything recently. Thus, the bard finds himself in quite a bind when Henslowe, desperate to stave off another round of application, stakes The Rose's solvency on Shakespeare's new comedy.

2. *Elizabeth: The Golden Age* (2007)

   The Golden Age is the sequel to the critically acclaimed 1998 film *Elizabeth*, which earned seven Academy Award nominations. The sequel follows the relationship between the queen and the dashing explorer Walter Raleigh, from their initial meeting to the magnificent victory over the Spanish Armada.

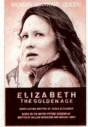

Book to read
Mistress Shakespeare by Karen Harper
It is a delicious and intriguing historical novel about the woman who was William Shakespeare's secret wife. The novel was written by *New York Times* best-selling author, Karen Harper.

Unit 9
The House of Stuart

> It is easier to get forgiveness than permission.
> —Stuart's Law of Retroaction

Unit Goals

- To know the English Civil War and its consequences
- To be familiar with the House of Stuart
- To learn the useful words and expressions that describe the English Bourgeois Revolution and improve English language skills
- To develop critical thinking and intercultural communication skills

Before You Read

(1) What do you know about the English Civil war?
(2) Have you ever heard of the "Short Parliament" and the "Long Parliament"? Share what you know with your classmates.
(3) You must have heard of Oliver Cromwell. What do you know about him? What was he best remembered for in history?
(4) Form groups of three or four students. Try to find, on the Internet or in the library, more information about the House of Stuart, which interests you. Get ready for a 5-minute presentation in class.

Start to Read

Text A　　The Age of Revolution

James I and the Gunpowder Plot

1. During the last years of Elizabeth's reign, relations between the monarchy and the bourgeoisie (with Parliament as its representative) were strained and problems cropped up.

2. After Elizabeth I died in 1603 without leaving an heir to succeed her, James VI of Scotland was welcomed to the English throne as James I in 1603. James was a Stuart—so Tudor England died on March 24th 1603 while the accession of James ushered in the era of the Stuarts.

3. James I was very unpopular because he insisted on the "Divine Right of Kings," believing that kings were only responsible to God and not to any Parliament. In his view, the king's will was the only law. He increased royal spending, went into debt and raised taxes. So he quarreled frequently with Parliament.

4. The accession of James I brought hope of victory for the Catholics in England. Catholics in England had expected James to be more tolerant of them. In fact, he had proved to be the opposite and had ordered all Catholic priests to leave England. This angered some Catholics and they decided to kill James. On November 5th, 1605, the infamous Gunpowder Plot took place in which some Catholics, most famously Guy Fawkes, plotted to blow up James I, the first of the Stuart kings of England. The Gunpowder Plot gave birth to the Guy Fawkes night bonfire which used to be one of the most regularly observed festivals in England. It befell on the fifth of November when bonfires were lit in the evening and many people got together in merry-making.

5. Though James I was called the wisest fool, he was quite learned and full of vigor. He managed to continue his reign with little help from Parliament until his death in 1625.

Charles I and the English Civil War

6. Upon the death of his father, James I, in 1625, Charles I ascended the throne. Like his father, he quarreled with Parliament too, and for eleven years (1629—1640) he ruled without Parliament. He persecuted the Puritans and

asked people for "loans". Many craftsmen, merchants and peasants went to the New World. Ordinary people as well as the bourgeoisie found the feudal oppression intolerable.

7. Charles I tightened his control not only over England but over Scotland as well. The Scots, of whom Charles was king, were really governed by their feudal aristocracy and bourgeoisie through the Church. Now Charles attempted to make the Church of Scotland into something like the Church of England. The Scots rose to defend their "true faith", and in 1639 their army crossed the border and invaded English territory.

8. Charles decided to fight the Scots. In April 1640 he summoned Parliament to raise money. Parliament demanded the punishment of royal favorites, but refused to supply money. It was dissolved in May. Hence its nickname was "Short Parliament". Forced by necessities, Charles summoned another Parliament in November 1640. This Parliament, with such eminent leaders as Pym and Hampden and Cromwell, was to play a great part in the revolution. It lasted until 1653. Hence the nickname was "Long Parliament".

9. By the time when the Long Parliament was called, London had become the centre of stirring activities. Backed by the masses, Parliament proceeded to struggle against the king. It was provided that the existing Parliament should not be dissolved without its consent.

10. Charles departed for the north, where he hoped to find supporters in the more backward districts. Thus began the Civil War. England was divided into two parts: feudal England and bourgeois England. The west and north were controlled by Charles, except some great industrial centers. The more notable sea-ports and the prosperous southeast stood for Parliament. The supporters of Parliament

were called Roundheads because the common people of London kept their hair cut short. The adherents of the King were called Cavaliers, which meant "proud, upper-class horsemen".

For the King	For Parliament
Catholics, most of the Nobles and the gentry, about half of all Members of Parliament, the poorer areas of the North and West.	Puritans, the more militant Members of Parliament, merchants, the richer areas of the South and East.

(Continued)

Cavaliers	Roundheads
The supporters of the king were called Cavaliers because many of them fought on horseback. The term comes from the French "chevalier" meaning "horse". Cavaliers had long hair and wore fancy clothes.	Parliamentarians were nicknamed "roundheads" because they cut their hair very short. They also wore very plain and simple clothes.

11. In the first years of the war, the parliamentary army suffered several defeats because of its poor organization. The tide turned when Oliver Cromwell started to organize the army, which was called "New Model Army". On June 14, 1645, the "New Model Army" scored a decisive victory at Naseby. 5000 royalist soldiers were taken prisoners. In March 1646 the Civil War was fundamentally concluded.

12. In 1649, Charles was deposed as "tyrant, traitor, murderer and a public and implacable enemy of the Commonwealth of England". In January 1649, his head was cut off. In March of 1649, the House of Lords and the office of the king were abolished and a Council of State was set up to carry out the executive work of the government. In May 1649, England was declared a Commonwealth.

Charles II and the Restoration

13. In 1658, Cromwell died, and his son Richard was declared Lord Protector. But Richard could not handle the affairs of government. General George Monck, the commander of the army in Scotland, arranged free election for a new Parliament, which immediately decided to bring back the rule of kings. In 1660, the monarchy was restored in England with Charles II ascending the throne.

14. Just eleven years after Charles I's death, in 1660 cheering crowds welcomed back his son as Charles II, and all the bells of London rang with joy. Charles II died in 1685. The period from 1660 to 1685 is known as the Restoration in history.

15. In the 1670s, the Cavaliers and the Roundheads had settled down to become two political parties: the former the Tories and the latter the Whigs. The Tory represented the conservative forces of the country and the Whig stood for the interests of bourgeoisie.

James II and the Glorious Revolution

16. Upon the death of Charles II in 1685, James II (brother of Charles II) ascended the throne. He was a Roman Catholic. He openly ignored laws passed by Parliament. People disliked his policies but were tolerant of him. They expected his Protestant daughter Mary to be the queen after his death. Being afraid of another revolution, the Whigs and Tories came together and precipitated a coup d'etat. James's daughter, Mary was  married to William of Orange. In June 1688 leaders of Parliament invited William to come and take the throne. James was deposed and William and Mary were recognized as joint-sovereigns. The quick change of rulers in 1688 is called "the Glorious Revolution" because it was bloodless and successful. It created a constitutional monarchy, which finally put the monarch under the control of Parliament.

17. When William died in 1702 with no heir, he was succeeded by his wife's sister, the second daughter of James II, Queen Anne. Anne was the last monarch of the House of Stuart. She died in 1714 and was succeeded by her distant German cousin, George, Elector of Hannover, as King George I of Great Britain and Ireland.

18. The English Revolution is an epoch-making event in the history of England. It concludes the medieval period—the period of feudalism, and marks the beginning of the period of capitalism.

After You Read

Knowledge Focus
1. **Pair Work**
   Discuss the following questions with your partner.
   (1) Who was the first king of Stuart family?
   (2) How do you understand the "Divine Right of Kings"? What is your comment on that?
   (3) Can you retell the story about the Gunpowder Plot?
   (4) Can you differentiate the "Short Parliament" from the "Long Parliament"?

(5) Who was the leader of "New Model Army"?
(6) How do you understand the religious belief—"Pleasure is sin"?
(7) What do you know about the origins of the political parties—the Tories and the Whigs?
(8) What do you know about "the Glorious Revolution"?
(9) Who was the last monarch of the House of Stuart?
(10) How do you account for the significance of the English Revolution?

2. **Solo Work**
   Tell whether and why the following are true or false according to the knowledge you have learned.
   ____ (1) The English Bourgeois Revolution broke out because the Wars of the Roses had greatly weakened the feudal noble class.
   ____ (2) The Reformation had criticized those religious beliefs which served feudal relations but remained the church of its lands and wealth.
   ____ (3) James insisted on the "Divine Right of Kings," believing that kings were only responsible to God and not to any Parliament. This makes him not very popular.
   ____ (4) Guy Fawkes shot down James I in the infamous Gunpowder Plot.
   ____ (5) Charles decided to fight the Scots to help the Scottish people defend their "true faith".
   ____ (6) Forced by necessities, Charles summoned another Parliament in November 1640, whose nickname was "Short Parliament".
   ____ (7) The Civil War broke out after Charles departed for the north, where he hoped to find supporters in the more backward districts. (   )
   ____ (8) In March 1646, the Civil War was fundamentally concluded. (   )
   ____ (9) In March of 1649, the House of Lords and the office of King were abolished and a Council of State was set up to carry out the executive work of the government. In May 1649, England was declared a Commonwealth. (   )
   ____ (10) Richard could not handle the affairs of government, so he decided to bring back the rule of kings. (   )

Language Focus
1. **Fill in the blanks with the following words or expressions you have learned in the text. Put them into appropriate forms if necessary.**

| dispossess | around the corner | strain | crop up | be tolerant of |
| infamous | eminent | proceed | depart for | adherent |

(1) You have to learn to deal with difficult situations when they _____.
(2) After such a serious earthquake, economic recovery is just _____ with the help of all walks of life.
(3) Dorothy _____ Germany last week, starting her life as an overseas student.
(4) This description bears marked similarities to those offered by a number of

_____ sociologists who adopt this approach.
(5) Many black South Africans had been _____ of their homes.
(6) Officers will _____ peaceful demonstrations.
(7) Unfortunately, they did not respond to the complaint and _____ to recruit new employees.
(8) The night club is named after New Orleans' _____ red light district.
(9) The incident has _____ relations between the two countries.
(10) The anti-globalization movement is attracting new _____ to its principles.

2. **Complete the following sentences with the proper forms of the words in the brackets.**
   (1) The geographical _____ (discover) of the New World was followed by foreign expansion and slave trade, speeding up "primitive accumulation of capital".
   (2) The _____ (access) of James I brought hope of victory for the Catholics in England.
   (3) You should be at the airport an hour before _____ (depart).
   (4) Ordinary people as well as the bourgeoisie found the feudal _____ (oppress) intolerable.
   (5) By the time when the Long Parliament was called, London had become the centre of _____ (stir) activities.
   (6) The west and north were controlled by Charles, except some great _____ (industry) centers.
   (7) The more notable sea-ports and the _____ (prosper) southeast stood for Parliament.
   (8) The Tory represented the _____ (conservation) forces of the country and the Whig stood for the interests of Bourgeoisie.
   (9) It created a _____ (constitute) monarchy, which finally put the monarch under the control of Parliament.
   (10) The English Revolution concluded the medieval period—the period of _____ (feudal), and marks the beginning of the period of capitalism.

3. **Find the appropriate prepositions that collocate with the neighboring words.**
   (1) The Enclosure had dispossessed many peasants _____ their lands and driven them _____ cities.
   (2) The geographical discovery of the New World was followed _____ foreign expansion and slave trade, speeding _____ the "primitive accumulation of capital".
   (3) A new class was rising in England. The bourgeois revolution was just _____ the corner.
   (4) During the last years of Elizabeth's reign, relations between the monarchy and the bourgeoisie were strained and problems cropped _____.

(5) James I was very unpopular because he insisted on the "Divine Right of Kings," believing that kings were only responsible _____ God and not to any Parliament.

(6) Catholics in England had expected James to be more tolerant _____ them.

(7) On November 5, 1605, the infamous Gunpowder Plot took place in which some Catholics, most famously Guy Fawkes, plotted to blow _____ James I, the first of the Stuart kings of England.

(8) Parliament proceeded to struggle _____ the king. It was provided that the existing Parliament should not be dissolved _____ its consent.

(9) Charles departed _____ the north, where he hoped to find supporters in the more backward districts.

(10) General George Monck, the commander of the army _____ Scotland, arranged free election _____ a new Parliament, which immediately decided to bring back the rule of kings.

Comprehensive Work

1. Group Work

Retell what you know about the Stuart kings with the aid of the following family tree. Discuss their governing policies and their relationship with the parliament within your group.

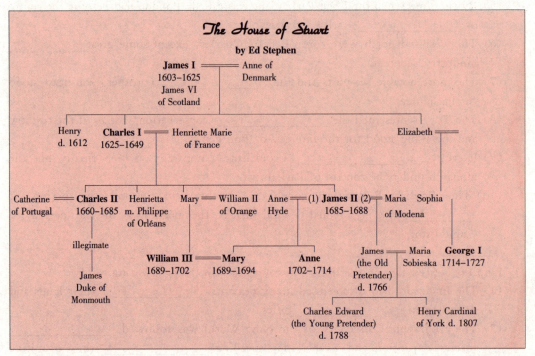

2. Writing Activity

James was a firm believer in the "divine right of kings". This was a belief that God had make someone a king. Do you think someone should have inborn privilege over others, due to his descent, gender or age? Comment on this topic and write an essay of around 300 words.

Read More

Text B King James VI and I

James's mother, Mary Queen of Scots, was removed from the throne and sent into exile when James was one year old. She fled to England but was put in prison there. After 19 years in prison, she was executed by the order of Queen Elizabeth I of England.

Baby James succeeded his mother as ruler of Scotland and was crowned King James VI of Scotland in 1567 at the age of 13 months.

While he was a child, rulers known as regents ran the country for him, and James was raised by tutors. They taught him everything a king needed to know, especially languages. James learned Greek, Latin, French, English, Scots, and more. Later, he would be able to consult with kings and queens of many countries in their own language.

When James reached the age of 19, he began to rule the country himself. He faced many challenges, including assassination attempts by his rivals.

Once he assumed control, James took steps to make the position of king a more powerful one. One important move that he made was an alliance with Queen of England.

Scotland and England had been rivals since ancient times, and Elizabeth I, the queen who had put James's mother to death, was still Queen of England. But James really wanted to extend his power to England, so despite all of this history, James forged an alliance with England's queen. They signed a treaty, the Treaty of Berwick. This treaty stated that James would become King of England when Elizabeth died.

Queen Elizabeth died in 1603, and King James VI of Scotland became King James I of England as well. He had already ruled Scotland for 36 years, but now he packed up and moved to England. For the rest of his life, 22 more years, he lived in England and ruled both countries.

James's years as ruler of England were often troubled years. There were times of corruption and conflicts. Conflicts between Catholics and Protestants continued. Conflicts also arose between Anglicans and Puritans. When King

James asserted that kings had a divine right to rule, he ran into conflicts with Parliament as well.

In 1605, he survived the famous Gunpowder Plot. When the plot failed, bonfires were lit in celebration. Today, this date is still celebrated in England as Guy Fawkes Day, named after the conspirator who was caught in the cellar with the gunpowder.

In 1611, James decided to take care of the problem with Parliament. He dissolved Parliament. In fact, he dissolved Parliament more than once over the next ten years, ruling much of the time without a lawmaking body.

King James played an important role in the Renaissance during his years as king. He was William Shakespeare's patron. Shakespeare wrote *Macbeth* while under King James' patronage. Shakespeare's company of actors was called the King's Men in honor of King James.

King James also authorized the publication of a new version of the *Bible* translated into English—the *King James Bible*.

The king himself was a writer as well. One of his most interesting essays is titled *A Counterblast to Tobacco*. In this essay, he wrote that smoking is "loathsome to the eye, hateful to the nose, harmful to the brain, and dangerous to the lungs".

He ruled during the years that England was establishing colonies in foreign lands. In fact, England's colonization of America began during his reign. He established the Colony of Virginia in America, which earned its money by raising tobacco.

King James VI and I died in 1625.

1. Finish the following multiple-choice questions according to Text B.

(1) King James was ruler of _____.
   A. Scotland   B. England
   C. both A and B   D. neither A nor B

(2) Mary Queen of Scots was _____.
   A. Queen of Scotland   B. executed by Queen Elizabeth I
   C. James' mother   D. all of the above

(3) King James made an alliance with _____.
   A. Queen of Scotland   B. Queen of England
   C. Guy Fawkes   D. all of the above

(4) King James died _____.
   A. as a result of the Gunpowder Plot
   B. by the order of Queen Elizabeth I
   C. in 1625
   D. both A and C

(5) King James was a patron of Renaissance artists, including _____.
   A. Shakespeare B. Rembrandt
   C. Guy Fawkes   D. Leonardo da Vinci
(6) King James ruled England _____ the time of the early American colonies.
   A. after   B. several centuries before
   C. during   D. one hundred years before

2. Discuss the following with your partners.
(1) Why is King James known as King James VI and I?
(2) What was King James's most important accomplishment?

Text C The English Civil War

How does a civil war start? In the case of the English Civil War, there was a series of small steps that increased tensions between two groups. Then all it took was a final spark to set off the war.

The situation in England changed rapidly in the years leading up to the war. Less than forty years earlier, the country was enjoying the reign of the popular Queen Elizabeth I. Nearly everyone was happy with the form of government in which a monarch made the decisions for the whole country. When Charles I took the throne, the country was still in a peaceful mood. Then things started to change. One event after another led to a bigger and bigger rift between the king and Parliament.

Charles I hoped to follow in his father's footsteps, and he began to take steps to recognize his father's dream of uniting England, Ireland, and Scotland. Charles believed that he had a Divine Right to rule and that his wishes should be obeyed. Parliament, however, was suspicious of King Charles' motives and of the effect that this might have on England. The steps towards a civil war had begun.

Then, Charles I married the Catholic princess, Henriette Marie de Bourbon. This stirred up new doubts and fears as the members of Parliament worried about the possibility of a Catholic prince who would one day inherit the throne.

Charles wanted England to continue fighting in the Thirty Years War in Europe. Like all wars, this one cost a lot of money. Soon, England was in financial difficulties, and more controversies between Charles and Parliament resulted.

King Charles also wanted a uniform Church of England throughout the British Isles. He introduced a new version of the prayer book, *the Book of*

Common Prayer. Violent protests broke out in Scotland. King Charles sent forces towards Scotland, but this time the conflict was settled by a truce.

In 1640, when King Charles was not able to get any more money from Parliament, he dissolved the Parliament. Later in 1640, a new Parliament was formed, but this one was even more hostile towards the king. At sessions of Parliament, they discussed their grievances against the king.

Then, in 1641, Parliament had Thomas Wentworth, Earl of Strafford, arrested for treason. Thomas Wentworth had worked for the same causes as other members of Parliament on many occasions, but at other times he had chosen to support the king. This time when he chose to support the king, he found that the tide had turned severely against King Charles. He was considered a traitor and was executed in 1641.

The next move would be made by King Charles. Parliament was now completely against him, and he was able to do nothing without their support. He sent three hundred troops to Parliament with the mission of arresting the five members of Parliament who were his biggest critics.

But Parliament had already received word of what was about to happen. The five members targeted by King Charles fled into the city of London and found places to hide safely.

Now, members of Parliament felt that no one was safe. King Charles felt that there was no turning back.

Six days later, King Charles left London to raise an army to go to war against the Parliament of his own country. The outcome of the war would tell whether or not the king could continue to rule England as a powerful monarch or whether Parliament would gain control.

The war took place over about nine years in three stages, also known as the First, Second, and Third Civil wars.

The First Civil War lasted from 1642 to 1646. Both sides had their moments, but in the end, Oliver Cromwell led the Parliamentarians, also known as the Roundheads, to victory.

The Second Civil War lasted from 1648 to 1649. In this war, King Charles joined sides with Scotland but still lost the war. King Charles was executed.

The Third Civil War lasted from 1649 to 1651. In this war, King Charles II invaded England in an attempt to take back control for the monarchy. He was defeated at the battle of Worcester, and the war ended.

The result of the war was that English monarchs could no longer rule with complete power. They now ruled with the consent of Parliament, not by divine right.

1. **Finish the following multiple-choice questions according to Text C.**
   (1) The English Civil War began after a series of conflicts between King Charles I and Parliament. The statement is _____.
       A. false   B. true
   (2) The war began during the reign of Queen Elizabeth I. The statement is _____.
       A. false   B. true
   (3) King Charles believed that the right of kings to rule came from _____.
       A. Parliament   B. God   C. the voters   D. the queen
   (4) Charles I's marriage to Princess Henriette Marie de Bourbon _____.
       A. led to an alliance between England and France
       B. made him even more popular
       C. led to further division between the king and Parliament
       D. helped to unite his country
   (5) King Charles' introduction of a new prayer book occurred _____.
       A. between the Second and Third Civil wars
       B. before the First Civil War
       C. before the reign of Queen Elizabeth I
       D. after the reign of King Charles II
   (6) After King Charles dissolved Parliament, a new Parliament was formed. This new Parliament had an attitude towards the king that was _____.
       A. accepting   B. friendly   C. indifferent   D. hostile
   (7) The English Civil War was made up of _____ shorter wars.
       A. four   B. two   C. seven   D. three
   (8) The outcome of the war determined that _____.
       A. kings ruled with the consent of Parliament
       B. kings ruled by divine right
       C. kings must be members of Parliament
       D. kings must now be elected by the voters

2. **Discuss the following questions with your partners.**
   (1) What were the steps that led up to the English Civil War? What was the final spark that started the war?
   (2) Can you think of another war that began after a series of steps that escalated the conflict between the two sides? Name the war and write about the steps that led up to the war.

Proper Names

Council of State 国务会议
Divine Right of Kings 君权神授
George Monck 乔治·蒙克

Gunpowder Plot 火药阴谋案
Guy Fawkes Day 盖伊·福克斯节
Lord Protector 护国公

Oliver Cromwell 奥利弗·克伦威尔
the Cavaliers 保王党成员（英国内战时期查理一世的支持者）
the constitutional monarchy 君主立宪政体
the Roundheads 圆颅党（17世纪中期，英国国会一知名党派）
the Tory 托利党
the Whig 辉格党

Notes

Divine Right of Kings：This was a political and religious doctrine of royal absolutism. It asserted that a monarch was subject to no earthly authority, deriving his right to rule directly from the will of God. The king was thus not subject to the will of his people, the aristocracy, or any other estate of the realm, including the church. The doctrine implied that any attempt to depose the king or to restrict his powers ran contrary to the will of God and might constitute heresy.

For Fun

Movies to see

1. *To Kill a King*（2003）

To Kill a King is a 2003 English Civil War film, directed by Mike Barker. It centers on the relationship between Oliver Cromwell and Thomas Fairfax in the post-war period from 1648 until the former's death, in 1658. At the end of the English Civil War, Sir Thomas Fairfax celebrates the Parliamentarian victory over the royalist Cavaliers with his colleague and fellow commander, Oliver Cromwell. Meanwhile, King Charles I, who has been captured and is held prisoner by the victors, tries to appeal to Fairfax's wife, Lady Anne. Soon, the trial of the king takes place, and Cromwell & Fairfax disagree over what to do, and from there, tensions rise.

2. *Gunpowder, Treason & Plot*（2004）

This BBC mini-series depicts the turbulent and bloody reigns of Scottish monarchs Mary, Queen of Scots and her son King James VI of Scotland who became King James I of England and foiled the Gunpowder Plot. The first film dramatizes the relationship between Mary and her third husband, James Hepburn, 4th Earl of Bothwell. Scottish actor Robert Carlyle stars as James VI in the second part of the series, which concentrates on the Gunpowder Plot, planned by Guy Fawkes, to blow up the Houses of Parliament in order to rid the nation

of a Protestant monarch to be replaced by a Catholic one.

Websites to visit
1. http://www.historylearningsite.co.uk/stuart_england.htm
   This page provides a large variety of hyperlinks with regard to the House of Stuart, including the monarchs, major historical events and great figures during this period.
2. http://www.historyonthenet.com/Civil_War/civilwarmain.htm
   This page contains a comprehensive listing of hyperlinks about the English Civil War.

Unit 10
The House of Hanover

> The true character of liberty is independence, maintained by force.
>
> —Voltaire (French philosopher and writer)

Unit Goals

- To know the line of succession of Hanoverians
- To learn about the history of England in the 18th century
- To be familiar with the struggle against Napoleonic France
- To learn the useful words and expressions that describe the House of Hanover and improve English language skills
- To develop critical thinking and intercultural communication skills

Before You Read

(1) Do you know that the first Hanoverian king of Great Britain could not speak English? Do you know why?
(2) Who was ruling England when the American War of Independence broke out? What was the situation in England then?
(3) Form groups of three or four students. Try to find, on the Internet or in the library, more information about the House of Hanover, which interests you. Get ready for a 5-minute presentation in class.

Start to Read

Text A   The Hanoverian Monarchs

1. Queen Anne died and the crown passed to her cousin George, Elector of Hanover—the first Hanoverian king of Great Britain. George I was born on May 28, 1660 in Hanover, Germany. In 1701, under *the Act of Settlement*, George's mother Sophia was nominated heiress to the English throne if the reigning monarch William III and his heir Anne died without issue. The Act sought to guarantee a Protestant succession and George's mother was the closest  Protestant relative although there were at least 50 Catholic relatives whose claims were stronger. The Electress Sophia and Anne died in quick succession and George became king in August 1714.

2. The following year George was confronted with a rebellion by the Jacobites, supporters of the Catholic James Stuart, who had a strong claim to the throne. This was concentrated mainly in Scotland, and was suppressed by the end of the year.

3. George I spoke no English. His lack of English even turned out to be a blessing. It prevented him from holding council and it led to the cabinet system of government. The cabinet is a council which contains the leaders of the biggest party in Parliament, and its chief is called the Prime Minister. The first Prime Minister was Robert Walpole, who gradually developed this system during his twenty-one years in office. Walpole led the Whig party, but he understood the Tories. His plan was "to let the sleeping dog lie": to do nothing that would stir up

 trouble. He was not a coward, but he knew that his country needed long years of peace to build up its strength. Under Walpole's leadership the English had complete freedom of speech, which no other country had.

4. George died on June 11, 1727 during a visit to Hanover and was succeeded by his son. George II was the second Hanoverian king of Great

Britain and Ireland. During the last decade of his life, George took little interest in politics. Britain was involved in the Seven Years' War (1756—1763). This period also saw the expansion of British influence in India and Canada with the military successes of Clive and Wolfe. George died on October 25, 1760. Frederick had died in 1751, leaving George II's grandson to inherit the throne.

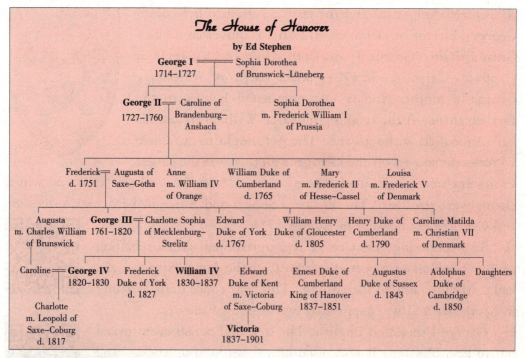

5. George III became heir to the throne on the death of his father in 1751, succeeding his grandfather, George II, in 1760. He was the third Hanoverian monarch and the first one to be born in England and to use English as his first language. George III is widely remembered for two things: losing the American colonies and going mad.

6. By the middle of the 18th century, most of the American colonies were in the hands of the Englishmen. The policy of England was to use the American colonies for her own interests. In 1765, the English parliament passed *the Stamp Act*, requiring the use of stamped paper for newspapers, pamphlets and legal documents in the colonies. This provoked anger and violence. In 1773, the Bostonians boarded an English tea ship and dumped cargos into water. The war broke out in April 1775. Delegates of the thirteen colonies met at Philadelphia and made George Washington commander-

in-chief of American armies. *The Declaration of Independence* was drawn up in 1776, which proclaimed the independence of thirteen American colonies.

7. The American war, its political aftermath and family anxieties placed great strain on George in the 1780s. After serious bouts of illness in 1788 and again in 1801, George became permanently deranged in 1810. He was mentally unfit to rule in the last decade of his reign; his eldest son—the later George IV—acted as Prince Regent from 1811. Some medical historians have said that George III's mental instability was caused by a hereditary physical disorder. George remained ill until his death at Windsor Castle on January 29, 1820.

8. In 1801, under *the Act of Union* Great Britain and Ireland were united into a single nation—the United Kingdom. George III was thus the first king of the new nation.

9. George IV was born on August 17, 1762, the eldest son of King George III and Queen Charlotte. In 1811, George became regent—with the duties but not yet the status of a king—after his father was declared insane. He was naturally gifted, was well taught in the classics, learned to speak French, Italian and German fluently, and had considerable taste for music and the arts; and in person he  was remarkably handsome. His tutor, Bishop Richard Hurd, said of him when he was fifteen years old that he would be "either the most polished gentleman or the most accomplished blackguard in Europe—possibly both".

10. During the reign of George IV, England was at war with France from 1793 to 1815. England's struggle against Napoleon was essentially a struggle for industrial and commercial supremacy. For the benefit of French industry, Napoleon endeavored to build up an economic empire in Europe, known as the Continental System. But in the long contest for supremacy, England had the better of France in many aspects. In 1805, the English fleet destroyed the combined French and Spanish fleets at Trafalgar and warded off Napoleon's attempted invasion of England. In 1815, Napoleon was ultimately defeated at Waterloo by Britain and her allies under the commandership of Duke of Wellington.

11. George IV died on June 26, 1830. His only child, Princess Charlotte had died in childbirth in 1817, so the crown passed to George's brother who became William IV.

12. William IV was King of Great Britain and Ireland from 1830. William was born at Buckingham Palace in London on August 21, 1765. He was the third son of King George III and Queen Charlotte and as such was not expected to

succeed to the throne. He was known as the "Sailor King", for he started his career in the Royal Navy at the age of thirteen. And he was nicknamed "Silly Billy", due to his habit of making rambling and intemperate speeches. William died on June 20, 1837, without surviving children. His niece Victoria succeeded him.

13. Queen Victoria was the longest reigning British monarch and the figurehead of a vast empire. She oversaw vast changes in British society and gave her name to an age—the Victorian Age.

After You Read

Knowledge Focus

1. **Pair Work**
   Discuss the following questions with your partner.
   (1) Why could George from Hanover succeed to the throne after the death of Anne?
   (2) Who were the Jacobites who rebelled against King George I?
   (3) Who was the first Prime Minister in the history of England?
   (4) Which king from the House of Hanover was the first one to be born in England and to use English as his first language?
   (5) George III became permanently deranged in 1810. There was another king in the history of England suffering from mental disorder. Who was that king?
   (6) During whose reign were the Great Britain and Ireland united into a single nation—the United Kingdom?
   (7) What do you know about the England's war against Napoleon?
   (8) What do you know about the Battle of Waterloo?
   (9) What were the nicknames of King William IV? How did he get the nickname "Silly Billy"?
   (10) Who was the last king of House of Hanover?

2. **Solo Work**
   Tell whether and why the following are true or false according to the knowledge you have learned.
   _____ (1) The Electress Sophia and Anne died in quick succession and George became king in August 1714.
   _____ (2) George I was too lazy to hold council and it led to the cabinet system of government.
   _____ (3) Robert Walpole's plan was "to let the sleeping dog lie": to do nothing that would stir up trouble because he was not courageous enough.
   _____ (4) George III was the third Hanoverian monarch and the first one to be born in

England but he, just like his father and grandfather, cannot use English as his first language.

____ (5) In 1765, the English Parliament passed the Stamp Act, requiring the use of stamped paper for newspapers, pamphlets and legal documents in the colonies. This provoked anger and violence.

____ (6) The Declaration of Independence was drawn up in 1776, which proclaimed the independence of thirteen American colonies.

____ (7) In 1801, under the Act of Union Great Britain and Ireland were united into a single nation—the United Kingdom. George II was thus the first king of the new nation.

____ (8) George IV's tutor, Bishop Richard Hurd, said of him when he was fifteen years old that he would be "either the most polished gentleman or the most accomplished blackguard in Europe—possibly both". because he could speak French, Italian and German fluently.

____ (9) For the benefit of French industry, Napoleon endeavored to build up an economic empire in Europe, known as the Continental System.

____ (10) William IV was known as the "Sailor King", for he started his career in the Royal Navy at the age of thirteen.

Language Focus

1. Fill in the blanks with the following words or expressions you have learned in the text. Put them into appropriate forms if necessary.

nominate	be confronted with	suppress	inherit	provoke
proclaim	aftermath	place strain on	endeavor	ward off

(1) The long working hours _____ employees.
(2) The present government _____ a state-dominated economy.
(3) Do not forget to use some insect repellent to _____ the mosquitoes.
(4) Customers _____ a bewildering amount of choice.
(5) The president _____ the republic's independence.
(6) The president has power to _____ people to certain key offices, including the judge of the Supreme Court.
(7) Were they talking about the _____ of the Napoleonic Wars?
(8) Police were accused of _____ evidence that might have proved that the men were innocent.
(9) The management control process should _____ to measure whether predetermined goals are being achieved.
(10) She hopes her editorial will _____ readers into thinking seriously about the issue.

2. Complete the following sentences with the proper forms of the words in the brackets.

(1) Most regions are enjoying rapid economic _____ (expand).
(2) Some applicants who meet the _____ (require) are rejected because

they are lacking in the most essential communication skills.

(3) Dad left me all his money when he died, which made me financially _____ (depend).

(4) The increase in the tax on heating fuel is causing a lot of _____ (anxious) among elderly people.

(5) After serious bouts of illness in 1788 and again in 1801, George became _____ (permanence) deranged in 1810.

(6) There are fears that political _____ (stable) in the region will lead to civil war.

(7) The recent slowdown in the US economy is likely to have a _____ (consider) impact on the rest of the world.

(8) The playwright has added a few characters and changed some names but _____ (essence) this is a true story.

(9) Napoleon was _____ (ultimate) defeated at Waterloo by Britain and her allies under the commandership of Duke of Wellington.

(10) William IV was nicknamed "Silly Billy", due to his habit of making _____ (ramble) and intemperate speeches.

3. Find the appropriate prepositions that collocate with the neighboring words.

(1) The Electress Sophia and Anne died _____ quick succession and George became king in August 1714.

(2) The following year, George was confronted _____ a rebellion by the Jacobites, supporters of the Catholic James Stuart, who had a strong claim to the throne.

(3) George I spoke no English, which prevented him _____ holding council and led to the cabinet system of government.

(4) Walpole led the Whig party, but he understood the Tories. His plan was "to let the sleeping dog lie": to do nothing that would stir _____ trouble.

(5) Britain was involved _____ the Seven Years' War (1756—1763).

(6) The policy of England was to use the American colonies _____ her own interests.

(7) The American war, its political aftermath and family anxieties placed great strain _____ George in the 1780s.

(8) Some medical historians have said that George III's mental instability was caused _____ a hereditary physical disorder.

(9) England's struggle _____ Napoleon was essentially a struggle for industrial and commercial supremacy.

(10) William IV was nicknamed "Silly Billy", due _____ his habit of making rambling and intemperate speeches.

Comprehensive Work
1. Cloze Activity

Below is a brief summary of the Seven Years' War. Please use the words in the box to fill in the blanks in the summary.

Europe	France	battles	Britain	fighting
North America	War	Washington	east	Revolution
Fort	died	1763	taxes	Pennsylvania

The French and Indian War (1756—1763) was a seven-year-long (1)_____ between (2)_____ and France (France was allied with the Indians). Although fighting began in 1754, the war did not officially begin until 1756. They were (3)_____ for the control of much of North America. This war was a part of a larger war that was going on in (4)_____.

At the beginning of the war, France controlled Canada and the Louisiana Territory. Britain controlled most of the (5)_____ coast of (6)_____. In one of the first (7)_____ of the war, Lieutenant Colonel George (8)_____ and his Virginia troops (fighting for the British) were sent to Pittsburgh, (9)_____, to remove the (10)_____ from their new (11)_____. Washington was defeated by the French, who soon controlled the entire region.

In 1756, the British began to defeat the French, especially in naval battles. In 1759, General James Wolfe's army defeated the French at Quebec (although both Gen. Wolfe and his French adversary Gen. Montcalm both (12)_____ during the battle).

The French lost the war, and the Treaty of Paris (signed in (13)_____) gave Britain control of Canada. Spain gave Florida to Britain, and received the former French areas west of the Mississippi River. As a result of the war, the English colonists became more independent from Britain. This war also resulted in higher (14)_____ paid to Britain. These influences eventually led to the American (15)_____.

2. Writing Activity

At the very beginning of this unit, you read a quote by a French philosopher and writer—Voltaire, which says "the true character of liberty is independence, maintained by force."

What's your view on this quote? What are your interpretations of "liberty" and "independence"? Do you think liberty or independence can never be achieved without force? Write an essay of around 300 words to illustrate your point.

Text B **Napoleon Bonaparte (1769—1821)**

Despite his many accomplishments, Napoleon Bonaparte may be best known for what he almost did. Napoleon almost, but not quite, became ruler of all of Europe.

Napoleon was born in 1769 on the island of Corsica which had just become a part of France. Napoleon learned French at an early age, and at the age of nine attended a French military school.

Upon his graduation from his first military school, he enrolled in the Ecole Royale Militaire in Paris where he was trained to become an artillery man. In that same year, Napoleon's father died, and Napoleon put all of his energies into his studies. He graduated from his artillery training in just one year, and he had made good use of his short time in the Ecole. Napoleon had studied all of the important military tactics and strategies. He stored the knowledge away for future use.

After his graduation, Napoleon was commissioned Second Lieutenant in an artillery regiment of the French Army. He was just sixteen years old.

Soon, the French Revolution broke out in France. Napoleon sided with the revolutionaries and joined the revolutionary group known as the Jacobins.

In the Revolution, Napoleon quickly made a name for himself when he faced down a rebellion against the new revolutionary leaders at Toulon. He set up his troops on high ground overlooking the harbor, and from there fired on the British ships which were supporting the rebels. Napoleon was victorious, and at the age of twenty four, he was named Brigadier General.

After the Revolution, Napoleon went on to more and more military campaigns. He fought many of the countries in Europe. For a while, he enjoyed more and more victories as well. He took control of much of Europe, some by military victories and some by alliances.

Napoleon crowned himself emperor.

During his time as ruler of France, Napoleon modernized and strengthened the French army. He became known as a great military strategist. His strategies and campaigns are still studied by historians and war buffs today.

He also instituted the system of laws known as the Napoleonic Code. It became the law in France, where it brought the government up to date and made it more efficient. It also became the law in many other countries of Europe.

The Napoleonic Code organized laws that were already in the books, and many of the laws went back to ancient Roman times. It also made the government more responsible to the citizens of the country. It made it easier for everyday people to own land. It provided for freedoms like freedom of religion. It set up basic rights including the right to vote. It also provided for a system of education so that boys could go to school. The Napoleonic Code also set up basic government systems like a parliament and a judicial system.

Napoleon married twice, first to Josephine and then to Marie-Louise. He had one son who was known as Napoleon II.

For the first part of the 19th century, Napoleon seemed invincible. Then, just as quickly as he had risen to power, it was all over. In 1815, he suffered his final military defeat at the Battle of Waterloo. For the last six years of his life, the once invincible emperor lived in exile. Today, he is remembered as the general who almost conquered all of Europe, but he is also recognized for his military strategy skills and for the Napoleonic Code.

1. **Finish the following multiple-choice questions according to Text B.**
    (1) Napoleon began his military training at the age of _____.
        A. 12   B. 6   C. 16   D. 9
    (2) While in military school, Napoleon studied _____.
        A. artillery   B. military tactics
        C. military strategies   D. all of the above
    (3) Napoleon began his military career as a(an) _____.
        A. Emperor   B. Brigadier general
        C. General   D. Second lieutenant
    (4) During the French Revolution, Napoleon sided with the _____.
        A. nobility   B. royalty
        C. revolutionaries   D. British
    (5) Napoleon's forces won a decisive battle of the French Revolution at _____.
        A. Paris   B. Elba   C. Toulon   D. Corsica
    (6) At the height of his power, Napoleon controlled _____.
        A. most of Europe   B. most of France
        C. all of Europe   D. France and England
    (7) Napoleon _____ the French army.
        A. disbanded   B. strengthened
        C. weakened   D. divided
    (8) Napoleon died _____.
        A. while he was ruler of much of Europe
        B. while he was married to Josephine
        C. in exile
        D. in battle

2. **Discuss the following question with your partners.**
    For which two events or accomplishments do you think Napoleon is remembered most? Tell why each of the two events or accomplishments is important.

Text C　King George III

Do you know that a king gets to be a king just by being born into a certain family? His family is a royal family, and he is part of it. From the time a prince, the young king, is born, he is trained and educated to be the ruler of the country. The family of King George III was the ruling family of England. By the time George was born, the people of England had taken some of the powers away from the ruling family in an uprising called the Glorious Revolution. A group of men, called Parliament, now had the final say in making laws for the government. That did not mean that the king could not make the rules; it was just harder for him to do so. From the time he became king, George tried his hardest to bring more power back to the king and leave less to Parliament.

George was born in 1738, the oldest son of the Prince of Wales. Doctors did not know that he was born with a disease which would eventually make him deaf, blind, and would cause him to lose his mind. The disease worked slowly. All through his life he had times when he could not control his temper. He had times when his thinking was not normal. There were times when he had to be locked in a room by himself for his own safety.

Whether it was the disease or just his personality, George did not like to learn. He was ten years old before he started to learn to read. In his older life, he was smart enough to surround himself with people who would do the things he wanted done. Charles Townshend was one of these men. The two men together were able to get laws passed that would tax the colonists in America.

George became King of England in 1760, right in the middle of a war the British were having with France. France and England wanted to own all of the land in the New World. When the war was over in 1763, England claimed all of the land from the Atlantic Ocean to the Mississippi River. They let Spain claim all the land from the Mississippi westward. It had cost England a lot of money to get this land for the colonists and protect them against the French, so King George felt that they should pay a large share of that cost. The colonists did not agree with the taxes King George wanted them to pay. It was not so much that they did not want to help pay their share; they just did not think it was fair for the king to make all the decisions without giving them some say. When the colonists refused to pay a tax, it made the king mad, and he created a new tax to replace it. This went on for several years until both sides were so mad at each other. They started fighting.

When the colonists accepted *the Declaration of Independence* on July 4, 1776, they sent a message to England and the entire world that they were going to start their own country. This had never been done to a king of England before. How did King George react? Well, history tells us that he kept a diary. In that diary the message he wrote on July 4, 1776, was, "Nothing of importance happened today". What do you think?

1. **Questions for discussion or reflection.**
   (1) What was George III best remembered for in history?
   (2) How do you comment on the message in the diary—"Nothing of importance happened today"?

Proper Names

Prime Minister（英国）首相
Prince Regent 摄政王
the Act of Settlement《嗣位法》或《王位继承法》
the Acts of Union《英苏合并法案》
the Declaration of Independence《独立宣言》

the Jacobites 詹姆斯二世党人；雅各布斯派（英王詹姆斯二世退位后的拥戴者）
the Stamp Act《印花税法案》
Waterloo 滑铁卢

Notes

1. ***The Act of Settlement***: This is an act of the Parliament of England, originally filed in 1700, and passed in 1701, to settle the succession to the English throne on the Electress Sophia of Hanover—a granddaughter of James I—and her Protestant heirs.

2. ***The Stamp Act***: It was imposed by the British Parliament on the colonies of British America. The act required that many printed materials in the colonies carry a tax stamp. The purpose of the tax was to help pay for troops stationed in North America following the British victory in the Seven Years' War. The British government felt that the colonies were the primary beneficiaries of this military presence, and should pay at least a portion of the expense.

3. ***The Acts of Union***: They were a pair of Parliamentary Acts passed in 1707 by the Parliament of Scotland and the Parliament of England to put into effect the terms of *the Treaty of Union* that had been agreed on July 22, 1706, following the negotiation between commissioners representing the parliaments of the two countries. The Acts joined the Kingdom of England and the Kingdom of Scotland into a single United Kingdom of Great Britain.

For Fun

Websites to visit

1. http://www.britannica.com/EBchecked/topic/254505/House-of-Hanover
   This Britannica online encyclopedia presents articles on House of Hanover, British royal house of German origin, descended from George Louis, etc.
2. http://www.great-britain.co.uk/history/georges.htm
   This is an introduction to the Britain from 1714 to 1815, ruled by House of Hanover.
3. http://www.encyclopedia.com/topic/house_of_Hanover.aspx
   This page provides information, facts, and pictures about House of Hanover.

Movie to see

The Madness of King George (1994)

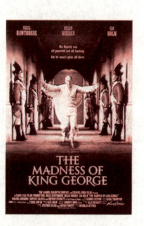

   This is a 1994 film directed by Nicholas Hytner and adapted by Alan Bennett from his own play *The Madness of George III*. It tells the true story of George III's deteriorating mental health, and his equally declining relationship with his son, Prince of Wales, particularly focusing on the period around the Regency Crisis of 1788. Modern medicine has suggested that the king's symptoms were the result of porphyria.

Unit 11
The Industrial Revolution

> Revolution is not the uprising against preexisting order, but the setting up of a new order contradictory to the traditional one.
> —Jose Ortegay Gasset

Unit Goals

- To be familiar with the situation before the Industrial Revolution
- To know the major advancements in the Industrial Revolution
- To understand the consequences of the Industrial Revolution
- To learn the useful words and expressions that describe the Industrial Revolution and improve English language skills
- To develop critical thinking and intercultural communication skills

Before You Read

(1) What was the situation before the Industrial Revolution started?
(2) Can you name some major inventions in the Industrial Revolution and their significance?

Invention	Inventor(s)	Significance

(3) Why did Britain become the "workshop of the world" after the Industrial Revolution?
(4) Form groups of three or four students. Try to find, on the Internet or in the library, more information about the Industrial Revolution. Get ready for a 5-minute presentation in class.

Start to Read

Text A   The British Industrial Revolution

1. After the Bourgeois Revolution in the second half of the 17th century, Britain saw great economic development which gave rise to the British Industrial Revolution and, in return, was greatly accelerated by it. The British Industrial Revolution has been understood to mean the invention and application of various machines in production and the changes which transformed Britain from a predominantly rural and agricultural country into a mainly urban and manufacturing one.

2. The British Industrial Revolution was a necessary result of the social development in Britain. The 1688 palace coup indicated the formal establishment of the constitutional monarchy in Britain, with the bourgeoisie holding an effective control of the state machine. The way to the establishment of capitalist relations of production was thus paved. Externally, Britain had got the upper hand of Spain, France and Holland in the contest to reign supreme on the sea. As a result, the English capitalists could move their goods abroad and plunder the world as freely as they could at home. An inviting chance to make money was what the capitalist economy needed.

3. The greedy English bourgeoisie had accomplished its "primitive accumulation of capital" through plunder and exploitation. They plundered the English peasants through the Enclosure. They plundered the church through Reformation. They plundered Africa and America through the notorious triangular trade. Through all these, the English merchants, manufacturers and other adventurers had accumulated a large sum of money. They were ready to invest in any enterprise that would pay well. Besides, there was no lack of cheap labor, for the Enclosure which had been going on in England for many years was now turning more and more peasants out of their lands. As a result, the English peasants disappeared as a class towards the end of the 18th century. These peasants would seek new employment for their daily bread.

4. English mentality had also undergone changes. The Renaissance had broken religious dogmas and awakened human initiative. It had become acceptable for one to make money and seek happiness. Interests on loans became acceptable and there appeared a nationwide banking system in the mid-18th century after the founding of the Bank of England in 1694. The banking system made it possible to raise a  large sum of money for enterprises. Francis Bacon's philosophical works helped to make the English more practical in doing things. The free competition and free trade doctrine, which were to appear soon, offered the middle class, the mercantile Puritans, the best opportunity to acquire and accumulate wealth.

5. All these factors combined made England the first country to undergo Industrial Revolution.

6. The Industrial Revolution in Britain first began in the textile industry. This was natural. Over several centuries beginning with the Enclosure, wool and then woolen cloth had been the principal exports of England. And cloth-making, though a domestic industry in the main, had the characteristic of capitalism which divided the employer from the employee and introduced the division of labor, such as carding, spinning, weaving and dyeing. With the enlarged market, there appeared a growing demand for cloth. But one person could only make one thread at a time. The lack of abundant yarn became the main obstacle to the mass-production of cloth. The general effort to improve thread-making technique led to the invention of the spinning jenny in 1764 by the English spinner Hargreaves. The new instrument enabled a single workman to spin eight or ten threads at once. Then Arkwright established a great factory by applying power-driven mules and became Father of Factory System in England. Before the end of the 18th century, power-driven machines spinning two hundred threads simultaneously had been introduced in production.

7. With the appearance of new and larger machines, new power had to be found. Wind, waterfalls, and the running stream could no longer satisfy growing demands. Efforts by mechanics to seek more reliable and stronger power led to the invention of the steam engine by James Watt. In 1785, his new steam engine was first used to furnish power for a spinning factory in Nottinghamshire. Very soon it was used all over the country. The invention of the steam engine marked a turning point. With it, there came the fast development of iron, steel and coal industries.

8. The increased production and trade promoted the transportation revolution. Stephenson built his first steam locomotive in 1814 and this marked the beginning of a new stage of the Revolution. Britain had already dug thousands of miles of canals to connect the different shires. Now the newly-built railways began to play a more important part than canals. By 1850 Britain had completed its railway system. Soon steam boats also plied rivers and the sea. Britain became the strongest sea power and had the largest commercial fleet in the world.

9. After the Revolution, Britain became the "workshop of the world". English products flooded the world market. The English bourgeoisie amassed large amounts of wealth through trade, plunder and colonization. No country was strong enough to match England in the 19th century.

After You Read

Knowledge Focus

1. **Pair Work**

    Discuss the following questions with your partner.

    (1) Can you name several important factors that gave rise to the British Industrial Revolution?

    (2) What made it possible for the English capitalists to move their goods abroad and plunder the world freely?

    (3) In what way did the English bourgeoisie accomplish its "primitive accumulation of capital"?

    (4) Why was labor not a problem to the capitalists?

    (5) What gave rise to the changes in English mentality?

    (6) What made it possible to raise a large sum of money for enterprises?

    (7) In which field did the Industrial Revolution in Britain first begin?

    (8) What led to the invention of spinning jenny?

    (9) Who invented the steam engine? What was the significance of such an invention?

    (10) How do you understand the "workshop of the world"?

2. **Solo Work**

    Tell whether and why the following are true or false according to the knowledge you have learned.

    ____ (1) The spinning jenny was invented by James Hargreaves.

    ____ (2) The Industrial Revolution in Britain first began in the clothing industry.

    ____ (3) During the Industrial Revolution, the free competition and free trade were unacceptable to the middle class.

    ____ (4) The importation of goods from British colonies and the exportation of these goods all over the world became the key to British prosperity.

____ (5) After the Industrial Revolution, Britain became the "workshop of the world".

Language Focus

1. **Fill in the blanks with the following words or expressions you have learned in the text. Put them into appropriate forms if necessary.**

| give rise to | accelerate | predominantly | external | plunder |
| undergo | principal | enable | reliable | amass |

(1) Your taxes depend on where your _____ residence is located.

(2) As a civil engineer, Susan will be competing in a _____ male profession.

(3) The president's absence has _____ speculation about his health.

(4) In those days, there was no _____ system of transportation between Alaska and the rest of the US.

(5) The rich provinces of the nation were _____ by the invaders.

(6) Under the old system, many women _____ secret savings unknown to their husbands.

(7) Without _____ pressure, it is unlikely that the civil rights abuses would have stopped.

(8) Recent innovations with computer-aided design _____ us to produce magazines which are more creative and efficient.

(9) The truck's wheels skidded on the snow as the driver _____ forward.

(10) At that time, she was _____ tremendous emotional problems following the breakup of her marriage.

2. **Complete the following sentences with the proper forms of the words in the brackets.**

(1) The way to the establishment of _____ (capitalize) relations of production thus paved.

(2) The _____ (greed) English bourgeoisie accomplished its "primitive accumulation of capital" through plunder and exploitation.

(3) English _____ (mental) had also undergone changes.

(4) One of Britain's most _____ (notoriety) criminals has escaped from prison.

(5) With the _____ (enlarge) market, there appeared a growing demand for cloth.

(6) Before the end of the 18th century, power-driven machines spinning two hundred threads _____ (simultaneity) had been introduced in production.

(7) Wind, waterfalls, and the running stream could no longer satisfy the _____ (grow) demands.

(8) Nothing's more _____ (invite) than a plump sofa or chair.

3. Find the appropriate prepositions that collocate with the neighboring words.

(1) Britain saw great economic development which gave rise _____ the British Industrial Revolution.

(2) France and Holland _____ the contest to reign supreme on the sea.

(3) The lack _____ abundant yarn became the main obstacle _____ the mass-production of cloth.

(4) They were ready to invest _____ any enterprise that would pay well.

(5) In 1785, the new steam engine was first used to furnish power _____ a spinning factory in Nottinghamshire.

(6) Interests _____ loans became acceptable and there appeared a nationwide banking system in the mid-18th century.

(7) The accused was furnished _____ a list of local solicitors.

(8) Clothing industry, though a domestic industry _____ the main, had the characteristic of capitalism.

Comprehensive Work

Solo Work

You are an investigative reporter working for a British newspaper that has decided to publish a special edition on the Industrial Revolution. You have been given the responsibility to head up this project. It will be up to you to research, write, and design the newspaper. In your report, you will provide your readers with the facts regarding the successes and failures of your country's move towards mechanization and mass-production. In the end, you will write an editorial giving your opinion whether this "progress" has benefited or harmed the society in which you live.

Your task: As the reporter for the local newspaper, you will be responsible for:

● researching and writing two news stories on different topics from the Industrial Revolution—unions and strikes, women, child labor, health and sanitation, life in the mines, textile mill conditions;

● spotlighting an Industrial Revolution inventor. You must give some basic biographical information, his main invention(s), and the impact the invention(s) have had on society then and now. This article should be at least 200 words;

● writing an editorial that defends or criticizes the effects the Industrial Revolution has had on British society as a whole;

● finding two or more images to supplement your articles;

● placing your stories and images together in a newspaper or magazine format.

Read More

Text B Machines for the Industrial Revolution

The Industrial Revolution began with inventors—people with ideas about how to make work more efficient.

The one invention that led most directly to the growth of industry was the steam engine. In 1698, Thomas Savery, an Englishman, had invented a simple steam engine. His original plan was to use it to pump water out of coal mines. Another English inventor, Thomas Newcomen, improved on Savery's steam engine and produced one that was actually used for the purpose of pumping water out of mines. A third inventor, a Scotsman by the name of James Watt, made more improvements to the steam engine. Watt's steam engines were more efficient than earlier models. Before too long, they were powering the machines in factory towns all over Europe and North America.

Other inventions led to the growth of industry, too, starting with the textile industry in England.

One of the inventors was an American—Eli Whitney, the inventor of the cotton gin. The cotton gin was a machine that automated the removal of cotton seeds from cotton fiber. Before the invention of the cotton gin, it took a day or more to remove the seeds from just one pound of cotton. With a cotton gin, fifty pounds of cleaned cotton could be produced in one day. Cotton produced by this faster method soon began to make its way back to England where it could be spun and woven into cloth.

James Hargreaves, a weaver from England, invented another useful machine, the spinning jenny, which he named after his daughter. The spinning jenny sped up the next step in the production of cotton cloth, the spinning of thread. Previously, this had been done by hand, one spindle of thread at a time. The original spinning jenny, while it was still operated by hand, produced eight spindles of thread at one time. Later models produced even more.

In 1768, Richard Arkwright, a wigmaker from England, invented a machine that further automated the process of making thread. His invention, called the water frame, was powered by a turning water wheel. It could be operated by a single unskilled worker. With its four rows of 32 spindles each, one water frame could produce 128 spindles of thread simultaneously.

Arkwright was not only an inventor; he was also an investor. He bought land and built a large factory where workers could produce huge amounts of cloth very quickly. He built a factory town full of houses to attract workers to his factory. He advertised for workers with large families. Men who could weave cloth and also had large families were often hired. While the men wove cloth, the wives and children as young as ten years old worked in the mills spinning all of the thread that the weavers would need.

Arkwright's model of a cotton mill soon spread, and sprawling mills with tall smokestacks sprang up all over England.

These inventions paved the way for the Industrial Revolution. They led to many unexpected results including child labor and the concentration of wealth in the hands of the few people who already had money to invest.

They also paved the way for our modern society in which people have a closet full of clothes instead of the few pieces that the average person once owned. They led to an increase in foreign trade and population booms in factory cities. As a matter of fact, there are few topics in modern history that cannot in some way be traced back to the inventions of the Industrial Revolution.

1. Finish the following multiple-choice questions according to Text B.
  (1) The inventions that began the Industrial Revolution were created mainly during the _____.
   A. 1800s   B. 1700s   C. 1600s   D. 1900s
  (2) All of the following were inventions that directly affected the Industrial Revolution in England EXCEPT the _____.
   A. water frame   B. spinning jenny
   C. steam engine   D. printing press
  (3) _____ invented the cotton gin.
   A. Newcomen B. Whitney   C. Savery   D. Watt
  (4) _____ invented the model of the steam engine that was used in factories during the Industrial Revolution.
   A. Watt   B. Savery   C. Whitney D. Newcomen
  (5) Before Richard Arkwright became an inventor and factory owner, he worked as a/an _____.
   A. weaver   B. investor C. farmer   D. wigmaker
  (6) A _____ separated cotton fiber from cotton seeds.
   A. water frame   B. steam engine
   C. spinning jenny   D. cotton gin

(7) Both the _____ and the _____ spun thread.
   A. water frame, steam engine
   B. steam engine, spinning jenny
   C. cotton jenny, water frame
   D. cotton gin, cotton jenny
(8) One negative effect of the Industrial Revolution was _____.
   A. the invention of the steam engine
   B. child labor
   C. the increase in trade
   D. the invention of the spinning jenny

2. **Discuss the following questions with your partners.**
   (1) What is the most significant invention of the Industrial Revolution? How did this invention affect people's lives?
   (2) Do you think that the inventions of the Industrial Revolution had an overall positive or negative effect? Give reasons for your answer.

Text C The Consequences of the Industrial Revolution

In the last part of the 18th century, a new revolution gripped the world that we were not ready for. This revolution was not a political one, but it would lead to many implications later in its existence. Neither was this a social or cultural revolution. This revolution was an economic one.

The Industrial Revolution, called by historians, changed the ways the world produced its goods. It also changed our societies from a mainly agricultural society to one in which industry and manufacturing dominated.

The Industrial Revolution first got its start in Great Britain, during the 18th century, which at the time was the most powerful empire on the planet. So, it was inevitable that the country with the most wealth would lead in this revolution. After its adoption in England, other countries such as Germany, the United States and France joined this revolution.

During this time there were also many new technological advance, socioeconomic problems, and cultural problems.

On the technology front, the biggest advancements were in steam power. New fuels, such as coal and petroleum, were incorporated into new steam engines. This revolutionized many industries including textiles and manufacturing. Also, a new communication medium called the telegraph was invented. This made communicating across the Atlantic much faster.

But, along with this great leap in technology, there was an overall downfall in the socioeconomic and cultural situation of the people. Growth of cities was one of the major consequences of the Industrial Revolution. Many people were driven to cities to look for work. With the new industrial age, a new quantitative and materialistic view of the world took place. This caused the need for people to consume as much as they could. This still happens today. Living on small wages required small children to work in factories for long days.

During this time, much international strife was also occurring. The American Revolution was occurring in the beginning of the Industrial Revolution. The French Revolution was in the process at the turn of the 19th century. This was a great time, and it resulted in newly found democratic rights that spread through Europe and North America.

The Industrial Revolution was not a good revolution for the planet. From the time of its start, the factories and the industry have increased the amount of carbon dioxide in the atmosphere by two folds. Also in our drive for consumerism, our planet's natural resources are being depleted at an alarming rate. Pollution by nuclear waste, pesticides and other chemicals are also the result of the Industrial Revolution.

1. Questions for discussion or reflection.
   (1) What was the biggest advancement on the technology front?
   (2) What influence did the Industrial Revolution exert on the socioeconomic and cultural situation of the people?
   (3) What were the negative impacts of the Industrial Revolution?

Proper Names

Arkwright 阿克赖特
Bank of England 英格兰银行
Bourgeois Revolution 资产阶级革命
British Industrial Revolution 英国工业革命
Francis Bacon 弗朗西斯·培根
James Hargreaves 詹姆斯·哈格里夫斯

James Watt 詹姆斯·瓦特
Nottinghamshire 诺丁汉
Renaissance 文艺复兴
Stephenson 斯蒂芬森
the spinning jenny 珍妮纺纱机

Notes

1. **Francis Bacon (1561—1626)**: He was one of the leading figures in natural philosophy and in the field of scientific methodology in the period of transition from the

Renaissance to the early modern era. As a lawyer, member of Parliament, and Queen's counsel, Bacon wrote on questions of law, state and religion, as well as on contemporary politics; he also published texts in which he speculated on possible conceptions of society.

2. **James Watt (1736—1819):** He was a Scottish mathematician and engineer whose improvements to the steam engine were a key stage in the Industrial Revolution. He was born in Greenock, Scotland, and lived and worked in Birmingham, England. He was a key member of the Lunar Society. Many of his papers are in Birmingham Central Library.

Websites to visit

1. **http://www.victorianweb.org/technology/ir/index.html**
   This page serves as an overview of the Industrial Revolution in Britain.
2. **http://plato.stanford.edu/entries/francis-bacon/**
   This page provides you with an introduction to Francis Bacon.

Movie to see

Modern Times (1936)

Modern Times is a 1936 comedy film by Charles Chaplin who has his iconic Little Tramp character, in his final silent-film appearance, struggling to survive in the modern, industrialized world. The film is a comment on the desperate employment and fiscal conditions many people faced during the Great Depression, conditions created, in Chaplin's view, by the efficiencies of modern industrialization. The movie stars Chaplin, Paulette Goddard, Henry Bergman, Stanley Sandford and Chester Conklin, and was written and directed by Chaplin. *Modern Times* was deemed "culturally significant" by the Library of Congress in 1989, and selected for preservation in the United States National Film Registry.

Book to read

What the Industrial Revolution Did for Us by Gavin Weightman

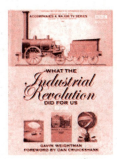

Gavin Weightman is a noted historian and film-maker. The book is made up of six detailed and beautifully illustrated chapters covering aspects of the Industrial Revolution including the invention of new machinery and technology, the changing face of the landscape and the improvement in transport; the working conditions of the poor and the changes in law, advances in medicine and the development of new military weaponry; the emergence of cotton and the arrival of tea.

Unit 12
The Victorian Age (1837—1901)

> The Victorian era was perhaps the last point in Western history when magic and science were allowed to coexist.
> —Jonathan Auxier

Unit Goals

- To be familiar with the Victorian Age
- To have a rough idea about the literary achievements in this period
- To know the important historical figures of the Victorian Age
- To learn the useful words and expressions that describe the Victorian Age and improve English language skills
- To develop critical thinking and intercultural communication skills

Before You Read

(1) Victoria is a beautiful name. What do you know about Queen Victoria and the Victorian era? Please share your knowledge with your partner.
(2) Do you know anything specific with regard to the Fabian Society?
(3) Brontë, Dickens, and George Eliot are household names in literary circle. You must be familiar with the characters in their novels. Share your knowledge with your partner.
Brontë: _____
_____
Dickens: _____
George Eliot: _____
(4) Form groups of three or four students. Try to find, on the Internet or in the library, more information about Queen Victoria. Get ready for a 5-minute presentation in class.

Start to Read

Text A Queen Victoria and Her Reign

1. The Victorian era is generally agreed to stretch through the reign of Queen Victoria (1837—1901). It was a tremendously exciting period when many artistic styles, literary schools, as well as social, political and religious movements flourished. It was a time of prosperity, broad imperial expansion, and great political reform. Without a doubt, it was an extraordinarily complex age, which has sometimes been called the Second English Renaissance. It was, indeed, the precursor of the modern era. If one wishes to understand the world today in terms of society, culture, science, and ideas, it is imperative to study this era.

2. Victoria's time was full of tremendous changes in almost every respect. The Industrial Revolution continued to develop in spite of the social evils that accompanied it. The emergence of locomotives threw Britain into a frenzy of railway building. Agriculture was further mechanized. Trade and commerce grew tremendously, driving more peasants, hand spinners and weavers to the crowded factories of the smoky cities. England was arriving at the age of machinery.

3. Development of productivity enlarged men's vision and increased their interest in scientific knowledge. In 1859, Darwin published his *Origin of Species* in which he proved that the physical species are not fixed, but changing by natural selection in which the fittest survive. His theory greatly shocked clergymen because it clearly contained the suggestion that man was descended from monkeys instead of God. It also provided material evidence to justify the theory of free competition, as had been raised by Adam Smith concerning production and trade. Free competition and individualism became a more important element in British values.

4. The change in outlook and eagerness to gain useful knowledge made it possible for a group of famous writers to appear, with Thackeray, the Brontës, Dickens, and George Eliot among the most famous. Their works either exposed social evils in an effort to promote social reforms, such as the novels of Dickens, or sought to establish guiding values for the relationship of the individual to himself, to other individuals and to society at large, such as *Jane Eyre* and *Wuthering Heights*. Their works played an important role in pushing forward social reforms and establishing the British values.

5. Charles Dickens did as much as any man to draw his country's attention to the needs of the poor. He was especially sorry for children who had no parents, or whose parents were in prison, for his own father had been in prison for debt. The characters of history and of most literature belong to the middle and upper classes of society, but Dickens writes of the poor and the humble. His first book took his middle-class Mr. Pickwick to prison and showed him the terrible conditions inside.

6. It was followed by sad but exciting stories of poor and fatherless children: *Oliver Twist*, *The Old Curiosity Shop*, *David Copperfield*, *Great Expectations* and many more. Such books had a great influence on those who pressed the parliament to improve conditions in factories and prisons, and to care for homeless children.

7. The 19th century produced great poetry too, but three of the greatest poets died young before Victoria became Queen: Byron in Greece, Keats and Shelley in Italy. All three were lovers of Greek and Roman art and thoughts; they aimed to express the ancient ideals of beauty in their own fresh English verse. Wordsworth shared their ideals and opened his countrymen's eyes to the beauty of nature.

8. Wordsworth's poetry attracted his readers to visit the Lake District where he lived, for the holiday habit was taking hold of the British people. Many factory workers, especially in the north, began to take their families to the seaside; the middle class went to the Lakes, to Cornwall, or to the Welsh and Scottish mountains; the upper class developed a fashionable colony on the south coast of France, which was then quiet and unspoilt.

9. Secret voting was introduced in 1872 and male members of the working class in the towns got the right to vote in 1876. The rural working class was also enfranchised in 1886. Compulsory education was adopted and universities began to admit women students. Oxford and Cambridge got their freedom to enroll students who were not Anglican Church believers and the college fellows

were allowed to get married.

10. The improved social conditions were manifested by the birth, in 1884, of the Fabian Society, with Bernard Shaw as one of its founders. The Society advocated changing the nature of government by way of permeating the ruling class and its organs. This English type of "socialism" based on class cooperation was later adopted by the Labor Party.

11. Britain's social changes at home were cause and effect of its foreign expansion during the same time. Britain suppressed the revolt of the Canadians. It started the Opium War against China in 1840 and put down a large-scale rebellion of the Indians. It fought the Russians in the Crimean War especially remembered for the sake of Florence Nightingale, founder of modern nursing. The war was the local effort by France and Britain to keep Russian influence out of the eastern Mediterranean. Generally speaking, Britain began to adopt a more flexible policy in its foreign expansion. Canada, Austria, and New Zealand were granted self-government. Victoria became Empress of India by taking over its control from the East India Company.

12. During the American Civil War, the English government was forced to give up supporting the South with which Britain had a closer tie. Because of industrial competition from Germany and the United States, Britain made more efforts to become the world's banker than to preserve its position as the workshop of the world. The English government, instead of reducing its foreign expansion, brought it to a new height. Queen Elizabeth had laid the foundation for the empire and its real establishment was achieved under the reign of Queen Victoria. Britain had reached its pinnacle and was going over to imperialism.

13. Victoria's reputation in Britain was also due to her personality. She set a very severe home discipline for her children. Any dishonesty, mischief, negligence or rude language might result in beatings for them. She herself was very careful about her behavior on public occasions. In addition, she maintained a very harmonious relation with her husband and almost set a standard for posterity.

14. Victoria's achievements were so popular in Britain and her personality was so widely esteemed and imitated by the middle class that the title "Victorian" was later applied to any person or time with the characteristics of decency, morality and self-satisfaction. Her time was thus called "the polite society" in English history. It cannot be said for sure that all these were in complete agreement with social facts, but it is true that her influence on life set a standard for the English middle class for many years to come.

After You Read

Knowledge Focus

1. Pair Work

   Discuss the following questions with your partner.
   (1) Why was the Victorian age called the Second English Renaissance?
   (2) What do you know about the theory put forward by Darwin?
   (3) Why did Darwin's theory shock the clergymen in Britain?
   (4) Can you name several famous writers and their works during the Victorian age?
   (5) Can you name those famous novels written by Charles Dickens?
   (6) What do you know about such poets as Byron, Keats, Shelley and Wordsworth?
   (7) Do you know why Wordsworth was called "Lake Poet"?
   (8) What do you know about the Fabian Society? Who was the most important founder?
   (9) Do you know Florence Nightingale? What was she famous for?
   (10) How do you describe Victoria's personality?

2. Solo Work

   Tell whether and why the following are true or false according to the knowledge you have learned.
   ____ (1) Victoria and Albert had nine children but they spent little time with them.
   ____ (2) Charles Dickens wrote about the social problems of the Victorian Age in his novels.
   ____ (3) Britain became the richest commercial nation under Victoria's reign. It produced machines, textiles and ships, and sold them to other countries.
   ____ (4) Florence Nightingale was generally regarded as founder of modern nursing.
   ____ (5) Three of the greatest poets died young before Victoria became Queen: Byron in Greece, Keats and Shelley in Italy.
   ____ (6) Wordsworth's poetry attracted his readers to visit the Lake District. And Wordsworth is known as a "Lake Poet".
   ____ (7) Victoria's reputation in Britain was also due to her personality.
   ____ (8) Victoria who ruled over the British Empire for 50 years was another well-known queen in English history.
   ____ (9) The improved social conditions were manifested by the birth, in 1884, of the Fabian Society, with Bernard Shaw as one of its founders.

____ (10) Victoria became Empress of India by taking over its control from the East India Company.

Language Focus

1. Fill in the blanks with the following words or expressions you have learned in the text. Put them into appropriate forms if necessary.

| precursor | imperative | frenzy | be descended from | justify |
| enroll | manifest | permeate | press...to... | posterity |

(1) Basic education remains a necessary _____ to behavior change, especially for the young.

(2) His parents _____ him in a military academy when he was only eight years old.

(3) The _____ of rebuilding is now past due to the implementation of the state policy.

(4) There is a culture of racism that _____ the entire organization.

(5) I do not think anyone can _____ spending so much money on weapons.

(6) The police _____ the witness _____ recall all the details after the assassination.

(7) When the writing begins, it is _____ that relevant research should be summarized.

(8) Mountain sickness is usually _____ as headache and tiredness.

(9) The spokesman of the executive office claims to _____ Abraham Lincoln.

(10) Perhaps she simply wanted to hear herself perform, unless of course she hoped to leave _____ an example of her playing.

2. Complete the following sentences with the proper forms of the words in the brackets.

(1) It was a tremendously exciting period when many _____ (art) styles, literary schools, as well as social, political and religious movements flourished.

(2) It was a time of prosperity, broad imperial _____ (expand), and great political reform.

(3) The potential application of this technology to monitoring environmental changes that could affect the _____ (emerge) of infectious diseases will be assessed.

(4) The application of his theory gave rise to high _____ (produce) in manufacturing.

(5) The convention brought money and media _____ (expose) to this small city.

(6) It was followed by sad but exciting stories of poor and _____ (father) children.

(7) The upper class developed a fashionable colony on the south coast of France, which

was then quiet and _____ (spoil).
(8) The significance of these comparatively simple provisions on open _____ (enroll) should not be overlooked.
(9) This latest outbreak of violence is a clear _____ (manifest) of discontent in the city.
(10) Any _____ (honest), mischief, negligence or rude language might result in beatings for them.

3. **Find the appropriate prepositions that collocate with the neighboring words.**
   (1) _____ a doubt, it was an extraordinarily complex age, which has sometimes been called the Second English Renaissance.
   (2) The Industrial Revolution continued to develop _____ spite of the social evils that accompanied it.
   (3) England was arriving _____ the age of machinery.
   (4) Development of productivity enlarged men's vision and increased their interest _____ scientific knowledge.
   (5) Man was descended _____ monkeys instead of God.
   (6) Their works played an important role _____ pushing forward social reforms and establishing the British values.
   (7) Charles Dickens did as much as any man to draw his country's attention _____ the needs of the poor.
   (8) He was especially sorry _____ children who had no parents.
   (9) Wordsworth shared their ideals and opened his countrymen's eyes _____ the beauties of nature.
   (10) The Society advocated changing the nature of government _____ way of permeating the ruling class and its organs.

Comprehensive Work

Group Work: A Symposium on the Victorian Era
You will work in small groups on projects to attend the Victorian Symposium. Each group will choose one topic from the options listed below.

Project Options
1. Literature in the Victorian Age: Who were the famous literary figures? You might stage a panel discussion or talk show of noteworthy individuals from the literary world. You could write a review to critique popular works of literature.
2. Women in Victorian Society: Research the lifestyles of women in the Victorian Age. What were the roles and responsibilities of women? What restrictions did women face? How did social class affect a woman's opportunities? Perhaps you could dramatize the lives of several representative women or stage a discussion among several individuals.
3. Victorian Education: Examine the British educational system. You will need to distinguish between education for the wealthy and education for the poorer classes. How did social class affect an individual's education and upbringing? What were the differences in education between men and women? You could write a school newspaper to distribute

to the class.

4. Victorian Manners and Etiquette: How did Victorian men and women behave in upper class society? What roles did women play? How was a true gentleman defined? You might have people like Ann Landers or Miss Manners debate the question.

5. Victorian Justice: You will explore the justice system, its criminals, and its punishments. How did the society attempt to solve its social problems in its justice system? What were the prisons like? How were the debtors treated? You might present case studies of imaginary (or real) criminals. Perhaps you could draw up a "Most Wanted" list.

6. Charles Dickens' Life: Your group will explore Charles Dickens' life. What were his most profound experiences? What types of literature did he write? How was his work published and illustrated?

Writing Practice

Choose one topic above and answer the corresponding questions in essay form.

Class Presentation

As with most symposia, you will present your project orally. You will need visual aids (handouts, pictures, models, drawings, etc.) and audio aids (music) if necessary.

Read More

Text B   Everyday Life in Victorian England

What was an ordinary day like back in Victorian England? More than anything else, the answer depended on what social class a person belonged to. Let's take a look at the daily routine of some women of the era. One woman is a member of the upper class; she is the lady of the house. The second woman lives in the same house and works as a housekeeper. The third woman also lives and works in the same house, and she is the children's nurse.

Upon rising, the lady of the house chooses the first of several outfits that she will wear that day. She will remain in her chambers until she is ready to call for her servant to help her dress.

She is in charge of the household and the children, but with servants to attend to the work; she can take care of her own responsibilities when it suits her.

In the afternoon, she visits the home of a neighbor. She stays for a short, sociable chat of perhaps half an hour, or if her neighbor is not at home, she leaves a calling card.

Later in the afternoon, she spends an hour with her children. She asks the nurse how their lessons are progressing. She eats dinner with her husband after he returns home from work while their children eat dinner in the nursery.

The nurse is responsible for caring for the children at nearly all time. She does not have a room of her own but sleeps in the nursery with the children. She helps the young children bathe, dress, and eat. She tutors them until they are old enough to go to school.

The nurse has little time for a life of her own. Living in someone else's house, she is not free to meet friends. Neither does she usually have time to go out. A few free hours every other Sunday provide little time for visiting friends or making new acquaintances. She spends her few vacation days each year visiting with her family. These days are never around holiday times, since she is always busy with the children then. She misses spending more time with her own family, especially on holidays.

The housekeeper has her own room in the attic, and she spends nearly all of her time waiting on the family as well. Her day begins early when she rises to light the fires in the fireplaces. On warm days, she opens the shutters to let in some fresh air.

The housekeeper also carries warm water up to the family members to wash or shave each morning. If the lady of the house wishes to have breakfast in her room, she will carry breakfast to her. When the lady is ready to dress, she will help her to dress.

There are certain chores that she does daily. These include sweeping, dusting, making the beds, and tending the fires. The parlor must be tidied up and the soot from the fires and the lamps must be wiped away. Other chores, like cleaning certain rooms or doing laundry might be done on one day each week. Her schedule shows that she has many responsibilities on each of the seven days of the week.

There are meals to plan, following her lady's wishes, and there is cooking to supervise. Meals must be prepared, not only for the owners of the house, but for the staff as well. The housekeeper and the other staff members, including the cook, the scullery maid, and the nurse, eat their meals in the kitchen.

One thing that all of the residents of the house enjoy is tea time. The lady of the house sips hers from an elegant tea service in the parlor. The staff take their tea, along with a few minutes to catch up on the latest gossip, in the kitchen.

The housekeeper's day does not end until around 11:00 at night. By then, the children are sound asleep, and so is their nurse. The family has gone to bed. It is time to tend to the fires one last time, check to make sure that the house is tidy, and turn in. In a few short hours it will be morning.

1. Finish the following multiple-choice questions according to Text B.
   (1) A person's daily routine depended mainly on what _____ he or she belonged to.
       A. dynasty   B. neighborhood   C. guild   D. class
   (2) The daily routine of the _____ included the most free time.
       A. lady of the house   B. scullery maid
       C. children's nurse   D. housekeeper
   (3) If the lady of the house visited at a neighbor's house but the neighbor was not at home, she would leave a _____.
       A. treat   B. calling card
       C. package   D. phone number
   (4) The _____ supervised the running of the household and the care of the children.
       A. the lady of the house   B. the man of the house
       C. the housekeeper   D. the oldest child
   (5) The lady of the house _____.
       A. dressed herself in a casual outfit each day
       B. dressed the children in three outfits each day
       C. helped to dress the children
       D. required help in dressing herself
   (6) The nurse helped the children _____.
       A. bathe   B. dress   C. eat   D. all of the above
   (7) The first and last duty of the housekeeper each day was to _____.
       A. tend the fires   B. clean the kitchen
       C. cook   D. dress the children
   (8) The job of a housekeeper included _____.
       A. mostly caring for children
       B. few responsibilities
       C. little work
       D. many responsibilities

2. Discuss the following questions with your partners.
   (1) Do you think that becoming a children's nurse was a good job for a young woman in Victorian times? Why or why not?
   (2) Why do you think social visits were an important part of the daily routine for the lady of the house?

Text C Charles Dickens (1812—1870)

Charles Dickens is much loved for his great contribution to classical English literature. He is the quintessential Victorian author: his epic stories, vivid characters and exhaustive depiction of contemporary life are unforgettable.

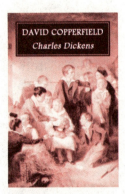

His own story is one of rags to riches. He was born in Portsmouth on February 7, 1812, to John and Elizabeth Dickens. The good fortune of being sent to school at the age of nine was short-lived because his father, inspiration for the character of Mr. Micawber in *David Copperfield*, was imprisoned for bad debt. The entire family, apart from Charles, was sent to Marshalseah. Charles was sent to work in Warren's blacking factory and endured appalling conditions as well as loneliness and despair. After three years he was returned to school but the experience was never forgotten and became fictionalized in two of his better-known novels *David Copperfield* and *Great Expectations*.

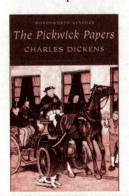

Like many others, he began his literary career as a journalist. His own father became a reporter and Charles began with *The Mirror of Parliament* and *The True Sun*. Then in 1833, he became a parliamentary journalist for *The Morning Chronicle*. With new contacts in the press he was able to publish a series of sketches under the pseudonym "Boz". In April 1836, he married Catherine Hogarth, daughter of George Hogarth who edited sketches by Boz. Within the same month came the publication of the highly successful *Pickwick Papers*, and from that point on there was no looking back.

As well as a huge list of novels he published autobiography, edited weekly periodicals including *Household Words* and *All Year Round*, wrote travel books and administered charitable organizations. He was also a theatre enthusiast, wrote plays and performed before Queen Victoria in 1851. His energy was inexhaustible and he spent much time abroad—for example lecturing against slavery in the United States and touring Italy with companions Augustus Egg and Wilkie Collins, a contemporary writer who inspired Dickens' final unfinished novel *Mystery of Edwin Drood*.

He was estranged from his wife in 1858 after the birth of their ten children, maintained relations with his mistress, the actress Ellen Ternan and died of a stroke in 1870. He is buried at Westminster Abbey.

1. Questions for discussion or reflection.
   (1) What is Charles Dickens much loved for?
   (2) What do you know about the childhood of Charles Dickens?
   (3) What influence did his childhood exert on his novels?

Proper Names

Adam Smith 亚当·斯密
American Civil War 美国南北战争
Bernard Shaw 萧伯纳
British Empire 大英帝国
Brontë 勃朗特
Byron 拜伦
Cornwall 康沃尔
Darwin 达尔文
David Copperfield《大卫·科波菲尔》
Dickens 狄更斯
East India Company 东印度公司
Fabian Society 费边社
Florence Nightingale 费洛伦斯·南丁格尔
Great Expectations《远大前程》
George Eliot 乔治·艾略特
Jane Eyre《简爱》
Keats 济慈
Lake District 湖区
Oliver Twist《雾都孤儿》
Opium Wars 鸦片战争
Origin of Species《物种起源》
Queen Elizabeth 伊丽莎白女王
Queen Victoria 维多利亚女王
Second English Renaissance 第二次英国文艺复兴
Shelley 雪莱
Thackeray 萨克雷
The Old Curiosity Shop《老古玩店》
Victorian era 维多利亚时代
William Wordsworth 威廉·华兹华斯
Wuthering Heights《呼啸山庄》

Notes

1. **The Victorian Era**: The Victorian Era of the United Kingdom was the period of Queen Victoria's reign from June 1837 to January 1901. This was a long period of prosperity for the British people, as profits gained from the overseas British Empire, as well as from industrial improvements at home, allowed a large, educated middle class to develop. Some scholars would extend the beginning of the period—as defined by a variety of sensibilities and political concerns that have come to be associated with the Victorians—back five years to the passage of *the Reform Act 1832*.

2. **The Opium Wars**: The Opium Wars, also known as the Anglo-Chinese Wars, lasted from 1839 to 1842 and 1856 to 1860, the climax of a trade dispute between China under the Qing Dynasty and the British Empire. British smuggling of opium from British India into China in defiance of China's drug laws erupted into open warfare between Britain and China.

3. **Byron**: George Gordon Byron was a British poet and a leading figure in Romanticism.

Amongst Byron's best-known works are the brief poems *She Walks in Beauty*, *When We Two Parted*, as well as the narrative poems *Childe Harold's Pilgrimage* and *Don Juan*. He is regarded as one of the greatest European poets and remains widely read and influential, both in the English-speaking world and beyond.

For Fun

Books to read

1. ***David Copperfield*** by Charles Dickens

   David Copperfield is a novel by Charles Dickens, first published in 1850. Many elements within the novel follow events in Dickens' own life, and it is probably the most autobiographical of all of his novels. In the preface to the 1867 Charles Dickens edition, he wrote, "... like many fond parents, I have in my heart of hearts a favorite child. And his name is David Copperfield". The story is told almost entirely from the point of view of the first person narrator, David Copperfield himself, and was the first Dickens' novel to do so. The story deals with the life of David Copperfield from childhood to maturity.

2. ***Jane Eyre*** by Charlotte Brontë

   Charlotte Brontë's impassioned novel is the love story of *Jane Eyre*, a plain yet spirited governess, and her arrogant, brooding Mr. Rochester. Published in 1847, under the pseudonym of Currer Bell, the book heralded a new kind of heroine—one whose virtuous integrity, keen intellect and tireless perseverance broke through class barriers to win equal stature with the man she loved. Hailed by William Makepeace Thackeray as "the masterwork of great genius," *Jane Eyre* is still regarded, over a century later, as one of the finest novels in English literature.

   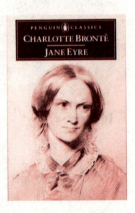

Websites to visit

1. http://www.bbc.co.uk/history/british/normans/after_01.shtml

   This BBC British history webpage provides a detailed account about the Victorian era.

2. http://www.britannia.com/history/h12.html

   This page is a comprehensive information resource of Queen Elizabeth and Queen Victoria.

Movies to see

1. Mrs. Brown (1997)

Queen Victoria is deeply depressed after the death of her husband, disappearing from public. Her servant Brown, who adores her, through caress and admiration brings her back to life, but that relationship creates scandalous situation and is likely to lead to monarchy crisis. The atmosphere in court is instantly tense and chilling. But the man, John Brown, has caught the queen's attention and cut through the miasma of two years' mourning for her beloved Prince Albert. The little woman—a plump pudding dressed all in black—looks up sharply, and a certain light glints in her eyes. Before long she is taking Brown's advice that she must ride out daily, for the exercise and the fresh air.

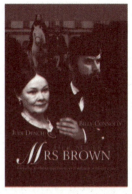

2. Victoria & Albert (2001)

The passionate love story was Queen Victoria and Prince Albert's lengthy marriage. Beginning in 1837, the year of King William IV's death and 18-year-old Victoria's ascension to the throne, the series charts the tumultuous period in 19th Century England where Victoria comes to terms with the enormous duties that lay ahead of her, while also falling deeply in love with her beloved Albert of Saxe-Coburg-Gotha. The marriage and birth of their nine children are featured, as is Albert's frustration by the inactivity he experienced in the early years of his role as Prince Consort.

3. The Young Victoria (2009)

On the eve of her 18th birthday and succession to the English throne, young Princess Victoria is caught in a royal power struggle. But, it is her blossoming relationship with Prince Albert that will determine the strength of her reign. Can she dedicate her life to her country and her heart to the one man she truly loves? Discover the passion and the romance behind one of history's greatest love stories.

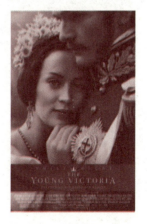

Song to enjoy

"Ribbons" by The Sister of Mercy

"Ribbons" is a song taken from the "Vision Thing" album of a band—The Sister of Mercy. It is a famous piece of Gothic Rock.

I'm lying on my back now	About Marx and Engels, God and Angels
The stars look all too near	I do not really know what for
Flowers on the razor wire	But she looked good in ribbons
I know you're here	So just walk on in
We are few	She looked good in ribbons
And far between	So just walk on in
I was thinking about her skin	
Love is a many splintered thing	Tie a red red red red red red ribbon
Do not be afraid now	Love is a many splintered thing
Just walk on in	Tie a red red red red ribbon
(Flowers on the razor wire)	Do not be afraid
(Walk on in)	Just walk on in
Her eyes were cobalt red	
Her voice was cobalt blue	Just walk on in
I see no purple light	(Incoming...)
Crashing out of you	(Incoming...)
So just walk on in	Just walk on in
(Flowers on the razor wire)	Just walk on in
(Walk on in)	Flowers on the razor wire
Her lovers queued up in the hallway	Just walk on in...
I heard them scratching at the door	INCOMING!
I tried to tell her	

Unit 13
The World at War

> All great civilizations, in their early stages, are based on success in war.
> —Kenneth Clark

Unit Goals

- To be familiar with the situation of the Great Britain in the two world wars
- To have a rough idea of the formation of the British Empire
- To explore the story about Winston Churchill and his achievements
- To learn the useful words and expressions that describe the Great Britain in the world wars and improve English language skills
- To develop critical thinking and intercultural communication skills

Before You Read

(1) How much do you know about the following questions? Share your knowledge with your partner.
   A. What was the situation before the First World War?
   B. What role did Winston Churchill play in the Second World War?

(2) Define the following terms.
   A. Adolf Hitler: _____
   _____
   B. Winston Churchill: _____
   _____
   C. The Treaty of Versailles: _____
   _____

(3) Form groups of three or four students. Try to find, on the Internet or in the library, more information about one important battle in the two World Wars. Get ready for a 5-minute presentation in class.

Start to Read

Text A   **The Great Britain in the World Wars**

1. In the late 19th century, Britain kept out of foreign politics as much as possible. Europe was divided into two camps: France and Russia in one, Germany, Austria and Italy in the other. Britain favored the second group so long as France threatened her interests in Africa and the Russians threatened her Indian border. But Germany was growing too strong. The various German states had been united under King of Prussia after his conquest of France in 1870. He was now Emperor of all Germany. He was Queen Victoria's son-in-law, but his ambition took no account of such a tie. Britain watched him with growing mistrust.

2. The Germans already had the best army in Europe. By 1901, when Victoria died, they had begun to build a very large navy to fight its British rival. Edward VII had never shared his mother's faith in the emperor's goodwill, and Britain now openly made friends with France. She could not make a defense treaty, but she showed that her sympathy would be with the French if the Germans attacked them. Plans were made for an army of 150,000 men which would be ready to cross the Channel at a moment's notice. When war came in 1914, this force managed to arrive just in time to save Paris.

3. Britain had no quarrel with Germany, and public opinion was divided on the question of supporting France. If the Germans had made a direct attack, they might have taken Paris before anyone interfered. But they attacked through Belgium. Their emperor did not believe that Britain would go to war for "a bit of paper", which was his scornful description of Palmerston's treaty. However, when he attacked Belgium, all Britain united against him, and half the nations of the world were soon fighting in the muddy ditches of France. Every part of the empire immediately joined the British side, and three years later the United States followed their example. When the war was won, both sides had suffered immense losses. The empire's forces had lost a million men, and Britain had spent all her wealth.

4. The war destroyed the power of the Liberal Party, which had been in office for eight years when fighting started. During that time it had done much to tax the rich and to help the poor, especially the old and the workless. It had introduced insurance against illness and industrial accidents, and it had arranged regular medical examination of children.

5. The House of Lords did not like the ever-increasing taxes. In 1909, they refused to pass the budget, which is the government's yearly plan for getting and spending money. It included a Land Tax which the Prime Minister, Lloyd George, had put in on purpose, knowing that the majority of land-owning lords would  resist it. It was a clever trap, and they fell straight into it. For centuries, customs had allowed them to refuse an ordinary bill; but this time they were refusing a budget because it was against their own interests. It was time that their power was reduced. The next year, Edward VII died, and a new election showed that people supported the government. Edward's son, now George V, had to make the lords change their minds. He threatened to make new Liberal Lords, just as William IV had done to pass Lord Grey's reform bill. The country was relieved to see that the royal power could still be used to support its will, and the position of the crown was strengthened.

6. The war had been won by a united Liberal-Conservative government under Lloyd George, but it was followed by an unwise peace treaty. The spirit of revenge ruled France, which had suffered most, and Lloyd George would not listen to his more moderate advisers. The Americans quickly stopped taking any interest in the matter. An international parliament, called the League of Nations, was formed in Geneva; but America and Russia refused to join it. The severe treatment of Germany helped Hitler's rise to power, which the League was unable to stop.

7. The question of Irish independence was settled at last. Protestant Ulster chose to remain in the United Kingdom. The rest of the island became a dominion until 1937, when it decided to leave the empire altogether and took the name of Eire. Eire kept out of the Second World War, but many of her men fought in the British forces.

8. The Irish settlement split Lloyd George's government, and in 1924 the Labor Party took office for the first time. But they tried to make friends with Communist Russia, and this was so unpopular that they were soon out of office. In 1929, they tried again. This time they lasted two years, but they had not the necessary experience to guide the country at a time when the entire world was in trouble. A new election gave them only a tenth of parliament's seats.

9. The whole country was now so anxious to return to normal conditions that it took little notice of events in Europe. Only Winston Churchill had the

courage to raise his voice in warning, but no one listened to him. The Americans still kept out of the League of Nations, which had no power to back up its views. Like everyone else, the British continued to believe Hitler's false promises of peace; Russia even made a treaty of friendship with him.

10. Hitler's broken promises included an attack on Poland, which Britain and France were bound by treaty to defend. But neither of them was armed in readiness for the Second World War, which began in September 1939. Within eight months, France had fallen, and only Britain stood against Hitler's armies. The empire supported her, but Russia and America still took no part in the struggle.

11. Then, in May 1940, Winston Churchill became Prime Minister of a government that combined all parties.

12. Later in the war, the army workshops had a saying: "Difficult repairs are done at once; impossible repairs take a little longer." Churchill had to make impossible repairs to his country's defenses, and he made them at once. The British army of a quarter of a million men was rescued from the shores of Dunkirk by hundreds of little boats that sailed from every harbor of the south and east. It had to leave its arms behind, and the German army waited eagerly for orders to cross the Channel and to seize the unarmed island.

13. But how could they cross while the Royal Navy still guarded the seas, and the Royal Air Force guarded the sky? Hitler did not dare to bring out his army. Instead, he sent his air force to destroy Britain's southern airfields and then London. He failed. In three months he lost over 2,000 airplanes. This was the Battle of Britain. It was won by the skill and courage of those who flew a few hundred Spitfire and Hurricane fighters against Germany's thousands  of more powerful machines. As Churchill said, "Never... has so much been owed by so many to so few".

14. But much was owed to Churchill himself. He formed a Home Guard. This was an army of citizens which would help to defend towns and villages if there was an enemy attack. At the same time, Churchill's stirring speeches gave new hope and courage to the nation. They also influenced President Roosevelt of America, who was already planning to help Britain by sending

arms.

15. Churchill was already planning the future. His aims, as he had said, were not only to defend Britain but also to set Europe free. While the German army waited to cross the Channel, he sent Britain's only armored army division round the south of Africa to the Suez Canal. Its duty was to prepare the way for those armies which would one day attack Hitler's empire from the south. The next year Hitler attacked Russia, and Japan attacked America; this gave Churchill two strong allies to help him finish the struggle.

16. When the war was over, Britain had to turn her attention to problems inside the empire. Many of the peoples, who had helped to win the war, now demanded their independence. Britain accepted their right to make this demand. She was already planning to turn the empire to a commonwealth of free and equal members. The word commonwealth explains itself, for its members are united for their common profits.

17. Religious problems caused India's division into two new independent states, India and Pakistan, in 1947. The next year Ceylon also became independent. Other countries needed an urgent development program to improve education, commercial production and public services before they were ready to stand on their own feet. With the British tax-payers' help, this program was implemented. One by one, the former colonies became independent members of the British Commonwealth, and took their seats among the United Nations.

After You Read

Knowledge Focus

1. **Pair Work**

    Discuss the following questions with your partner.
    (1) How did Britain take part in the First World War?
    (2) What was the aftermath of the First World War?
    (3) What was the background before the Second World War and how did Britain get involved in the war?
    (4) What was the impact of the Second World War on Britain?
    (5) Which countries were involved in the First World War?

2. **Solo Work**

    Tell whether and why the following are true or false according to the knowledge you have learned.
    ____ (1) An international parliament, called the League of Nations, was formed in

Geneva.

_____ (2) With the formation of the League of Nations, America and Russia immediately joined it.

_____ (3) Britain had quarrels with Germany, and public opinion was divided on the question of supporting France.

_____ (4) In the early 19th century, Britain kept out of foreign politics as much as possible.

_____ (5) The various German states had been united under King of Prussia after his conquest of France in 1870.

_____ (6) By 1901, when Victoria died, they had begun to build a very large navy to fight its British rival.

_____ (7) The war had been won by a united Liberal-Conservative government under Lloyd George, but it was followed by an unwise peace treaty.

_____ (8) The question of Irish independence was settled at last. Protestant Ulster chose to remain in the United Kingdom.

Language Focus

1. Fill in the blanks with the following expressions you have learned in the text. Put them into appropriate forms if necessary.

| so long as | keep out of | take no part in |
| take no account of | be anxious to | the rest of |

(1) In the late 19th century, Britain _____ foreign politics as much as possible.

(2) Britain favored the second group _____ France threatened her interests in Africa and the Russians threatened her Indian border.

(3) He was Queen Victoria's son-in-law, but his ambitions _____ such a tie.

(4) _____ the island became a dominion until 1937, when it decided to leave the empire altogether and took the name of Eire.

(5) The whole country _____ return to normal conditions that it took little notice of events in Europe.

(6) The Empire supported her, but Russia and America still _____ the struggle.

2. Complete the following sentences with the proper forms of the words in the brackets.

(1) He was arrested for _____ (threat) behavior and using abusive language.

(2) It's a _____ (faith) reproduction of the original picture.

(3) My friends were all extremely _____ (sympathy) when they heard I'd lost my job.

(4) He remained _____ (scorn) of religion and its influence over people.

(5) Your shoes are really _____ (mud)—take them off before you come in.

(6) Think how time flies in periods of intense and _____ (purpose) activity.
(7) The games can help _____ (relief) the boredom of long car journeys for kids.
(8) The entire _____ (divide) of 18,000 troops will be home in about a month.

3. **Find the appropriate prepositions that collocate with the neighboring words.**
   (1) Europe was divided _____ two camps at that time: France and Russia in one, Germany, Austria and Italy in the other.
   (2) The various German states had been united _____ King of Prussia _____ his conquest of France in 1870.
   (3) Edward VII had never shared his mother's faith _____ the emperor's goodwill.
   (4) She showed that her sympathy would be _____ the French if the Germans attacked them.
   (5) Plans were made for an army of 150,000 men which would be ready to cross the Channel _____ a moment's notice.
   (6) Public opinion was divided _____ the question of supporting France.
   (7) Their emperor did not believe that Britain would go to war _____ a "a bit of paper".
   (8) Half the nations of the world were soon fighting _____ the muddy ditches of France.
   (9) The war destroyed the power of the Liberal Party, which had been _____ office for eight years when fighting started.
   (10) It was a clever trap, and they fell straight _____ it.

Comprehensive Work
1. Group Work: Debate and Writing

The WWII brings about advances in technology and weapons. Read the following paragraph, and have a debate on "Is advanced weapon a blessing or a curse?"

During the war, aircraft continued their roles of reconnaissance, fighters, bombers and ground-support from World War I, though each area was advanced considerably. Two important additional roles for aircraft were those of the airlift, the capability to quickly move high-priority supplies, equipment and personnel, albeit in limited quantities; and of strategic bombing, the targeted use bombs against civilian areas in the hopes of hampering enemy industry and morale. Anti-aircraft weaponry also continued to advance, including key defenses such as radar and greatly improved anti-aircraft artillery, such as the German 88mm gun. Jet aircraft saw their first limited operational use during World War II, and though their late introduction and limited numbers meant that they had no real impact during the war itself, the few which saw active service pioneered a mass-shift to their usage following the war.

Write a passage about 300 words, summarizing your view on this topic.

2. Discussion

The impact of WWII is devastating to most of the world. It is a nightmare which took away 60 million lives. Please make a list about "How did WWII influence the world economically, socially, ecologically, psychologically, culturally etc.?" And then share your views with your classmates.

Read More

Text B　　Causes of World War I

Many people did not want a war to begin. Mothers and fathers all over Europe hoped for good lives for their sons who were just becoming adults. Young men hoped to begin their adult lives by going to work, getting married, and raising families. Instead, in 1914, many of them went to war.

Some of the leaders in Europe did not want the war to begin either. They tried to convince others not to go to war. Instead, one country after another declared war.

How did it happen? What caused World War I?

There were several causes of World War I. The most immediate cause was the assassination of Archduke Francis Ferdinand of Austria-Hungary. Austria-Hungary decided that Serbia was to blame for the assassination and declared war on Serbia.

Before the assassination, there were other things going on in Europe that led up to the war. One thing was an increase in the feeling of nationalism in many European countries. Nationalism is something like patriotism, so you may be surprised to hear that it was one cause of the war, but nationalism does not just mean supporting your own country. Nationalism means putting the interests of your own country above everything else and ignoring the rights of people in other countries.

Another cause of the war was military alliances. When two or more countries make an alliance, they agree to support each other if a war begins. Germany formed an alliance with Austria-Hungary, and Great Britain formed alliances with France and Russia.

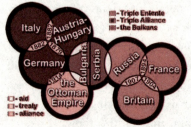

The alliance made countries on both sides feel powerful. With their allies, they felt safe from attack. The alliances were a cause of the war because, once countries felt safe from attack, they also felt free to take actions that might anger other countries. Tensions built up among the countries of Europe.

As tensions built up, countries in Europe began to make more and more weapons. Each side wanted to be in a position of power, just in case.

With all these going on, can you see why parts of Europe were referred to as a "powder keg"? The situation in Europe had made it a place that could explode at any moment, just like a barrel full of gunpowder.

The assassination of the archduke was the spark that set off the powder keg. Feelings of nationalism made countries decide to fight. Alliances brought in more countries. With stockpiles of weapons, a war could begin right away. World War I was the largest and most horrible war that had ever happened up to that time.

Did it all have to happen? Suppose the Archduke had never been shot. Do you think the countries of Europe might have found other ways to solve their problems? Do you think they might have made some different choices before it was too late?

1. Finish the following multiple-choice questions based on the information in Text B.

(1) World War I began in _____ in _____.
   A. Europe, 1814   B. the United States, 1914
   C. France, 1914   D. Europe, 1914

(2) World War I was fought _____.
   A. for freedom
   B. to save Austria-Hungary from a Serbian attack
   C. to end slavery
   D. as the result of several problems in Europe

(3) The first country to declare war was _____.
   A. Great Britain   B. Serbia
   C. Austria-Hungary   D. Germany

(4) The word that means an agreement among countries to support each other in time of war is _____.
   A. tension   B. alliance
   C. nationalism   D. arms race

(5) Which of the following term means "too much patriotism"?
   A. Nationalism.   B. Arms race.
   C. Tension.   D. Alliance.

(6) In the early 1900s, countries in Europe were producing more and more weapons in order to be more powerful than their neighboring countries. This could be called a/an _____.
   A. nationalism   B. tension

  C. alliance   D. arms race
(7) One conclusion that you could draw about the beginning of World War I is _____.
  A. the buildup of weapons was the main cause of the war
  B. all of the countries of Europe wanted to fight
  C. only Serbia and Austria-Hungary wanted to fight
  D. a combination of causes drew many countries into the war

2. Questions for discussion or reflection.
(1) This article discusses four causes of World War I—one immediate cause, and three underlying causes. What was the immediate cause of the war? What were the three underlying causes?
(2) The assassination of Archduke Ferdinand has been called the spark that set off World War I. Can you think of another situation that was set off by a "spark"? Describe the situation, and tell how you think it might have been resolved if the "spark" had never occurred.

Text C   Winston Churchill

  The story is told of a young man who had just been elected to the British House of Commons. During one long meeting, the man lit his thick cigar and listened quietly. Slowly, the cigar burned. Soon House members around him noticed the cigar and the growing length of ash hanging on the end. People around him began to notice the ash and watched to see how long it would get before falling. The young man appeared to be oblivious to the attention. Eventually, almost as many people were watching the cigar as were listening to the speech. So began the political career of Winston Churchill.

  Born in Blenheim Palace in Oxfordshire, England on November 30, 1874, Winston came from a mixed family. His father, Lord Randolph Churchill, came from a long line of military heroes. His mother, Jennie, was the daughter of an American financier.

  In spite of the fact that he was from a wealthy family, his childhood was not happy. He was neglected by everyone but his nurse, and this showed up in his performance at school. He had poor grades at Harrow and had to take the entrance exams for Sandhurst three times before finally passing. While he was there, his interest in the military peaked, and he began to prove he had a fine mind. He eventually graduated 20th in his class of 130 students.

  In 1895, his father died, and Churchill joined the army. Like many young men of the time, he sought adventure and the opportunity to show what he was made of in battle. The only real war at the time was the Cuban war for independence. Unable to join in as a soldier, he took two months leave from the army and went down as a reporter.

The next year, Churchill was sent to India. There he fulfilled dual duties as both a soldier and reporter. In 1898, his stories were expanded and became the "Story of the Malakand Field Force". It attracted a lot of attention to his writing. Soon he was made part of Lord Kitchener's expedition to the Nile. Churchill continued his writing. He produced *The River War* in 1899 and *Savrola* in 1900.

In 1899, Churchill was tired of military life and opted to try his hand at politics. He lost his first election and decided to go to South Africa until the next one. The Boer War was in full swing, and journalists were needed.

A month after arriving at the bottom of the Dark Continent, Churchill found himself helping with the rescue of an armored train from the Boers. He was captured and held prisoner for a month before escaping. His status as a military hero and prominent figure in the news was well assured.

At the turn of the century, Churchill again ran in the regular election for the same seat in the House of Commons and this time, won. He soon earned the reputation for being a powerful speaker. While he was not good at speaking informally, he was very good at writing and giving set speeches.

In 1904, Churchill found his own beliefs at odds with his political party. As a man of strong ideas, he could not abandon his beliefs in free trade to support his party's push for tariffs. He left the Conservative Party and joined the Liberals.

When the next election came around in 1906, Churchill found himself re-elected and made a cabinet member, this time for the Liberal Prime Minister. Five years later, he was instrumental in helping to push through reforms for the House of Lords. These reforms curbed the political power of the aristocracy. This won him much popular approval.

It was later that same year that Churchill became convinced that Germany was building up to start a major war. He saw the build-up of naval power and determined that it would never become greater than Britain's.

In August 1914, before World War I began, no one was more determined than Churchill in the need to oppose Germany. He mobilized the navy, so that they would be ready when the war was finally declared.

In 1915, his support of action in the Dardanelles turned sour. Following political attacks for his position, he resigned from office.

A man of vision, Churchill was tired of being blocked from what he considered effective action. Instead, he returned to active service in the army in 1915 and saw action in France. After a short time, he found that serving in the army had lost most of its luster. The next year, he ran again for public office and won his seat. It was through his efforts that the tank was rushed through final development and shipped to the western front.

After losing the election in 1922, Churchill occupied himself by writing and painting. He used earnings from his book on the history of the war *The World Crisis* to purchase Chartwell, an estate in Kent.

In 1924, Churchill was back in the Conservative party and won back his seat in the House of Commons. A strong anti-socialist, he tried to steer Britain away from high taxation spending.

The year 1929 was the start of political hard times for Churchill. The Conservative party was out of power, and he disliked the Labor party. He was excluded from office and was considered a loose cannon by most of the major party leaders.

Always acutely aware of the world around him, Churchill was soon concerned about the growing menace of Adolf Hitler. He tried to make the leaders of the British government sit up and take notice, but they chose not to believe him.

Churchill decided to take matters into his own hands. He and a small number of supporters built up his country home, Chartwell, into a private intelligence center. It was even superior to the one the government had. When Stanley Baldwin became the new Prime Minister in 1935, he would not allow Churchill to have a position in the new government. However, Baldwin did allow him to see some research about the air defenses of Britain. Churchill's driving goal was not personal power, but the containment of Germany.

When Neville Chamberlain became Prime Minister, he also disregarded Churchill's warnings, even though they had been proved right time after time. It was not long before people began to see that Churchill had the right position, and in 1939 they began to press for his return to office. Chamberlain ignored them because he thought that peace should be maintained at all cost, even if it meant looking the other way when Hitler invaded other countries.

That changed on September 3, 1939, when Great Britain finally declared war on Germany, and Churchill returned to his old job in the Admiralty. The war effort did not really take off until after May 10, 1940, after Germany invaded the Low Countries (Holland and Belgium). At that point, Chamberlain resigned from office. Churchill became Britain's new Prime Minister.

As a war-time Prime Minister, Churchill was outstanding. He was uniquely suited for the job. His attention to detail, his raw energy, intense patriotism, long years of preparation, and a dedication to defeating Hitler made him the man of the hour.

Churchill immediately formed a new government with elements from all the parties. The central ruling group, the Cabinet of five, would direct the war effort. The new Prime Minister took leadership of the House of Commons and the Ministry of Defense in addition to his other duties. Always glad to delegate authority, Churchill kept in constant contact with his people so that he knew what was going on all the time.

When France collapsed under the German invasion, Churchill warned Parliament that it was a threat and that England had to take it seriously. To keep the Germans from gaining control of the French fleet, he had the ships destroyed by the British navy. He also made use of American war ships through a program called "lend-lease", which allowed the British to use the ships even though the United States was not involved in the war.

Churchill was determined to develop a relationship with President Roosevelt of the U.S. They met at Placentia Bay, Newfoundland in August 1941. Between them, they wrote the Atlantic Charter. The attack on Pearl Harbor on December 7, 1941 brought the United States into World War II.

A year later, the Allies had seen many losses, and Churchill was criticized at home for doing a poor job. His leadership was challenged, but he managed to maintain his position as Prime Minister.

As part of his efforts to keep himself informed about every aspect of the war, Churchill traveled constantly, even to the Mediterranean. He met constantly with other Allied leaders as they devised plans for crushing the Axis threat. He was sick with pneumonia when he met with Stalin and Roosevelt in Cairo, Egypt in November 1943. He was not completely well again until the next January.

During the July 1945 Potsdam Conference, Churchill had to leave suddenly. The different British parties scented victory in the air, and they wanted to abandon the coalition government in favor of gaining individual power. They pushed for an early election, and Churchill lost.

That loss shocked him. He did not care for his position as leader of the opposition party. It was not until 1951, that he again became Prime Minister. At that point he immediately tried to re-establish British relations with the United States since those relations had been allowed to slide.

In 1953, Queen Elizabeth II was crowned. Churchill received a knighthood and the Nobel Prize for literature. In June, Churchill suffered a stroke with some paralyses, which meant canceling a Bermuda meeting with President Eisenhower. He recovered in time for the meeting to be held the following December. He hoped to get the U.S. to agree to summit talks with Russia, but it did not work.

By 1955, it became obvious that Churchill's health was failing. He'd passed his 80th birthday the year before. In April he resigned his position as Prime Minister. He kept his seat in the House of Commons. In 1963, the United States Congress gave him honorary citizenship. He died January 24, 1965.

1. Finish the following multiple-choice questions according to Text C.
  (1) What did Churchill do when he went to Cuba during its war for independence?
      A. Medic.   B. Journalist.   C. Sugar cane cutter.   D. Fight.
  (2) What major piece of war machinery was pushed through by Churchill so it could have an effect on WWI?
      A. Big Bertha. B. Planes.   C. Armored cars.   D. Tanks.
  (3) What program allowed Britain to use American warships before America joined WWII?
      A. Purchase order.   B. Purchase-lease.
      C. Atlantic Charter.   D. Lend-lease.

2. **Questions for discussion or reflection.**
   (1) Why do you think Churchill alternated between politics and the army?
   (2) How did his actions during the Boer War help him at home?
   (3) How did Churchill's strong personal beliefs affect his political life?
   (4) How did Churchill start WWI?
   (5) Why was 1929 the start of ten years of political hard times for Churchill?
   (6) What are two of the qualities of Churchill that made him uniquely suited to lead Britain during WWII?

Proper Names

Belgium 比利时
Dunkirk 敦克尔克
Edward VII 爱德华七世
Geneva 日内瓦
George V 乔治五世
Hitler 希特勒
House of Lords 英国上议院
League of Nations 国际联盟
Liberal Lords 自由党上议院
Liberal Party 自由党
Liberal-Conservative 自由保守

Lloyd George 劳埃德·乔治
Palmerston 帕麦斯顿岛
Protestant Ulster 北爱尔兰新教徒
Queen Victoria 维多利亚女王
Royal Air Force 英国皇家空军
Royal Navy 皇家海军
Second World War 第二次世界大战
the English Channel 英吉利海峡
William IV 威廉四世
Winston Churchill 温斯顿·丘吉尔

Notes

1. **House of Lords**: The House of Lords is the upper house of the Parliament of the United Kingdom and is also commonly referred to as "the Lords". The Parliament comprises the Sovereign, the House of Commons (which is the lower house of Parliament and referred to as "the Commons"), and the Lords.

2. **League of Nations**: The League of Nations was an inter-governmental organization founded as a result of the *Treaty of Versailles* in 1919—1920. The League's goals included disarmament, preventing war through collective security, settling disputes between countries through negotiation, diplomacy and improving global quality of life.

3. **Hitler (1889—1945)**: He was an Austrian-born German politician and the leader of the National Socialist German Workers' Party, popularly known as the Nazi Party. He was the ruler of Germany from 1933 to 1945, serving as chancellor from 1933 to 1945 and as head of state (Führer und Reichskanzler) from 1934 to 1945. He was named by *Time Magazine* as one of the 100 most influential people of the 20th century.

4. **Royal Navy**: The Royal Navy of the United Kingdom is the oldest of the British armed

services (and is therefore known as the Senior Service). From the mid-18th century until well into the 20th century, it was the most powerful navy in the world, playing a key part in establishing the British Empire as the dominant world power from 1815 until the early 1940s. In World War II, the Royal Navy operated almost 900 ships. During the Cold War, it was transformed into a primarily anti-submarine force, hunting for Soviet submarines. With the collapse of the Soviet Union, its role for the 21st century has returned to focus on global expeditionary operations.

For Fun

Websites to visit

1. http://www.worldwar1.com/
   This is a comprehensive page, which presents the "past and present" of World War I.
2. http://www.firstworldwar.com/
   This website provides an overview of the First World War.

Movies to see

1. *A Farewell to Arms* (1932)

   This movie is the original film version of Ernest Hemingway's novel about the tragic love affair between an American ambulance driver and an English nurse during the Italian campaign of WWI. The novelist disavowed the ambiguous ending, but the public loved the film. The movie boasts fine performances and cinematography.

2. *Doctor Zhivago* (2002)

   This mini-series version of the Pasternak novel focuses more on the story's romantic difficulties and slightly less on the politics of the Russian revolution. Noble doctor/poet Yury Zhivago marries his childhood sweetheart and cousin, Tonya, but falls madly in love with beautiful Lara. As if this affair were not dramatic enough, Lara is the obsession of the powerful Kormarovsky, who is determined to keep her as his possession and who is much more capable of bending with the changing political winds than the idealistic Yury.

Books to read

1. *The Winds of War* by Herman Wouk
   This multimillion-copy bestseller captures all the drama, romance, heroism, and tragedy of the Second World War.
2. *Treason & Triumph* by Bonnie Toews
   This is an exciting mystery thriller set during the traumatic days of World War II.

Combining romance and espionage, Toews' story unfolds over nine years in war-torn Europe. Lady Catherine Rushmore is a gifted concert pianist and Marla Franklin is an American journalist. So similar in looks, the two women's lives are forever intertwined when they become involved in a great scheme to protect the world from atomic destruction. Bonnie Toews has received high praise for her meticulously accurate research into the time period, and then events surrounding the setting of *Treason & Triumph*. She proves herself a master of surprises, and the twists and turns of her story are never quite expected.

Song to enjoy

"Heal the World" by Micheal Jackson

"Heal the World" is a song featured on Michael Jackson's hit album, "Dangerous", released in 1991. It is one of the most famous anti-war songs in the world.

The song starts with a monologue of a little boy from slum: "Think about the generations and they say we want to make it a better place for our children and our children's children. So that they know it's a better world for them and think if they can make it a better place". The little boy's voice also appears in the ending part, singing repeatedly about the same theme.

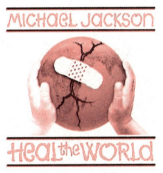

In a 2001 Internet chat with fans, Jackson said "Heal the World" was the song he was most proud to have created.

There's a place in
Your heart
And I know that it is love
And this place could
Be much
Brighter than tomorrow
And if you really try
You'll find there's no need
To cry
In this place you'll feel
There's no hurt or sorrow

There are ways
To get there
If you care enough
For the living
Make a little space
Make a better place...

Heal the world
Make it a better place
For you and for me

And the entire human race
There are people dying
If you care enough
For the living
Make a better place
For you and for me

If you want to know why
There's a love that
Cannot lie
Love is strong
It only cares for
Joyful giving
If we try
We shall see
In this bliss
We cannot feel
Fear or dread
We stop existing and
Start living

Then it feels that always

Loves enough for
Us growing
So make a better world
Make a better world...

Heal the world
Make it a better place
For you and for me
And the entire human race
There are people dying
If you care enough
For the living
Make a better place
For you and for me

And the dream we were
Conceived in
Will reveal a joyful face
And the world we
Once believed in
Will shine again in grace
Then why do we keep
Strangling life
Wound this earth
Crucify its soul
Though its plain to see
This world is heavenly
Be gods glow

We could fly so high
Let our spirits never die
In my heart
I feel you are all
My brothers
Create a world with
No fear
Together we cry
Happy tears
See the nations turn
Their swords
Into plowshares

We could really get there
If you cared enough
For the living
Make a little space
To make a better place...

Heal the world
Make it a better place
For you and for me
And the entire human race
There are people dying
If you care enough
For the living
Make a better place
For you and for me

Unit 14
Towards the New Millennium

> "I declare before you all that my whole life, whether it be long or short, shall be devoted to your service and the service of our great imperial family to which we all belong."
>
> —Queen Elizabeth II

Unit Goals

- To be familiar with the House of Windsor
- To learn about the story of Elizabeth II
- To learn the useful words and expressions that describe the House of Windsor and improve English language skills
- To develop critical thinking and intercultural communication skills

Before You Read

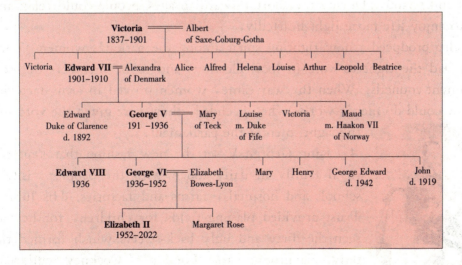

(1) Take a look at the family tree above and figure out which of the above kings and queens are mentioned in Text A. Share your knowledge about the House of Windsor with your classmates.
(2) Form groups of three or four students. Try to find, on the Internet or in the library, more information about Queen Elizabeth II. Get ready for a 5-minute presentation in class.

Start to Read

Text A   House of Windsor

1. Victoria died in 1901 after sixty-four years as Queen. She had given the country a new idea of royalty. It was proud of her, as the head of a world-wide family of nations, but it also liked her simple tastes and orderly habits. Politically, her relations with the cabinet were correct and formal. She demanded to be kept informed of all that her government was doing. She discussed it with them. She objected to what she did not like. Often ministers accepted her advice, which was based on greater experience than theirs, but she left the decisions to them. It was fortunate for Britain that the growth of popular government was supported by closer understanding between crown and people.

2. Edward VII had been refused any share of royal duties by his mother while he was Prince of Wales. He now brought a new feeling of fashionable gaiety to public life. The Victorians had many good qualities, but they were inclined to be dull and serious. During the short Edwardian age, people could relax and begin to enjoy life more light-heartedly.

3. It also produced a new fighting spirit among the nation's women. They already had the right to vote in local elections and to be members of local government councils. When the war came, women proved in arms factories that they could do men's work; when it ended, they were given the vote and the right to enter the parliament.

4. King George V set the new fashion that kept the royal family in daily touch with the people—visiting schools and hospitals, farms and factories. His Jubilee Trust provided playing-fields for children, for he had seen the dirty and ugly back-streets which formed the only playground for London's Cockney children.

London now has more than eight million people, but it has no more cheerful citizens than the Cockneys, who are the natives of London's east end. In the worst moments of the last war, when their homes were destroyed by nightly air attacks, they still managed to keep their sense of humor.

5. When George VI was a young man, he used to run boy's holiday camps. He himself had only two daughters, Elizabeth and Margaret. He was quiet by nature and he never expected to become king. But his elder brother, Edward VIII, wanted to marry an American woman, who had already been married twice. Since she could not be Queen, Edward did not want to be King. In December 1936, before he had been crowned, he left the country and his brother George took his place. Then the war came. In spite of the government's advice, George VI refused to leave London. His daily visits to the forces, the factories and the damaged towns cheered his people everywhere, but he always returned to Buckingham Palace, his London home.

6. Elizabeth II was visiting Kenya when she became Queen in 1952 on her father's death. Like her father and grandfather, she has travelled all over the world to meet her many peoples. She was brought up simply but carefully. Both she and her sister were Girls Guides, and during the war she received training in the women's branch of the army. Her marriage to Prince Philip of Greece in 1947 was extremely popular.

7. Philip was a descendant of Queen Victoria. He was brought up in Britain and during the war he served in Royal Navy. On his marriage he was given the title of Duke of Edinburgh. His great interest in science and industry, as well as in youth and sport, had fitted him to give the country a bold lead in matters outside politics.

8. Meanwhile, what was happening inside politics? The Labor party had become full-grown, and immediately after the war it had six years in office. It introduced a national health service, which had already been planned under Churchill's wartime government. It put the coal-mines and railways under state control, and it aimed at extending this control to banking, insurance and all essential industry. The country liked many Labor's ideas, but it did not quite trust the party to put them into practice without harmful effects. It was suspicious of interference with personal freedom. It saw that state control meant an army of government officials, with much waste of public money. After this first taste of Labor's rule, the country put their Conservative rivals back into power for thirteen years before it let them try again. By then they had adopted more moderate ideas on government control.

9. The good wages and free social services have given the British worker a

comfortable standard of living. His house may contain electric machines to wash clothes, to cook, to keep food cold, and to heat the room. He can afford to wear good clothes, to drive car, and to take his family for holidays abroad.

10. Such holidays travel has given him a closer personal interest in the affairs of other European countries, and this interest is reflected in the national press and in the schools. European languages—French, German, Spanish, Italian and Russian—are being more widely taught, not only in schools but in worker's evening classes.

11. Independence has loosened the ties of trade between the former colonies and Britain. This gives her the chance to play a fuller part in the commercial and industrial life of Europe. But her people are anxious not to weaken their friendship with the old dominions of Canada, Australia and New Zealand, which still attract many new British settlers every year.

12. In the meanwhile, Britain's children are growing up with a new outlook. To them, the empire is past history. They want Britain to be strong and respected, but they have no wish to be a World Power or to be responsible for keeping the peace in far-off places. Their international consciousness is expressed in support of world-wide causes like "Save the Children", but their direct interests remain nearer home. Their future lies in closer union with the rest of western Europe, where the English language is already valued as a basis of commercial and political understanding between the nations of the world. In the common search for peaceful progress, they have much to offer and much to learn.

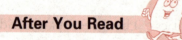

After You Read

Knowledge Focus

1. Pair Work

   Discuss the following questions with your partner.
   (1) How long did Victoria rule the nation as a queen?
   (2) How do you describe Victoria's relations with the cabinet?
   (3) What was the change in public life during Edward VII's reign?
   (4) How did women's role in politics alter during the Edwardian age?
   (5) Who are the Cockneys?
   (6) Can you name the only two daughters of George VI?
   (7) When did Elizabeth II become Queen?
   (8) What do you know about the Prince Philip of Greece?

Language Focus

1. **Fill in the blanks with the following words or expressions you have learned in the text. Put them into appropriate forms if necessary.**

inform...of...	object to	be inclined to	(be) suspicious of
moderate	afford (to do)	consciousness	manage (to do)

   (1) Thomas finally _____ to find an apartment near his office.
   (2) Commandos _____ shoot first and ask questions later.
   (3) Many smaller companies simply cannot _____ to buy health insurance for employees.
   (4) Please _____ me _____ any change of address as soon as possible.
   (5) New studies show that _____ drinking is good for you.
   (6) The committee strongly _____ the report's recommendations.
   (7) The death of President Kennedy almost 40 years ago still lives in the national _____ .
   (8) His employer became _____ the amount of money he was claiming for expenses.

2. **Complete the following sentences with the proper forms of the words in the brackets.**

   (1) Police said it was an _____ (order) demonstration and there were no arrests.
   (2) The production of this toy stopped in the 80s when they became _____ (fashion).
   (3) Teachers simply do not have the time or the _____ (incline) to investigate these matters.
   (4) The First Lady was _____ (cheer) and energetic during the press conference.
   (5) Essential oils are _____ (harm) to skin, provided they are used correctly.
   (6) A full murder inquiry was launched after the company chairman died in _____ (suspect) circumstances.
   (7) Although she was not a professional politician, her views were _____ (influence) in shaping government policy.
   (8) Congress has _____ (loose) some of the restrictions on immigration.
   (9) This will increase public _____ (conscious) of the pollution issue.
   (10) I knew I had to give a speech, but the thought filled me with _____ (anxious).

3. **Find the appropriate prepositions that collocate with the neighboring words.**

   (1) Queen Victoria demanded to be kept informed _____ all that her government was doing.
   (2) Queen Victoria discussed it with the cabinet. She objected _____ what she did

not like.

(3) It was fortunate _____ Britain that the growth of popular government was supported by closer understanding between crown and people.

(4) His Jubilee Trust provided playing-fields _____ children, for he had seen the dirty and ugly back-streets which formed the only playground for London's Cockney children.

(5) _____ spite of the government's advice, George VI refused to leave London.

(6) Her marriage _____ Prince Philip of Greece in 1947 was extremely popular.

(7) Philip was a descendant of Queen Victoria. He was brought _____ in Britain and during the war he served in Royal Navy.

(8) His great interest _____ science and industry, as well _____ in youth and sport, had fitted him to give the country a bold lead in matters outside politics.

(9) Some of his colleagues at work became suspicious _____ his behavior.

(10) _____ the meanwhile, Britain's children are growing up with a new outlook.

Comprehensive Work

1. Class Activity: What Identifies Britain?

In this activity, you would come across both commemorative and definitive stamps. Commemorative stamp means a stamp issued to mark a particularly important event, whereas the definitive stamp is standard stamp on sale for an unlimited period of time. Suppose you are British.

(1) Think about how you would define yourselves and the groups to which you belong. These groups could have something to do with: religion, gender, ethnicity, sport, social activities, musical interests, etc.

(2) Think about how you would represent these identities pictorially e.g. if you are interested in music, you could use a picture of a guitar; if you like sport, a tennis racket etc.

(3) Imagine how, if you were a king or queen, you would want to represent your personalities on a definitive stamp.

(4) Discuss what you think are the most important identities in Britain today. Do you think that the monarch is still an adequate icon to represent this country and the diversity within the country? Share your views in class.

2. Writing Activity

Imagine that you have suddenly been made King or Queen. Write a journal page describing your first day in office.

Read More

Text B   Queen Elizabeth II

Many of us dream of being named King or Queen, even for a day. We'd love to have people bow to us. We can see ourselves nodding nobly to our subjects. We'd really like telling people what to do. But what's it like to be royal for real? Life as a real king or queen might not be quite what we imagine.

Queen Elizabeth II should know. She is the longest reigning British monarch in history. She was Queen of the United Kingdom for 70 years. In fact, she was Queen of 16 countries called the Commonwealth Realms. Living in these countries are around 128 million people.

How do you get to be Queen? Most royalty comes through family lines. In London on April 21, 1926, the Duchess of York gave birth to a daughter. Elizabeth Alexandra Mary Windsor was born into a royal family. The tiny girl was the granddaughter of King George V. Her father, the Duke of York, was the second son of the king.

It is always the oldest son who inherits the throne. The duke's big brother, Edward, would become king at his father's death. Edward was not married at the time. It was assumed, however, that he would marry and have children. Upon his death, the crown would then pass to his first son. Girls did not get to be queen unless there were no boys to be king. They could also be Queen if they married a king.

Baby Elizabeth grew up as any child of the British royal family would. She and her family lived in one of the royal houses. She was cared for by a nanny. She was the favorite of her grandfather, King George V. He called the cute toddler "Lilibet".

The people of the UK watched Elizabeth grow. When she was three, *Time Magazine* put her picture on its cover. She was educated by private tutors. Still, she was not a child of the oldest son. No one expected her to become Queen.

When Elizabeth was 10, the king, her beloved "Grandpa England," died. Her Uncle Edward became king. Then, a surprising turn of events changed everything. Edward fell in love with an American woman named Wallis Simpson. The romance caused an uproar. Simpson had been married before. Church rules would not allow the king to marry a divorced woman.

Edward decided he would rather marry his sweetheart than be king. He abdicated the throne. As the next male heir, Elizabeth's father was crowned king. Suddenly, Elizabeth was next in line for the crown! After that she was called "Her Royal Highness, The Princess Elizabeth".

As a teenager, Elizabeth saw the world go through WWII. Nazi bombers attacked Britain. The war took a brutal toll on the British nation. The girl who would be Queen wanted to do her part. Finally, her father gave his consent. The princess put on a khaki uniform and was trained as a lorry driver. It was Elizabeth's first time in a classroom. She loved learning with other girls.

At war's end, the British people celebrated the victory. Elizabeth and her younger sister celebrated with the crowds of joyful citizens. On her 21st birthday, Elizabeth gave a speech. She pledged her life to help the people of the British Empire.

"I declare before you all that my whole life whether it be long or short shall be devoted to your service and the service of our great imperial family to which we all belong," she vowed.

Later that year, Elizabeth married. Her husband Philip was also from a royal family, an heir to the throne of Greece. Before the wedding, Philip had given up his right to the Greek crown. Elizabeth's father made him Duke of the British Realm. The couple's first

son, Prince Charles, was born a year later. A couple of years after that, a daughter, Princess Anne, came along. Eventually two more sons, Andrew and Edward, were born.

Elizabeth got some practice at royal tasks when her father, King George VI, became ill. She often represented him at public affairs. Then, in February 1952, Elizabeth and Philip were touring Kenya when they learned that the king died. With her father's passing, Princess Elizabeth had become Her Majesty Queen Elizabeth. Since he did not come from the royal line, Philip did not become king. Instead, his title was His Royal Highness, The Prince Philip, Duke of Edinburgh.

Elizabeth's coronation came a year later. The queen and her family moved into Buckingham Palace. From that time, Elizabeth has traveled far and wide. She has made it

her job as Queen to maintain contact between the nations of the Commonwealth and the rest of the world.

1. **Questions for discussion or reflection.**
   (1) What is a monarch?
       A. A special crown.
       B. The ceremony where a king or queen is formally crowned.
       C. A ruler.
       D. The second son in a royal family.
   (2) Elizabeth became queen because she was the oldest child of an oldest child and entitled to the throne. The statement is _____.
       A. true   B. false
   (3) When someone abdicates the throne, they _____.
       A. treat the crown disrespectfully
       B. treat the crown respectfully
       C. coldly claim their right to it
       D. give up being king or queen
   (4) On her 21st birthday, Princess Elizabeth _____.
       A. gave a speech vowing to serve her people
       B. went out to a bar since she could legally drink alcohol
       C. gave a party
       D. became queen

2. **Can you explain how Elizabeth helped her country during WWII?**

Text C   Margaret Thatcher

When Margaret Hilda Roberts was born, no one would have suspected that she would grow up to be the political leader of Great Britain. After all, a woman had never been Prime Minister of the country before. Why would anyone think that a woman would lead the country in the future? Margaret was born on October 13, 1925. Her parents lived in Grantham, a town in Lincolnshire, England. Her father was a grocer. He was also very active in local politics. Margaret grew up hearing politics discussed in her home.

Margaret did well in school. In 1944, she entered Somerville College. This college was part of Oxford University. At Somerville, she studied chemistry. After graduating, she went on to work as a research chemist. One of her first projects was to come up with a way to preserve ice cream for longer periods of time. She eventually worked with a team of scientists who developed the first soft serve frozen ice cream.

During the early 1950s, Margaret became involved in politics herself. She was unsuccessful in getting herself elected to office at the time. She was successful in meeting and marrying Sir Denis Thatcher. Sir Denis was wealthy enough so that Margaret could stop working as a chemist and go to law school. She became a British barrister in 1953. The same year, she gave birth to twins, Carol and Mark.

Mrs. Thatcher continued her quest to become part of the British political scene after the birth of her children. In 1959, she was finally elected to the British House of Commons. The House of Commons is comparable to the House of Representatives in the United States Congress. Her first speech in the House of Commons led to the passing of a bill forcing local councils to open up their meetings to the public.

Margaret Thatcher soon made a name for herself in Parliament. She was assigned to several committees throughout the next several years. In 1970, she became the Secretary of State for Education and Science. Not all of her decisions were popular ones. She was forced to make cuts in spending that did not make every citizen happy. When she ruled that no more free milk could be given to elementary aged children, she was given the nickname "Mrs. Thatcher, Milk Snatcher".

In 1976, Mrs. Thatcher received another nickname that stuck with her through her career. In January of that year, Mrs. Thatcher gave a speech that was a direct attack on the government of the Soviet Union. She accused them of finding more importance in building a military arsenal than in caring for the people of the country. One of the Russian newspapers that reported her speech dubbed her the "Iron Lady". Mrs. Thatcher rather liked the name because she thought it was a compliment to her courage and will to stand up to what she felt was wrong.

History was changed for Great Britain in 1979. In a general election, Thatcher's Conservative Party was voted into office. She was elected to the post of Prime Minister of the United Kingdom. This was the first time in history that a woman had held this job.

Life was not always easy for Prime Minister Thatcher. She had to deal with growing problems in Ireland. In 1984, she barely missed being killed or seriously injured when a bomb was set off in a hotel where she was attending a conference. The Provisional Irish Republican Army took credit for the attack. If the Prime Minister had not been delayed in reaching the bathroom she was headed for, she might not have been so lucky.

Thatcher had to deploy British troops to the Falkland Islands in 1982. A military force from Argentina invaded the islands in an attempt to capture them. She interceded in strikes by mineworkers in her own country in 1984 and 1985. Problems in South Africa took her attention in 1984. Thatcher supported the United States in its Cold War with the Soviet Union. Where trouble arose in the world, Margaret Thatcher's support and advice were sought.

Prime Minister Thatcher decided that it was time to resign from her job in 1990. Her party was losing support. She did not want to be the reason that the Conservatives lost their control of Parliament. John Major stepped into the leadership of Great Britain. Margaret Thatcher has remained busy since her retirement. She was given the title Baroness Thatcher in 1992. She has written two books and become a "geopolitical consultant" who travels the world speaking to leaders and citizens who want to make the world a better place.

1. **Finish the following multiple-choice questions according to Text C.**
   (1) Margaret Thatcher was the first female Prime Minister of Great Britain. This statement is _____.
       A. false   B. true
   (2) What did Mrs. Thatcher go to college to study?
       A. Political Science.   B. Education.
       C. Mathematics.   D. Chemistry.
   (3) As a _____, Margaret Thatcher helped create _____.
       A. teacher, a history test
       B. politician, a new country
       C. chemist, soft serve ice cream
       D. student, a new theory of relativity
   (4) Mrs. Thatcher was almost killed by the bomb set off by the army of _____.
       A. Scotland   B. Argentina
       C. Soviet Union   D. Ireland
   (5) What job did Mrs. Thatcher do after retiring?
       A. Member of Parliament.   B. Teacher.
       C. Geopolitical consultant. D. Lawyer.
   (6) What political party did Mrs. Thatcher represent?
       A. Republicans.   B. Conservatives.
       C. Liberals.   D. Democrats.

2. Discuss the following with your partners.
   (1) What two nicknames did Margaret Thatcher have? How did she get them?
   (2) How did Mrs. Thatcher become interested in politics?
   (3) Can women lead countries? Why or why not?

Proper Names

Duke of Edinburgh 爱丁堡公爵
Jubilee Trust 禧年信托基金
Kenya 肯尼亚

Prince Philip of Greece 菲利普亲王（1921 年生于希腊，伊丽莎白的丈夫，曾在 1940—1952 年服役英国皇家海军）
Royal Navy 皇家海军

Notes

1. **Edward VII**：(November 9, 1841—May 6, 1910) He was King of the United Kingdom and the British Dominions and Emperor of India from January 22, 1901 until his death on May 6, 1910. He was the first British monarch of the House of Saxe-Coburg and Gotha, which was renamed the House of Windsor by his son, George V.

2. **Edward VIII**：(June 23, 1894—May 28, 1972) He was King of the United Kingdom from January 20, 1936 until his abdication on December 11, 1936. After his father, George V, he was the second monarch of the House of Windsor, his father having changed the name of the royal house from Saxe-Coburg and Gotha in 1917.

3. **King George V**：(June 3, 1865—January 20, 1936) He was the first British monarch belonging to the House of Windsor, which he created from the British branch of the German House of Saxe-Coburg and Gotha. As well as being King of the United Kingdom and the other Commonwealth Realms, George was the Emperor of India and the first King of Ireland post-independence. George reigned from 1910 through World War I (1914—1918) until his death in 1936.

4. **George VI**：(December 14, 1895—February 6, 1952) He was King of the United Kingdom and the British Dominions from December 11, 1936 until his death. He was the last Emperor of India until 1947 and the last King of Ireland until 1949, and the first Head of the Commonwealth.

5. **Queen Victoria**：(May 24, 1819—January 22, 1901) Victoria was, from June 20, 1837, the Queen of the United Kingdom of Great Britain and Ireland, and from May 1, 1876 the first Empress of India of the British Raj until her death. Her reign as the queen lasted 63 years and seven months, longer than that of any other British monarch

before her. The period centered on her reign is known as the Victorian era, a time of industrial, political, and military progress within the United Kingdom.

6. **Save the Children**: This is a leading international organisation helping children in need around the world. It was first established in the United Kingdom in 1919, and then separate national organizations have been set up in more than twenty-eight countries, sharing the aim of improving the lives of children through education, health care and economic opportunities, as well as emergency aid in cases of natural disasters, wars and conflicts.

Book to read

The Decline and Fall of the House of Windsor by Donald Spoto

The author of this book is the biographer of Elizabeth Taylor, Marlene Dietrich and Marilyn Monroe. He has skillfully assembled what could be entitled "Windsor 101". All those Edwards and Georges are sorted out neatly and laid before us, each with his idiosyncrasies. And, clearly, one of their strengths is their women.

Websites to Visit

1. http://www.royal.gov.uk/

   This official website of British Monarchy offers the early life, education, marriage and family, accession and coronation, public life of the monarchy.

2. http://www.britroyals.com/windsor.htm

   This page presents the family tree of House of Windsor.

Movies to See

1. **The Queen** (2006)

   This movie is an intimate behind-the-scenes glimpse at the interaction between Elizabeth II and Prime Minister Tony Blair during their struggle, following the death of Diana, to reach a compromise between what was a private tragedy for the royal family and the public's demand for an overt display of mourning.

2. **Windsors: A Royal Family** (1994)

   This is an in-depth look at the British royal family's House of Windsor, which goes back five generations, using interviews and archival footage. Highlighted are Edward VIII's abdication in 1936. It offers a full description of Wallis Simpson and the crowning of Elizabeth II after her father, George VI's death.

3. *The King's Speech*(2010)

This movie is based on the incredible true story of King George VI, whilst it is not completely historically accurate. With many of the events added for entertainment value it is still a wonderfully British drama, which touches on themes of friendship, love and overcoming the odds. With various embezzlements to make the protagonist far more likeable than he was it makes the audience fall in love with the main character the king overcomes his stutter in a brave feat.

Unit 15

Wales, Scotland and Ireland

> There is no sunlight in the poetry of exile. There is only mist, wind, rain, the cry of the curlew and the slow clouds above damp moorland. That is the real Scotland; that is the Scotland whose memory rings the withers of the far-from-home; and, in some way that is mysterious, that is the Scotland that even a stranger learns to love.
>
> —H. V. Morton

Unit Goals

- To learn about the history of Wales
- To have a rough idea of the English conquest of Scotland
- To have a glimpse of the history of Ireland
- To learn the useful words and expressions that describe the history of Wales, Scotland and Ireland and improve English language skills
- To develop critical thinking and intercultural communication skills

Before You Read

(1) What do you know about the Norman invasion of Wales?
(2) Have you ever read Shakespeare's play—*Macbeth*? Please share your knowledge about *Macbeth* with your classmates.
(3) Do you remember Edward I who conquered Wales through three major campaigns? Please figure out the details of these three campaigns while reading Text A.
 ◇ The First Campaign: _____
 _____
 ◇ The Second Campaign: _____
 _____

◇ The Third Campaign：_____

(4) Form groups of three or four students. Try to find, on the Internet or in the library, more information about Llewelyn ap Gruffydd and his death. Get ready for a 5-minute presentation in class.

Text A The English Conquest of Wales

1. Unlike their invasion of England, the Norman penetration of Wales took place very gradually after 1066.

2. The new King of England, William I quickly secured his English kingdom by establishing earldoms along the Anglo-Welsh borders at Hereford, Shrewsbury and Chester. But it was not long before the new Norman lords began to look at expanding their lands west into Wales.

3. William himself led a military expedition across south Wales in 1081, and is said to have founded Cardiff on the way. England's King Henry I, William's youngest son, encouraged large-scale Norman settlement in south Wales, building the first royal castle at Carmarthen in 1109. The Welsh princes refused to submit however, and took the opportunity to reclaim land from the Normans, following the death of King Henry I in 1135.

4. The Welsh were truly united when Llewelyn the Great became Prince of Wales in 1194. Llewelyn and his armies drove the English from North Wales in 1212. Not content with this, he reversed the trend of conquering, taking the English town of Shrewsbury in 1215. During his long reign through to 1240, Llewelyn resisted several attempts at re-invasion by English armies dispatched by the then English King, Henry III. Following his death, Llewelyn was succeeded by his son Dafydd, Prince of Wales from 1240—1246, and then his grandson, Llewelyn II ap Gruffydd from 1246.

5. The really bad event for Wales happened in 1272 when following the death of King Henry III, his son Edward I became the new king of England. Edward I appeared to have a disliking for Celts in general, and Llewelyn ap Gruffydd in particular. Edward I achieved the conquest of Wales through three major campaigns and

on a scale that he knew that the Welsh could not hope to match.

6. The first invasion in 1277 involved a massive English army together with heavily armed cavalry that pushed along the north Wales coast. Llewelyn's support was limited in comparison, and he was forced into accepting Edwards' humiliating peace terms. In 1282, the Welsh, led by Llewelyn's brother Dafydd, were provoked into revolt against the English in northeast Wales. Edward responded with a further invasion, and this time Llewelyn was killed on the 11th December 1282. Llewelyn's brother Dafydd continued the Welsh resistance through into the following year. He obviously lacked the charisma of his brother, as his own countrymen handed him over to Edward in June 1283. He was later tried and executed. The Welsh ruling dynasties were in tatters, and Wales virtually became an English colony.

7. Shortly thereafter, the *Statute of Rhuddlan* united Wales to England and divided it into counties. The king's son Edward II became Prince of Wales in 1301. Nevertheless, revolts against English rule continued, notably under Owen Glendower, whose uprising against Henry IV lasted from 1400 to 1409.

8. Relations between Wales and England took a new direction during the late 15th century. The Tudors were a Welsh dynasty and fought on behalf of the House of Lancaster in the Wars of the Roses. One member of this house ascended the throne of England in 1485 as King Henry VII. Wales was brought into a legal and administrative union with England by his son King Henry VIII between 1534 and 1536. However, many Welsh continued to remain bitterly opposed to this union, and a powerful nationalist movement continues to quietly battle for independence to this very day.

Text B The Story of Scotland

The Roman Emperor Hadrian built a wall which ran across north England from Carlisle to Newcastle. It was intended to keep out the wild Scottish tribes. The Saxons crossed this wall and took possession of Northumberland. Their new border ran roughly from Carlisle to the River Tweed, as it does today.

Another Roman Emperor built a wall across the narrowest part of Scotland which separated the highlands from lowlands. These two halves of the land still reflect the differences of a thousand years of history. The highlands were always fiercely independent and resisted the influences of English civilization. As a result, their country remains the most unspoiled, the most beautiful and the poorest part of the island. The lowlands, however, have played a part in

English history since the days of Macbeth, whose name has been made famous by Shakespeare's play.

When King Duncan of Scotland was killed by Macbeth, his young son Malcolm escaped to England, where he was given a friendly welcome. Seventeen years later, in 1057, he drove out his father's murder with English help. He then welcomed many English families who escaped the Norman Conquest and settled in the lowlands, where their language quickly spread.

His sons realized that the only way to keep out the Normans was to adopt their feudal system of defense; so they invited the Norman knights across the border and gave them lands. These knights built castles and ruled the countryside with their cavalry. They became royal Scots, and some of their names, like Balliol, Bruce and Wallace, are among the most famous in Scottish history.

In 1286 the crown passed to Margaret, the daughter of King of Norway. Arrangements were made for her to marry the eldest son of Edward I, which would have united the kingdoms of England and Scotland. But her ship was wrecked on the way from Norway and she was drowned. Edward now supported the claim of her cousin, John Balliol, whose father had built Balliol College at Oxford to house Scottish students.

The new king was at first grateful for Edward's support, but he soon found that he had little real power. When he tried to act independently, Edward seized him and took him to London. But Scotland would not suffer such treatment for long, and her spirit was stirred by two great leaders, William Wallace and Robert Bruce. It was Bruce who defeated a much larger English force under Edward II in the great Scottish victory of Bannockburn in 1314.

For the next two hundred years, Scotland remained free but desperately poor. Universities were opened at St. Andrews, Glasgow and Aberdeen, but education without commerce could not raise the standard of living. Only union with England could bring commercial progress.

In 1513, the English took their revenge for Bannockburn; at the battle of Flodden, King of Scotland was killed with many of his noblemen and ten thousand of his soldiers. Catholic church leaders then held power until they married their young Queen Mary to King

of France, and a French army took control of Scotland. This was more than national pride could bear. A rising was led by the Protestant preacher John Knox, who was supported by most of the remaining noblemen. With Elizabeth's help they drove away the French and gained control of the weak parliament in Edinburgh. Then, like Henry VIII, they cut all ties with Rome.

We all know what happened to Mary. Her son James was only one year old when he was crowned in Edinburgh, but he grew up with the firm intention of being crowned in London, too. With this object, he did his utmost to follow Elizabeth's religious policy and to keep extreme Protestants under control. He brought peace and order to the countryside, and made the highland chiefs responsible for their people.

When Elizabeth died, the English Parliament accepted James as their king; but they were not yet ready for political union with such a poor and unsettled country as Scotland. For another century the two countries remained separate, though loyalty to the crown brought peace and encouraged trade between them. Scotland profited so greatly by arrangement that in 1707 she agreed to complete union under the Parliament at Westminster, whoever England's future kings might be.

After You Read

Knowledge Focus
1. **Pair Work**
   Discuss the following questions with your partner.
   (1) Why did William establish a series of earldoms in the borderlands?
   (2) What happened after King Henry I's death in 1135?
   (3) Who made Wales truly united? List at least two of his main contributions.
   (4) Why was it considered as bad news to Wales that Edward I became the new king of England after the death of King Henry III?
   (5) What were the three major campaigns that contributed to Edward's conquest of Wales?
   (6) Who brought Wales into a legal and administrative union with England?
   (7) What does the author mean by saying "the two halves of the land still reflect the differences of a thousand years of history"?
   (8) What do you know about William Wallace and Robert Bruce? What contributions did they make to bring freedom to Scotland?
   (9) What happened at the battle of Flodden? And who took control of Scotland?
   (10) Why did James do his utmost to follow Elizabeth's religious policy and to keep extreme Protestants under control?

2. Solo Work

Tell whether and why the following are true or false according to the knowledge you have learned.

____ (1) Just like the invasion of England, the Norman penetration of Wales took place very quickly after 1066.

____ (2) The first royal castle was built at Carmarthen in 1109 by King Henry I to encourage large-scale Norman settlement in south Wales.

____ (3) Upon Henry's death in 1135, revolts once again broke out in parts of Wales.

____ (4) The Welsh were truly united when Llewelyn the Great became King of Wales in 1194.

____ (5) Edward conquered Wales, because he disliked Celts in general, and Llewelyn II ap Gruffydd in particular.

____ (6) Even though Wales was brought into a legal and administrative union with England by his son King Henry VIII, many Welsh still continued to remain opposed to the union.

____ (7) In order to keep out the wild Scottish tribes, the Roman Emperor Hadrian built a wall which separates the highlands from lowlands.

____ (8) The lowlands were always fiercely independent and resisted the influences of English civilization.

____ (9) The crown passed to Margaret's cousin John Balliol after she was drowned in the sea. But Edward refused to support him, so Edward seized him and took him to London.

____ (10) James followed Elizabeth's religious policy and kept extreme Protestants under control.

Language Focus

1. Fill in the blanks with the following expressions you have learned in the text. Put them into appropriate forms if necessary.

| take revenge for | (be) content with | be stirred by | in particular |
| on behalf of | provoke...into... | do one's utmost | (be) lacking in |

(1) He was a strong, vital man, successful and _____ his life.

(2) Mary loves most classical music, _____ Bach and Vivaldi.

(3) He spoke _____ all the members of the faculty and staff.

(4) The *Times* was much _____ Humboldt's death and gave him a double column spread.

(5) Now that you put your hand to the work, you should _____ to finish it.

(6) The students tried every possible means to _____ the teacher _____ losing his temper.

(7) Members of the party are _____ the assassination of their leader.

(8) He is a television journalist, recently divorced, intelligent, good with women, somewhat _____ confidence.

Unit 15 Wales, Scotland and Ireland

2. Complete the following sentences with the proper forms of the words in the brackets.

(1) Military sources reported several enemy _____ (penetrate) of U.S. airspace.

(2) There were only a few scattered _____ (settle) of squatters by the river.

(3) Some analysts fear that increasing desperation could lead to a military _____ (invade) of the country's southern neighbors.

(4) He was an outgoing man. In _____ (compare), his brother was rather shy.

(5) Any policy that creates unemployment is likely to meet with strong _____ (resist).

(6) When disturbed they roll up so tightly that it is _____ (virtual) impossible to unroll them.

(7) There are additional _____ (administrate) functions, such as the submission of a statement of affairs and the making of reports on specified matters.

(8) The president has not been _____ (force) enough in changing the judicial system.

(9) The tutor discussed her own _____ (religion) beliefs openly with the students.

(10) Although he was only fifteen at the time of his father's death, he soon showed himself to be a cunning and unscrupulous _____ (politics).

3. Find the appropriate prepositions that collocate with the neighboring words.

(1) Dafydd obviously lacked the charisma of his brother, as his own countrymen handed him _____ to Edward in June 1283.

(2) The Welsh ruling dynasties were _____ tatters, and Wales virtually became an English colony.

(3) The Tudors were a Welsh dynasty and fought _____ behalf of the House of Lancaster in the Wars of the Roses.

(4) Welsh continued to remain bitterly opposed _____ this union, and a powerful nationalist movement continues to quietly battle _____ independence to this very day.

(5) The Roman Emperor Hadrian built a wall which ran _____ north England from Carlisle to Newcastle.

(6) Malcolm escaped to England, where he was given a friendly welcome. Seventeen years later, in 1057, he drove _____ his father's murder with English help.

(7) Scotland would not suffer such treatment for long, and her spirit was stirred _____ two great leaders, William Wallace and Robert Bruce.

(8) We all know what happened to Mary. Her son James was only one year old when he was crowned _____ Edinburgh, but he grew _____ with the firm intention of being crowned in London too.

Comprehensive Work

1. Group Work: Scottish place names

You must have encountered many ancient Gaelic and Norse place names. Many of the names have not changed over the centuries.

In the following guidelines, you are given the ways in which people remember and preserve the past.

You are involved in recognizing and then placing these names correctly. By finding out the origins of and then placing these names, you can discover that the Scottish heritage is preserved in place names in every part of the country.

Many Scottish place names have their roots in either the Gaelic, Pictish, or Norse language. Here are some examples.

Gaelic

Many Scottish place names have their origins in the Gaelic language, e.g.

"Inver"—meeting of the waters: Inverness and Inverkip,

"Tigh"—house: Tighnabruaich and Tyndrum,

"Dun"—fortress or castle: Dundee and Dunkeld,

"Cill"—chapel or church: Kildonan, Kilconquhar, Kilkenneth.

Pictish

Many Scottish place names have their origins in Pictish times. Some are:

"Pett"(pit)—portion or share: Pittenweem and Pitlochry (Some include people's names e. g. Pitcarmick, Pitewan, Pitcalman or their jobs e. g. Pitskelly which means the storyteller's share or place),

"Carden"—thicket: Kincardine and Urquhart,

"Aber"—river mouth: Aberdeen and Aberdour.

Norse

There are many Scottish place names which have Norse origins. Norse names are mostly found round the coast as the Norse arrived by boat and stuck mostly to coastal regions. Some are:

"dalr"(-dale)—valley: Brosdale, Helmsdale, and Laxdale (2 Norse words together),

"Lax"—salmon: Laxay and Laxdale (Both are villages in Lewis),

"Vik"(wick)—a bay: Wick, Lerwick and Uig.

---

2. Writing Activity

Which one of the British monarchs impressed you most? What qualities in him/her or what historical event in his/her reign made such enduring impression on you? Write an essay of about 300 words, summarizing your view.

Read More

Text C   The Ties between Ireland and the Great Britain

Ireland had not been troubled by the Romans or Saxons, though Danes had settled on the east coast and built towns like Dublin. The Irish themselves had no towns; each man lived on his farm and passed his days happily in raising his own cattle or stealing his neighbors. They were simple people who only wanted to be left in peace.

They were too simple, in fact, to resist either the greed of the feudal ages or the heartless politics of modern times. St. Patrick had brought them Christianity in the 5th century, but they were not united in Church or State. Their clan system was not as well organized as in Scotland, though even today one finds that many people in a district seem to have the same name. Thus they were defenseless against the private army of Norman cavalry and Welsh longbow men who seized the land in 1169. The leaders of this army were border lords who had mixed with the Welsh and so had no difficulty in settling down among the Celtic Irish.

King Henry II then took official possession of the island. The Danes were driven out and Dublin was given to the citizens of Bristol; its castle became the seat of government until the 20th century. The district around Dublin came under direct royal rule. The rest of the island remained under Irish clan chiefs in the west and under Normans in the east, but they soon married Irish girls and lost touch with their own people.

For a while there was peaceful development. Dublin and Cork became busy ports. After Bannockburn, the victorious Scots landed in the north and took possession of the Ulster district, but England was too busy with her wars to attend to Irish affairs for the next two centuries. Her language and civilization were unknown in Ireland beyond Dublin.

Henry VIII did not understand the Irish. He did not realize that the new learning of the renaissance had never reached them; that the Catholic Church was still popular and socially useful; and that its abbeys had no wealth which he could use to keep their schools going. His interference with the Church in Ireland was a mistake for which both countries have suffered ever since. All Ireland except Ulster was now united in loyalty to Rome and in hatred of England.

Henry tried to fit the clan chiefs into a new system of government. This might have been possible before the Reformation, but in the heat of religious quarrels it was hopeless. The violent extremes of Edward and Mary only made things worse so that Elizabeth was faced with a serious problem. The southern Irish were especially friendly with Spain, and she realized that Spain could easily take the island and use it as a base for attack on England.

Peaceful agreement was clearly necessary to solve this problem, but no such agreement was ever reached. Spanish armies twice landed in Ireland and were destroyed by Elizabeth's forces. To guard against this danger, she colonized all the south with Englishmen, who were given land for settlement. She also opened a university in Dublin and encouraged education. Meanwhile thousands of Protestant Scots were settling in Ulster to escape the rule of James.

In the 17th-century quarrel between the king and the parliament, Catholic Ireland supported the king, but it was defeated and severely punished. The whole island was handed over to Protestant settlers, except for the parts west of the River Shannon. The 18th century passed peacefully, but Napoleon's wars raised the old problem of defense. This led to the union of the two islands in 1801 under one parliament at Westminster, where Irish members joined those of Wales and Scotland. But the parliament was still blinded by religious prejudice and failed to reach any fair solution to Irish problems. In the end, Catholic Ireland became an independent country, called Eire; but Protestant Ulster chose to remain part of the United Kingdom.

In spite of everything, the ties of blood and language still hold Eire close to Britain, where she is regarded as a sister country rather than a foreign one.

1. Questions for discussion or reflection.
   (1) Who brought the Irish Christianity in the 5th century?
   (2) What happened to Ireland after Henry II took official possession of the island?

Proper Names

Bannockburn 班诺克伯恩
Cardiff 卡迪夫
Dafydd 戴维德
Emperor Hadrian (古罗马)帝王哈德良
Northumberland 诺森伯兰郡
King Duncan of Scotland 苏格兰邓肯一世
Llewelyn ap Gruffudd 卢埃林·阿普·格鲁菲德

Macbeth 麦克白(苏格兰国王邓肯的表弟)
Owen Glendower 欧文·格伦德尔
Robert Bruce 罗伯特·布鲁斯(罗伯特一世,1306年任苏格兰国王)
River Tweed 特威德河(苏格兰边区的一条河流)
The Statute of Rhuddlan《罗德兰法令》
William Wallace 威廉·华莱士

Notes

The Statute of Rhuddlan: The Statute of Rhuddlan was enacted on March 3, 1284 after the military conquest in 1282—1283 of the Principality of Wales. The statute assumed the lands held by Princes of Gwynedd under the title Prince of Wales as legally part of the lands of England under Edward I. Some of the claimed lands such as the south of the Kingdom of Powys had apparently already been surrendered. These territories did not include a substantial swathe of land from Pembrokeshire through south Wales to the Welsh borders which was largely in the hands of the Marcher Lords.

For Fun

Book to read

Welsh Family History: A Guide to Research by Rowlands John
This handbook on Welsh genealogy deals primarily with those aspects of family history unique to Wales. It is considered the best book ever written on Welsh genealogy. It is certainly a very comprehensive handbook, with over twenty chapters treating the essential elements of Welsh genealogy.

Websites to visit

1. **BBC Wales History**
   http://www.bbc.co.uk/wales/history/
   This BBC Wales' guide features Welsh history, genealogy, myths, legends, Celtic peoples and languages.
2. **Scotland History**
   http://www.scotlandhistory.net/
   This website serves as a Scotland resource guide for Scottish history, religion, music, battles, royalty and much more.
3. **Scottish History**
   http://www.electricscotland.com/history/
   This Scottish history site offers information in general and Highland history, battles, culture, clan histories and more.

Movie to see

Braveheart (1995)
　　This is a 1995 historical action-drama movie produced and directed by Mel Gibson, who also starred in the title role. The film was written for screen and then novelized by Randall Wallace. Gibson portrays a legendary Scot, William Wallace, who gained

recognition when he came to the forefront of the First War of Scottish Independence by opposing Edward I of England and subsequently abetted by Edward's daughter-in-law Princess Isabelle and a claimant to the Scottish throne, Robert the Bruce.

Song to enjoy

Auld Lang Syne

Lyric by Robert Burns

Should auld acquaintance be forgot,
And never brought to min'?
Should auld acquaintance be forgot,
And days o' lang syne?
We twa ha'e run about the braes,
And pu'd the gowans fine,
But we've wandered mony a weary foot,
Sin' auld lang syne.
We twa ha'e paidl'd i' the burn,
Frae mornin' sun till dine,
But seas between us braid ha'e roared,

Sin' auld lang syne.
And surely ye'll be your pint-stowp,
And surely I'll be mine;
And we'll tak a right gude-willie waught,
For auld lang syne.
And there's a hand, my trusty fiere,
And gie's a hand o' thine;
And we'll tak a cup o' kindness yet' For auld lang syne.
For auld lang syne, my dear,
For auld lang syne, And we'll tak a cup o' kindness

Appendixes

Appendix 1: Kings and Queens of England and Britain

English Monarchs
Saxon Kings
Egbert 827—839   Egbert was the first monarch to establish a stable and extensive rule over Anglo-Saxon England. He is buried at Winchester.
Aethelwulf 839—858—son of Egbert   King of Wessex, son of Egbert and father of Alfred the Great. In 851 Aethelwulf defeated a Danish army at the Battle of Oakley while his eldest son Althelstan fought and beat the Danes at sea off the coast of Kent in what is believed to be the first naval battle. In 855, Aethelwulf travelled to Rome with his son Alfred to see the Pope.
Aethelbald 858—860   The eldest son of Aethelwulf of Wessex, Aethelbald was born in around 834 and became King of Wessex after forcing his father to abdicate. Married his widowed stepmother Judith but the marriage was annulled.
Aethelbert 860—865   After the death of his father Aethelwulf in 858, Ethelbert ruled Kent, Surrey, Sussex, and Essex, and he reunited them with Wessex when in 860 he succeeded his brother Aethelbald. Like his brother and his father, Ethelbert of Wessex was crowned at Kingston-Upon-Thames. Viking raids in Kent and Northumberland. He is buried at Sherborne Abbey, Dorset. 
Aethelred 865—871   King of Wessex and Kent and the elder brother of Alfred the Great.
Alfred the Great 871—899—son of Aethelwulf   Born at Wantage, Oxfordshire around 849. Well educated, he is said to have visited Rome on two occasions. Devout Christian and scholar. He was a fine king, strong in battle against the Danes and a wise ruler, although perhaps he is best known for "burning the cakes". Began *the Anglo-Saxon Chronicles* (detailing life between the 9th and 12th centuries) Originated the Royal Navy.
Edward the Elder 899—924   Son of Alfred. Retook the northern counties from the Danes.
Athelstan 924—939

(Continued)

Edmund 939—946
Assassinated (stabbed by a robber) in his hall whilst celebrating the feast of Augustine.
Eadred 946—955
Eadwig 955—959
Edgar 959—975
Edward the Martyr 975—978
Assassinated by followers of his brother, Ethelred, at Corfe Castle, aged about 15 years old.
Ethelred II the Unready 978—1016
Unable to organize resistance against the Danes hence his nickname "The Unready". Became King aged about 10, fled to Normandy in 1013 when Sweyn, King of the Danes had over-run the country. Returned after Sweyn was killed by a fall from his horse.
Edmund the Ironside 1016—1016
Son of Ethelred. Made a pact with Canute to divide England, but died soon afterwards.
Canute (Cnut) the Dane 1017—1035
Son of Sweyn, he ruled well and with fairness. Well known for trying to control the power of the sea. Divided England into four earldoms.
Harold I 1035—1040
Son of Canute.
Hardicanute 1040—1042
Son of Canute. Died drunk, aged 24.
Edward the Confessor 1042—1066
Founded Westminster Abbey. Died eight days after building work on the Abbey was finished.
Harold II 1066
Defeated the Norwegians at the Battle of Stamford Bridge in Yorkshire, then marched south to confront William of Normandy who had landed in Sussex. The death of Harold at the Battle of Hastings meant the end of the English Saxon kings and the beginning of the Normans.
Norman Kings
William I (the Conqueror) 1066—1087  Also known as William the Bastard. Reigned from 1066—1087. William came to England from Normandy and beat Harold at the Battle of Hastings in 1066. In 1085 the Domesday survey was begun and all England was recorded so William knew exactly what his new kingdom contained. He also created The New Forest as a Game Park for hunting. After losing his devoted wife, Matilda of Flanders, William had few friends. He died at Rouen in 1087.

(Continued)

William II (Rufus) 1087—1100

William was not a popular king, given to extravagance and cruelty. He never married and was killed in the New Forest by a stray arrow while out hunting, maybe accidentally. There is some doubt about this. Walter Tyrrell, one of the hunting party, was blamed for the deed. The Rufus Stone in The New Forest marks the spot where he fell.

Henry I 1100—1135

Henry Beauclerc was the fourth son of William I. Well educated, he founded a zoo at Woodstock to study animals. He was called the "Lion of Justice" as he gave England good laws even if the punishments were ferocious. His two sons were drowned in the White Ship so his daughter Matilda was made his successor. She was married to Geoffrey Plantagenet. When Henry died the Council considered a woman unfit to rule so offered the throne to Stephen, a grandson of William I.

Stephen 1135—1154

Stephen was a very weak king and the whole country was almost destroyed by the constant raids by the Scots and the Welsh. During Stephen's reign the Norman barons wielded great power, extorting money and looting towns and countries. A decade of civil war ensued when Matilda invaded from Anjou. A compromise was decided, Matilda's son was to be the king when Stephen died.

Plantagenet Kings

Henry II 1154—1189

Henry of Anjou was a strong king. A brilliant soldier, he extended his French lands until he ruled most of France. He laid the foundation of the English Jury System and raised new taxes from the landholders to pay for a militia force. Henry is mostly remembered for his quarrel with Thomas Becket, and Becket's subsequent murder in Canterbury Cathedral on 29th December 1170. His sons turned against him, even his favorite son John.

Richard I (The Lionhearted) 1189—1199

Richard was the second son of Henry II. He was thought to be homosexual. He spent almost all of his reign abroad, fighting in the Third Crusade. He had no children. Richard died from an arrow-wound, far from the Kingdom that he so rarely visited.

John 1199—1216

John Lackland was the fourth child of Henry II. Short and fat, he was jealous of his dashing brother Richard I whom he succeeded. He was cruel, self-indulgent, selfish and avaricious, and the raising of punitive taxes united all the elements of society against him. The Pope excommunicated him. On 15th June 1215 at Runnymede the barons compelled John to sign *Magna Carta*, *the Great Charter*, which reinstated the rights of all his subjects. He has been termed "the worst English king".

Henry III 1216—1272

Henry was 9 years old when he became king. Brought up by priests he became devoted to church, art and learning. He was a weak man, dominated by churchmen and easily influenced by his wife's French relations. In 1264 Henry was captured during the rebellion of barons led by Simon de Montfort and was forced to set up a "parliament" at Westminster, the start of the House of Commons. Henry was the greatest of all patrons of medieval architecture and ordered the rebuilding of Westminster Abbey in the Gothic style.

Edward I 1272—1307

Edward Longshanks was a statesman, lawyer and soldier. He formed the Model Parliament in 1295, bringing together the knights, clergy, nobility and burgesses of the cities, bringing Lords and Commons together for the first time. Aiming at a united Britain, he defeated the Welsh chieftains and created his eldest son Prince of Wales. He was known as the "Hammer of the Scots" for his victories in Scotland and brought the famous coronation stone from Scone to Westminster. He died on the way to fight Robert Bruce.

Edward II 1307—deposed 1327

Edward was a weak and incompetent king. He had many "favorites", Piers Gaveston being the most notorious. He was beaten by the Scots at the Battle of Bannockburn in 1314. Edward was deposed and held captive in Berkeley Castle in Gloucestershire. His wife joined her lover Mortimer in deposing him: by their orders he was murdered in Berkley Castle—so legend has it, by having a red-hot poker thrust up his anus! His beautiful tomb in Gloucester Cathedral was erected by his son, Edward III.

Edward III 1327—1377

Son of Edward II, he reigned for 50 years. His ambition to conquer Scotland and France plunged England into The Hundred Years' War, beginning in 1338. The two great victories at Crecy and Poitiers made Edward and his son, the Black Prince, the most renowned warriors in Europe, however the war was very expensive. The outbreak of bubonic plague, the "Black Death" in 1348—1350 killed half the population of England.

Richard II 1377—deposed 1399

The son of the Black Prince, Richard was extravagant, unjust and faithless. In 1381 came the Peasants Revolt, led by Wat Tyler. The rebellion was put down with great severity. Queen Anne's sudden death completely unbalanced Richard and his extravagance, acts of revenge and tyranny turned his subjects against him. In 1399 Henry of Lancaster returned from exile and deposed Richard, becoming elected King Henry IV. Richard was murdered in Pontefract Castle in 1400.

House of Lancaster

(Continued)

Henry IV 1399—1413

Henry's brief reign was one of rebellions. Richard's half brothers rose immediately on his behalf and in Wales Owen Glendower led a national uprising that was not finally quelled until 1410. Henry, the first Lancastrian king, died of leprosy in 1413 at the age of 45.

Henry V 1413—1422

Henry was a pious, stern and skilful soldier. He pleased the nobles by renewing the war with France and in the face of tremendous odds beat the French at the Battle of Agincourt in 1415. On a second expedition Henry captured Rouen, was recognized as the next King of France and married Catherine, the daughter of the lunatic king of France. Two years later he died.

Henry VI 1422—deposed 1461　Beginning of the Wars of the Roses

Gentle and retiring, he came to the throne as a baby and inherited a losing war with France, The Hundred Years' War finally ending in 1453 with the loss of all French lands except for Calais. The king had an attack of mental illness that was hereditary in his mother's family in 1454 and Richard Duke of York was made Protector of the Realm. The House of York challenged Henry VI's right to the throne and England was plunged into civil war. The Battle of St Albans in 1455 was won by the Yorkists. Henry was restored to the throne briefly in 1470. Henry's son, Edward, Prince of Wales was killed at the Battle of Tewkesbury one day before Henry was murdered in the Tower of London in 1471. Henry founded both Eton College and King's College, Cambridge, and every year the Provosts of Eton and King's College lay roses and lilies on the altar which now stands where he died.

House of York

Edward IV 1461—1483

He was the son of Richard Duke of York and Cicely Neville, and not a popular king. His morals were poor (he had many mistresses and had at least one illegitimate son) and even his contemporaries disapproved of him. Edward had his rebellious brother George, Duke of Clarendon, murdered in 1478 on a charge of treason. During his reign the first printing press was established in Westminster by William Caxton. Edward died suddenly in 1483 leaving two sons aged 12 and 9, and five daughters.

Edward V 1483—1483

Reigned for only two months. Elder son of Edward IV. Succeeded to the throne at the tender age of 13. He and his brother Richard were murdered in the Tower of London — it is said on the orders of his uncle Richard Duke of Gloucester. Richard declared the brothers illegitimate and named himself rightful heir to the crown.

(Continued)

Richard III 1483—1485 End of the Wars of the Roses

Brother of Edward IV. The murders of his nephews and the ruthless extinction of all those who opposed him made his rule very unpopular. In 1485 Henry Richmond, descendant of John of Gaunt, father of Henry IV, landed in west Wales, gathering forces as he marched into England. At Market Bosworth in Leicestershire he defeated and killed Richard in what was to be the last important battle in the Wars of the Roses.

The Tudors

Henry VII 1485—1509

When Richard III fell at the Battle of Bosworth, his crown was picked up and placed on the head of Henry Tudor. He married Elizabeth of York and so united the two warring houses, York and Lancaster. He was a skilful politician but avaricious. The material wealth of the country increased greatly. During Henry's reign playing cards were invented and the portrait of his wife Elizabeth has appeared eight times on every pack of cards for nearly 500 years.

Henry VIII 1509—1547

The best known fact about Henry VIII is that he had six wives. Most school children learn the following rhyme to help them remember the fate of each wife: "Divorced, Beheaded, Died; Divorced, Beheaded, Survived". His first wife was Catherine of Aragon, his brother's widow, whom he later divorced to marry Anne Boleyn. This divorce caused the split from Rome and Henry declared himself the head of the Church of England. The Dissolution of the Monasteries began in 1536, and the money gained from this helped Henry to bring about an effective Navy. In an effort to have a son, Henry married four further wives, but only one son was born, to Jane Seymour. Henry had two daughters. Both became rulers of England—Mary, daughter of Catherine of Aragon, and Elizabeth, daughter of Anne Boleyn.

Edward VI 1547—1553

Son of Henry VIII and Jane Seymour, Edward was a sickly boy; he had, it is thought, tuberculosis. Edward succeeded his father at the age of 9, the government being carried on by a Council of Regency with his uncle, Duke of Somerset, styled Protector. Even though his reign was short, many men made their mark. Cranmer wrote *the Book of Common Prayer* and the uniformity of worship helped turn England into a Protestant State.

After Edward's death there was a dispute over the succession. As Mary was Catholic, Lady Jane Grey was named as the next in line to the throne. She was proclaimed Queen but Mary entered London with her supporters and Jane was taken to the Tower. She reigned for only 9 days. She was executed in 1554, aged 17.

(Continued)

Mary I (Bloody Mary) 1553—1558

Daughter of Henry VIII and Catherine of Aragon. A devout Catholic, she married Philip of Spain. Mary attempted to enforce the wholesale conversion of England to Catholicism. She carried this out with the utmost severity. The Protestant bishops, Latimer, Ridley and Archbishop Cranmer were among those burnt at the stake. The place, in Broad Street Oxford, is marked by a bronze cross. The country was plunged into a bitter blood bath, which is why she is remembered as Bloody Mary. She died in 1558 at Lambeth Palace.

Elizabeth I 1558—1603

Daughter of Henry VIII and Anne Boleyn, Elizabeth was a remarkable woman, noted for her learning and wisdom. From first to last she was popular with the people and had a genius for the selection of capable advisors. Drake, Raleigh, Hawkins, the Cecils, Essex and many more made England respected and feared. The Spanish Armada was decisively defeated in 1588 and Raleigh's first Virginian colony was founded. The execution of Mary Queen of Scots marred what was a glorious time in English history. Shakespeare was also at the height of his popularity. Elizabeth never married.

British Monarchs

The Stuarts

James I and VI of Scotland 1603—1625

James was the son of Mary Queen of Scots and Lord Darnley. He was the first king to rule over Scotland and England. James was more of a scholar than a man of action. In 1605 the Gunpowder Plot was hatched: Guy Fawkes and his friends, Catholics, tried to blow up the Houses of Parliament, but were captured before they could do so. James's reign saw the publication of the *Authorized Version of the Bible*, though this caused problems with the Puritans and their attitude towards the established church. In 1620 the Pilgrim Fathers sailed for America in their ship The Mayflower.

Charles I 1625—1649   English Civil War

Son of James I, Charles believed that he ruled by Divine Right. He encountered difficulties with Parliament from the beginning, and this led to the outbreak of Civil War in 1642. The war lasted four years and after the defeat of Charles by the New Model Army, led by Oliver Cromwell, Charles was captured and executed at Whitehall in 1649.

The Commonwealth   Declared on May 19, 1649

(Continued)

Oliver Cromwell, Lord Protector 1653—1658

Cromwell was born at Huntingdon, north of Cambridge in 1599, son of a small landowner. He entered Parliament in 1629 and became active in events leading to the Civil War. A leading Puritan figure, he raised cavalry forces and organized the New Model Army, which he led to victory over the Royalists at Naseby in 1645. Failing to gain agreement on constitutional change in government with Charles I, Cromwell was a member of a "Special Commission" that tried and condemned the king to death in 1649. Cromwell declared Britain a republic "The Commonwealth" and he went on to become Lord Protector. Cromwell went on to crush the Irish clans and the Scots loyal to Charles II between 1649 and 1651. In 1653 he finally expelled the corrupt English Parliament and with the agreement of army leaders became Lord Protector (King in all but name).

Richard Cromwell, Lord Protector 1658—1659

The Restoration

Charles II 1660—1685

Son of Charles I. Known as the Merry Monarch. After the collapse of the Protectorate following the death of Oliver Cromwell and the flight of Richard Cromwell to France, the Army and Parliament asked Charles to take the throne in 1660. Although very popular he was a weak king and his foreign policy was inept. He had 13 known mistresses, one of whom was Nell Gwyn. He fathered numerous illegitimate children but no heir to the throne. The Great Plague in 1665 and the Great Fire of London in 1666 took place during his reign. Many new buildings were built at this time. St. Paul's Cathedral was built by Sir Christopher Wren and also many churches still to be seen today.

James II and VII of Scotland 1685—1688

Brother of Charles II. A Catholic, he was very unpopular because of his persecution of the Protestants, and he was hated by the people. Following the Monmouth uprising (Monmouth was an illegitimate son of Charles II and a Protestant) and the Bloody Assizes of Judge Jeffries, the Parliament asked William of Orange to take the throne. William was married to Mary, James's daughter. William landed in England and James fled to France where he died in exile in 1701.

William III 1689—1702/ Mary II 1689—1694

William and Mary were to reign jointly, and William was to have the Crown for life after Mary died in 1694. James plotted to regain the throne and in 1689 landed in Ireland. William defeated James at the Battle of the Boyne and James fled to France once again.

Anne 1702—1714

Anne was the second daughter of James II. She had 17 children but all died. Anne was a close friend of Sarah Churchill, Duchess of Marlborough. Anne was a staunch, high church Protestant and the victories of the Duke of Marlborough abroad gave the country an influence never before attained in Europe. After Anne's death the succession went to the nearest Protestant relative of the Stuart line. This was Sophia, daughter of Elizabeth of Bohemia, James I's only daughter.

(Continued)

The Hanoverians

George I 1714—1727

Son of Sophia and Elector of Hanover, great-grandson of James I. George never learned English so the conduct of national policy was left to the government of the time. Sir Robert Walpole became England's first Prime Minister. In 1715 the Jacobites (followers of James Stuart, son of James II) attempted to supplant George, but the attempt failed. George spent little time in England—he preferred his beloved Hanover.

George II 1727—1760

Only son of George I. He was more English than his father, but still relied on Sir Robert Walpole to run the country. George was the last English king to lead his army into battle at Dettingen in 1743. In 1745 the Jacobites tried once again to restore a Stuart to the throne. Prince Charles Edward Stuart, "Bonnie Prince Charlie" landed in Scotland. He was routed at Culloden Moor by the army under the Duke of Cumberland, known as "Butcher Cumberland".

George III 1760—1820

He was a grandson of George II and the first English-born and English-speaking monarch since Queen Anne. His reign was one of elegance and the age of some of the greatest names in English literature—Jane Austin, Byron, Shelley, Keats and Wordsworth. It was also the time of great statesmen like Pitt and Fox and great captains like Wellington and Nelson. In 1773 the "Boston Tea Party" was the first sign of the troubles that were to come in America. The American colonies proclaimed their independence on July 4th 1776. George suffered from a mental illness due to intermittent porphyria and eventually became blind and insane. His son ruled as Prince Regent after 1811 until George's death.

George IV 1820—1830

Known as the "First Gentleman of Europe". He had a love of art and architecture but his private life was a mess, to put it mildly. He married twice, once in 1785 to Mrs. Fitzherbert, secretly as she was a Catholic, and then in 1795 to Caroline of Brunswick. Mrs. Fitzherbert remained the love of his life. Caroline and George had one daughter, Charlotte in 1796 but she died in 1817. George was considered a great wit, but was also a buffoon and his death was hailed with relief.

William IV 1830—1837

Known as the "Sailor King" (for 10 years the young Prince William, brother of George IV, served in the Royal Navy), he was the third son of George III. Before his accession he lived with Mrs. Jordan, an actress, with whom he had ten children. When Princess Charlotte died, he had to marry in order to secure the succession. He married Adelaide of Saxe-Coburg in 1818. He had two daughters but they did not live. He hated pomp and wanted to dispense with the coronation. The people loved him because of his lack of pretension. During his reign England abolished slavery in the colonies in 1833. *The Reform Act* was passed in 1832; this extended the franchise to the middle classes on a basis of property qualifications.

(Continued)

Victoria 1837—1901

Victoria was the only child of Princess Victoria of Saxe-Coburg and Edward Duke of Kent, fourth son of George III. The throne Victoria inherited was weak and unpopular. Her Hanoverian uncles had been treated with irreverence. In 1840 she married her cousin Albert of Saxe-Coburg. Albert exerted tremendous influence over the Queen and until his death was virtual ruler of the country. He was a pillar of respectability and left two legacies to England, the Christmas Tree and the Great Exhibition of 1851. With the money from the Exhibition several institutions were developed, the Victoria and Albert Museum, the Science Museum, Imperial College and the Royal Albert Hall. The Queen withdrew from public life after the death of Albert in 1861 until her Golden Jubilee in 1887. Her reign saw the British Empire double in size and in 1876 the Queen became Empress of India, the "Jewel in the Crown". When Victoria died in 1901, after the longest reign in English history, the British Empire and British world power had reached their highest point. She had six children, 40 grand-children and 37 great-grandchildren, scattered all over Europe.

Edward VII 1901—1910

A much loved king, the opposite of his dour father. He loved horse-racing, gambling and women. This Edwardian Age was one of elegance. Edward had all the social graces and many sporting interests, yachting and horse-racing—his horse Minoru won the Derby in 1909. Edward married the beautiful Alexandra of Denmark in 1863 and they had six children. The eldest, Edward Duke of Clarence, died in 1892 just before he was to marry Princess Mary of Teck. When Edward died in 1910 it is said that Queen Alexandra brought his current mistress Mrs. Keppel to his bedside to take her farewell. His best known mistress was Lily Langtry, the "Jersey Lily".

House of Windsor—Name changed in 1917

George V 1910—1936

George had not expected to be king, but when his elder brother died he became the heir-apparent. He had joined the Navy as a cadet in 1877 and loved the sea. In 1893 he married Princess Mary of Teck, his dead brother's fiancée. His years on the throne were difficult; the First World War in 1914—1918 and the troubles in Ireland which led to the creation of the Irish Free State were considerable problems. In 1932 he began the royal broadcasts on Christmas Day and in 1935 he celebrated his Silver Jubilee. His latter years were overshadowed by his concern about the Prince of Wales and his infatuation with Mrs. Simpson.

Edward VIII   June 1936—abdicated December 1936

Edward was the most popular Prince of Wales England had ever had. Consequently when he renounced the throne to marry Mrs. Wallis Simpson the country found it almost impossible to believe. The people as a whole knew nothing about Mrs. Simpson until early in December 1936. Mrs. Simpson was an American, a divorcee and had two husbands still living. This was unacceptable to the Church as Edward had stated that he wanted her to be crowned with him at the coronation to take place the following May. Edward abdicated in favor of his brother and took the title, Duke of Windsor. He went to live abroad.

Appendixes

(Continued)

George VI 1936—1952

George was a shy and nervous man with a very bad stutter, the exact opposite of his brother the Duke of Windsor, but he had inherited the steady virtues of his father George V. He was very popular and well loved by the English people. The prestige of the throne was low when he became king but his wife Elizabeth and his mother Queen Mary were outstanding in their support of him. The Second World War started in 1939 and throughout the King and Queen set an example of courage and fortitude. They remained at Buckingham Palace for the duration of the war in spite of the bombing. The Palace was bombed more than once. The two Princesses, Elizabeth and Margaret, spent the war years at Windsor Castle. George was in close touch with the Prime Minister, Winston Churchill throughout the war and both had to be dissuaded from landing with the troops in Normandy on D-Day. The post-war years of his reign were ones of great social change and saw the start of the National Health Service. The whole country flocked to the Festival of Britain held in London in 1951, 100 years after the Great Exhibition during Victoria's reign.

Elizabeth II 1952—2022

Queen of the United Kingdom from 1952 to 2022. She became heir presumptive when her uncle, Edward VIII, abdicated and her father became king as George VI. In 1947 she married her distant cousin Philip, duke of Edinburgh (1921—2021), with whom she had four children, including Charles, who succeeded her in 2022. She became queen on her father's death in 1952. Increasingly aware of the modern role of the monarchy, she favoured simplicity in court life and took an informed interest in government business. In the 1990s the monarchy was troubled by the highly publicized marital difficulties of two of the queen's sons and the death of Diana, princess of Wales. In 2002 the queen's mother and sister died within two months. Elizabeth became the longest-reigning monarch in British history in 2015, and she celebrated 70 years on the throne with a "Platinum Jubilee" in 2022.

Charles III 2022—present

King of the United Kingdom of Great Britain and Northern Ireland from September 8, 2022. He is the eldest child of Queen Elizabeth II and Prince Philip, Duke of Edinburgh.

Appendix 2: Genealogy of the Monarchs of England
by Ed Stephen

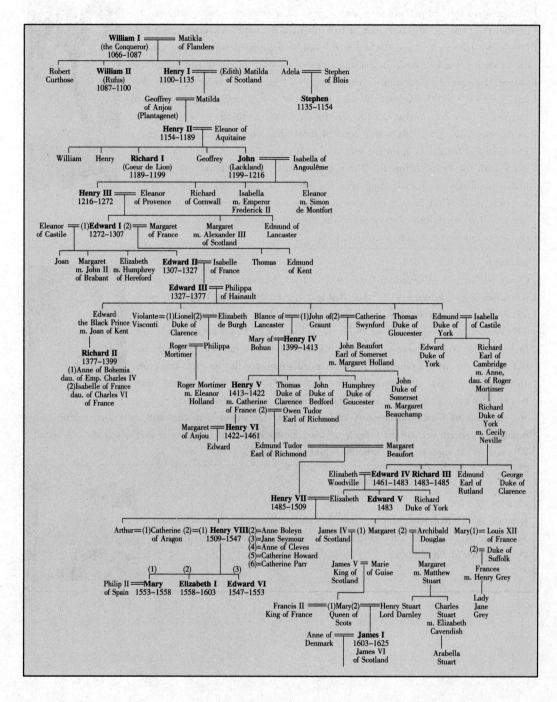

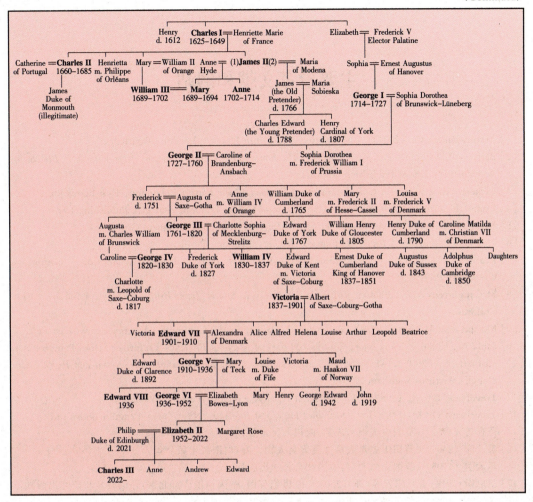

Appendixes (Continued)

主要参考文献和网站

[1] Arnold-Baker, C. (2001). *The Companion to British History*. London: Routledge.
[2] Berton, P. (1953). *The Royal Family: The Story of the British Monarchy from Victoria to Elizabeth*. Westminster: Knopf Publishing Group.
[3] Dickens, C. (2008). *A Child's History of England (New Edition)*. London: Icon Books Ltd.
[4] Evans, E. (2007). *British History: An Illustrated Guide*. London: Star Fire Publishing Ltd.
[5] Eyre, A. G. (1971). *An Outline History of England*. London: Longman Group Ltd.
[6] Fraser, R. (2004). *A People's History of Britain*. London: Pimlico.
[7] Kearney, H. (2006). *The British Isles: A History of Four Nations*. Cambridge: Cambridge University Press.
[8] McCaughrean, G. (2004). *Britannia: 100 Great Stories from British History*. London: Orion Children.
[9] Morton, A. Morton. (1979). *A People's History of England*. London: Lawrence & Wishart Ltd.
[10] Saul, N. (2000). *The Oxford Illustrated History of Medieval England*. Oxford: Oxford Paperbacks.
[11] Shahrad, C. (2007). *Secrets of the Royal Family: A Fascinating Insight into Present and Past Royals*. Slough: Arcturus foulsham.
[12] Trevelyan, G. M. (1967). *English Social History*. London: Penguin Books Ltd.
[13] Trevelyan, G. M. (1994). *A Shortened History of England*. New York: Penguin Books Ltd.
[14] 范存忠(1982)《英国史提纲》,成都:四川人民出版社。
[15] 郝 澎(2007)《英国历史重大事件及著名人物》,海口:南海出版公司。
[16] 蒋孟引(1995)《英国史》,北京:中国社会科学出版社。
[17] 凯尼斯·摩根(著),宋云峰(译)(2008)《20世纪英国:帝国与遗产》,北京:外语教学与研究出版社。
[18] 来安方(2004)《英美概况》,郑州:河南人民出版社。
[19] 钱乘旦(1998)《20世纪英国》,南京:南京大学出版社。
[20] 钱乘旦(2002)《英国通史》,上海:上海社会科学院出版社。
[21] 王觉非(1996)《近代英国史》,南京:南京大学出版社。
[22] Britain Express: http://www.britainexpress.com/History/index.htm
[23] Britannia: http://www.britannia.com/index.html
[24] British History Online: http://www.british-history.ac.uk/
[25] British Royal Family History: http://www.britroyals.com/
[26] English Monarchs: http://www.englishmonarchs.co.uk/index.htm
[27] Historic UK: http://www.historic-uk.com/index.shtml
[28] History Learning Site: http://www.historylearningsite.co.uk/
[29] The Official Website of British Monarchy: http://www.royal.gov.uk/
[30] Thinking History: http://www.thinkinghistory.co.uk/Index.html